CECIL SHARP

Da Capo Press Music Reprint Series

MUSIC EDITOR

BEA FRIEDLAND
Ph.D., City University of New York

CECIL SHARP

By A. H. FOX STRANGWAYS

In collaboration with MAUD KARPELES

DA CAPO PRESS · NEW YORK · 1980

Library of Congress Cataloging in Publication Data

Fox-Strangways, Arthur Henry, 1859-
  Cecil Sharp.

  (Da Capo Press music reprint series)
  Reprint of the ed. published by Oxford University
Press, London.
  "Cecil Sharp's publication": p.
  Includes index.
  1. Sharp, Cecil James, 1859-1924. I. Karpeles,
Maud, joint author.
ML423.S53F6 1980   784.4'92'4 [B]   79-24412
ISBN 0-306-86019-3

This Da Capo Press edition of *Cecil Sharp*
is an unabridged republication of the first
edition published in London in 1933.
It is reprinted by arrangement with Oxford University Press.

Published by Da Capo Press, Inc.
A Subsidiary of Plenum Publishing Corporation
227 West 17th Street, New York, N.Y. 10011

CECIL SHARP

CECIL J. SHARP
From a portrait by SIR WILLIAM ROTHENSTEIN
Reproduced by permission of the artist and The English Folk
Dance and Song Society

CECIL SHARP

By A. H. FOX STRANGWAYS

In collaboration with MAUD KARPELES

MCMXXXIII

OXFORD UNIVERSITY PRESS

LONDON : HUMPHREY MILFORD

*OXFORD
UNIVERSITY PRESS
Amen House, E.C. 4
London   Edinburgh   Glasgow
Leipzig   New York   Toronto
Melbourne   Capetown   Bombay
Calcutta Madras Shanghai*
HUMPHREY MILFORD
*Publisher to the
University*

PRINTED IN GREAT BRITAIN

$\mathcal{D}$EAR Countrymen, whate'er is left to us
    Of ancient heritage—
    Of manners, speech, of humours, polity,
    The limited horizon of our stage—
    Old love, hope, fear,
    All this I fain would fix upon the page;
    That so the coming age,
        Lost in the Empire's mass,
    Yet haply longing for their fathers, here
        May see, as in a glass,
    What they held dear—
May say, ' 'Twas thus and thus
    They lived'; and, as the time-flood onward rolls,
    Secure an anchor for their souls.

          T. E. BROWN
       Foc's'le Yarns (second series)

PREFACE

MISS MAUD KARPELES knew Cecil Sharp intimately for thirteen years; during twenty-two years I was a slight acquaintance of his, a haphazard correspondent, a familiar friend. In the spring of 1931 we fell to talking of him, and I found her to be oppressed with the fear that she would never be able to get down on paper the image of him that was in her mind. I proposed that we should write his biography together. This book is the result. Her collaboration has consisted in giving most of the story of his life, the planning of the book in detail, and two complete chapters. A pervasive sense of humour was included in it; pertinent criticism and obstinate argument were not excluded.

Mr. A. P. Oppé, who collaborated with Sharp in *The Dance* (1924), and Dr. Vaughan Williams, who more than any one has in word and in deed made Sharp's cause his own, have both read a draft of this book, and have taken trouble to tell us frankly, as few will do, what was wrong, or even right, in it. A great many of Sharp's friends have hunted out letters and in other ways helped to make these pages a truthful account.

A. H. FOX STRANGWAYS

LONDON,
Dec. 1933

CONTENTS

Contents

LIST OF ILLUSTRATIONS

xi

List of Illustrations

CHAPTER I

1859–1891

BOYHOOD AND EARLY MANHOOD

> I travelled among unknown men,
> In lands beyond the sea;
> Nor, England! did I know till then
> What love I bore to thee.
>
> W. WORDSWORTH.

CECIL JAMES SHARP was born on St. Cecilia's Day, November 22nd, 1859, at Denmark Hill, and died on Midsummer Eve, June 23rd, 1924, at 4 Maresfield Gardens, Hampstead.[1]

His father, James,[2] was born in 1827, and died on November 1st, 1903. He was a slate-merchant in Tooley Street, and retired from business before he was fifty; whether because, as he said, slates had come to be replaced by tiles, or because, as he probably thought, neither of them quite supplied all he expected of life, is not clear. He had a taste for old furniture, glass, and coins; for archaeology, especially when it led him to visit famous spots; for architecture, and, in particular, for cathedrals, to which he often took Cecil, who kept up the practice, after his father's death, with friends; and he loved the oratorios of Handel and operas of Mozart, which his wife played to him. Having entered business unexpectedly on the death of an elder brother, he had had little regular education; he gained from his business relations a quiet tolerance and a sense of humour. Cecil loved and admired him; he spoke of him in his later letters as 'the General'.

James Sharp married Jane Bloyd, the youngest daughter of Joseph Bloyd, a lead-merchant in the City. Joseph

---

[1] For his age at different dates it is convenient to remember that he was forty years old at the turn of the century.

[2] A medallion of him is shown in Evelyn Sharp's *Unfinished Adventure*.

Bloyd was a Welshman, and his wife, Elizabeth Angell, was of Italian extraction. Cecil's mother, tall, of fine carriage, with Italian features and lovely hands as she spread them on the keyboard, seemed to have the secret of youth up till her death at ninety. She loved music, as was natural, since in her Wales and Italy met; and it was the one taste she shared with her husband throughout a happy married life. She was a graceful hostess and fond of society. She died on February 12th, 1915.

Cecil was the third child and eldest son; he had four brothers and four sisters, and there were two boys who died as babies. Llewellyn (Lewen), the brother who came next to him, was an architect in good practice. He built some attractive houses in Brook Green, and the Apollo Theatre, recently reconstructed. He took pains with what he did, and was pleasant company. He reviewed and rejected, in his capacity of Chairman of the Fire Brigade Committee of the London County Council, a great number of sound-producers, before he selected the bell now in use on the London fire-engines. He died in October, 1914.

In this large family, the father's pride, there was an elder and a younger group, and between them Lewen was a kind of *liaison* officer. To the elder group belonged Mabel, who helped her mother with the younger ones, and Ethel (Mrs. Malcolm McCall), who was often, with Cecil, at the pianoforte; when they played at 'Church', for instance, Mabel said prayers, Ethel played 'the organ', and Cecil wrote and preached the sermon for the junior congregation. Cecil could also be naughty; he refused boiled mutton, one day, and sulked upstairs. When the mutton followed him, he still refused, and declared that when he grew up and had children, they should never be made to eat what they did not like—a vow he kept.

His youngest sister, Evelyn (Mrs. H. W. Nevinson), has made fame by her writing. She is the friend of the ugly duckling. As she walks—in 'Nicolette', or 'Who was Jane', or 'Wymps'—through the tangle of life, she instinctively turns up the stones to see how the wood-lice are getting on, or stoops to put the caterpillar back on his cool leaf, without missing the quarter of an hour of sunset that lights up the hill. She knows her slums, and without any illusions believes in them, in their promise, and their lack of promise. She writes words which are deeds she has been a part of. Her message is that of her brother Cecil: he was only working in a different medium. It is, on the whole, that there are a good many things and people about us every day that we could understand if we would try.

Cecil went to school when he was 'rising eight' at Miss Bennett's, Lansdowne House, Brighton. Two letters of his are printed here exactly as he wrote them.

October 4th 1867

My dear Mama

I felt rather lonely the first day but now I am very happy indeed. I had a piece of my cake for my luncheon and I gave a piece to each of the boys and they said they had never tasted such a nice one   All my things they like much better than theirs send my best love to believe me your affectionate son

Cecil James Sharp

(Undated and unsigned; probably enclosed with the preceding letter.)

My dear Ethel

I wish you many happy returns of the day. Tell Mamma I am very happy A boy has just come for some string I must go and give him some all the boys come and crowd round me for string and they say Sharp or new fellow give me some of your nice useful string will you and I say yes of course. I regocnised Goss directly I saw him I do like him so and I like Authur Pitman I am so fond of him I send you this little Mother of pearl knife. I thank you very much for your kind letter   Believe me

Thus to his mother and sister at eight years old; and thus to his son, at fifty-eight:

I am glad you are going to Brighton, which at this time of year

[April] ought to be very jolly—though ordinarily I hate the place. I have pleasant memories because my parents, being then in the fashion, usually spent Oct.–Dec. there, and took me out 3 or 4 times a week from the dame's school where I suffered an ignoble existence for two years—108 Lansdowne Place, by the way, was its beastly address. Look it up, and throw a stone through the window if it is still a school!

He was a nervous boy. He had a constant fear of spilling ink, because the penalty was to take a dirty rag out of a dark cupboard to wipe it up. One day the penalty was incurred and his terror was doubled by his finding a beetle in the rag. And he was a sensitive boy. An early and vivid recollection was the sound of a brass band in the street when he was in bed; in his ecstasy he wept. He had also, through life, a physical dread of noises: railway whistles made him jump, loud voices left him irritable.

Cecil's musical predilections, inherited from his mother, fostered by his sister Ethel, and encouraged by his father, had probably already secured recognition; it is possible also that he was regarded as not being very strong. At any rate he was sent to Uppingham, which Edward Thring had now made, from insignificance, into one of the healthiest and best-equipped schools of England; and it was the only school where music, under Paul David, was taken seriously. He entered the lower school in 1869 and the upper in 1872. He left, probably on account of weak health, in 1874. Nothing is now known of his school career beyond a dubious hint of his taking a solo at some concert. A tablet in the Chapel commemorates 'the Writer and Musician, Collector of English Folk Songs'.

The Heppel family, old friends of Cecil's father and mother, lived in Tooley Street. Through them Mr. Sharp came to know of a Mr. George Heppel, of Highfield, Weston-super-Mare, who had a coaching establishment for the Army and University. Cecil was sent there on May 18th, 1874; he passed the Cambridge local, and was then prepared for the University; Mr. Heppel thought well of his mathematics. He became intimate with the family during one holiday when he was laid up with a broken collar-bone, and this intimacy led to a good deal of concerted music-making and private theatricals. To the music-making came Constance Birch, the second daughter of a neighbouring family, who becomes later on of importance to this history. She was a tall and beautiful girl with brown, wavy hair, and, behind some unfortunate glasses, brown eyes: she could sketch successfully, sing, and play the violin. In the theatricals Cecil acted Antonio (*Merchant of Venice*), Nick Bottom, and Sarah Gamp; and in the intervals distinguished himself as handy man. We hear also of a bout of hay-fever, the precursor of the asthma that plagued him to the end.

After a few years at Weston he was sent to the Rev. J. T. Sanderson at Royston to be regularly coached for Cambridge. He entered at Clare College in October 1879, where he read mathematics. He was secretary of the debating society; although he did not find speaking easy, he used to propose annually 'that the House of Lords be abolished', but got no support. He rowed in the second and the first Clare boat; the record is given below.[1]

Looking back (14.4.24) on those days, he said:

Rowing was a great pleasure to me at Cambridge, though I did not get further than my first College eight, then eighth on the river.

Part of his enjoyment was expressed in limericks. He wrote one on each member of the crew; to which T. R.

[1] Dec. 1880. Stroked one of the College trial eights to victory. From the Captain's book:—Sharp (stroke). Capital worker, 2nd year man. Rowed in last year's 2nd. About the best man in trials: very keen.
Lent 1881. 2nd boat. Sharp (11 st. 10) started at No. 5, raced as No. 7. They made a bump. Captain's comment:—Works hard, but a bad seven; fair at five or three; better on stroke side.
May 1881. 1st boat. Sharp No. 3. They were bumped twice. Comment:—No. 3 was useless after Grassy.
(N.B. It does not mean, as two who have read it have thought, that there was a falling off.)

5

Wardale, afterwards Tutor, replied on their behalf with one quite as opprobrious, and honours were easy.

His life there is described in a communication from Henry J. Ford, the painter.

We got to know each other at Clare as freshmen of the same standing. Sharp at once became a leader of the musical men: I was *not* musical, though I liked to listen well enough. We had three good musicians in that year: Cecil, Fred T. MacDonnell—a really fine dramatic baritone and *musical* (horrid word!) to the core, as any one could see—and Fred Bagnall who possessed a very sweet high tenor voice and sang with it like a bird. Sharp could sing a little, and could play the pianoforte well enough to accompany adequately. I don't think he was at all a real pianist, though very useful: but his enthusiasm and high idealism and knowledge of music were, I fancy, unquestioned by those who knew.[1]

He at once became an important figure in our college society. His good humour was unfailing, also his high spirits and love of good company. He seemed a bit older in mind than those of us who were fresh from school. He had left Uppingham for a year or so before coming up,[2] and had had more opportunities of seeing life. He was almost as enthusiastic about his mathematics as about Wagner, the new and enormous star on the heavens of music. Much did he discourse on these subjects, of which I lay in wondering and somewhat contemptuous ignorance.

He worked harder at his music than at his mathematics. He got up concerts with MacDonnell, W. H. Wing, Bagnall, and Oliver Puckridge—people's concerts, I think they were—and he gave, among other things, a performance on the ocarina; and another on a row of bits of glass which you hit with a hammer (an instrument which, as far as I am concerned, has no name, neither does it deserve one).[3] He got tremendous encores for a spirited if barbaric performance.

---

[1] He had rooms out of College, in Tennis Court Road, so as to be able to make as much music as he liked.   [2] Five years.

[3] A few years later he made a xylophone himself, cutting the wood from the trees in his father's garden. This instrument made its appearance afterwards for the music of the 'tongs and bones' in Granville Barker's production of *A Midsummer-Night's Dream* (1914). He also taught himself the banjo when convalescing from typhoid, and, later on, the pipe and tabor.

We differed somewhat in religion and politics: he, a Freethinker in the early days and a Radical; I, a wavering Christian and uncertain Conservative, much shaken up, I remember, by *Alton Locke* in politics, and by *Religion and Dogma* when it came to religion. In after years he returned to the bosom of the Church. Talking our old talk over, I asked how it was that he had so changed, and he had the effrontery to say that it was such Christians, professing ones, as I that drove him into the hostile camp. Of course that was nonsense and only an attempt to score off me. The thing that brought him back to Christianity (though in fact he was, of course, always the best of Christians in the broad and human sense) was, he told me, seeing a young parson in Australia sitting on a fence telling fairy stories to a lot of children.

The fact is, Sharp was a happy, emotional creature, and he was never afraid of obeying the call of his emotions. He was excitable and warm-hearted, and a strong, full-blooded man, full of kind thoughts about others, and eager to enjoy, and help others to enjoy, everything in life that is enjoyable.

Sharp went all out for everything that interested him, was eager, argumentative, a fighter, but always a jovial good fellow. He used to sing a comic song—'The Emu': words by Bret Harte:

> Where's that specimen pin
> Which I gaily did win
> In raffle, and gave unto you—
> Not a word said the guilty Emu.

to a tune of his own.

He had, as you know, a handsomely Roman nose, somewhat ruddy in tone, and it became a commonplace to speak of him— 'Punch' was his nickname—as 'rubescing', when he grew warm in argument—which happened often. A very vital personality in our little world; a foretaste of what he became afterwards in everybody's big world.

But his views seemed to me to be founded not on the deeps, but on the shallows—netted with sun and shade, and showing bright fish darting about and lovely weeds and flashing dragon-flies—of passion and human sympathies and antipathies. However I doubt whether this is worth remarking, as it is the same with us all, at least all of us who are at all nice to be with.

7

After Henry Ford, one of his best friends was W. H. Wing, the possessor of a baritone voice with a real ring in it, knowledgeable about music, a coiner of the happy phrase, and one who left a room merrier than he found it. In after years he used to sing in an informal, open-hearted way, which just suited Sharp's views, in illustration of his lectures. Another friend was Sir Owen Seaman of *Punch*. Another was Edward D. Rendall, who conducted the 'Concordia' (men's voices) at Trinity, to which Stanford lent his help: Sharp was among the first tenors. Rendall was the composer of a setting of 'The Compleat Angler' and other pleasing and sincere music; he had charge of the music at Dulwich College and subsequently at Charterhouse. There was also a deaf friend for whose sake Sharp learned finger-language, in which he conversed with rapidity, and even devised improvements on the usual form. Another friend at this period was Dr. James Kingston Barton; Sharp, together with George Bernard Shaw, Charles Hayden Coffin, and others, was a constant visitor at his musical 'At Homes' in South Kensington.

When Sharp came down from Cambridge in 1882 his father seems to have told him that he must seek his own fortune, and that it would be best to try the colonies, probably Australia. Sharp's own account is given by Henry Ford:

> He said he knew nothing at the time of his departure about the geography of Australia, so he took a map and saw the name of Adelaide. That set him thinking of his adored Beethoven song, 'Adelaïde', and this was ample reason to our 'Punch' to decide on his future habitat. Such his merry, happy-go-lucky nature!

His father gave him his ticket and £10 or £20, and he sailed in October. He found chess useful as an escape from the gambling, drink, and quarrelling on board, and made a good many friends. He fell in with a wise man who advised him when he got out to take any job that came his way, and tell his employer that he knew how to do it. So when he landed the first job he took was washing hansom-cabs in a mews in Adelaide. He watched some man washing the wheels and spinning them, and apparently the important thing to do was to hiss loudly. There was no difficulty about that, he thought, for an experienced player of the ocarina, so he answered an advertisement and took the post.

Sharp reached Adelaide in November 1882, and early in 1883 he had found an occupation as a clerk in the Commercial Bank of South Australia. The typewriter was then new to banking circles, and this bank was the first to use it in Adelaide; Sharp worked it, though imperfectly, it is said. He also taught the violin. One of his colleagues wanted to learn it, and Sharp, to whom a fee would have been useful just then, after telling him to spread out his hands on the desk, said: 'Look, boy, go out and buy a small hammer and play on an anvil; that's all the music you have in you.'

From the bank he read with C. C. Kingston, and he assimilated enough legal knowledge to become in April 1884 Associate to Sir Samuel James Way, Bart., Chief Justice of South Australia (1876–1916) and Clerk of Arraigns. This position of Associate offers a special opportunity to those who wish to rise at the Bar; they hear not only the cases and decisions, but day to day comments on the pleadings and criticism of the pleaders. There was a brief period when Sharp thought of entering the South Australian Bar. Sir Samuel was a brilliant lawyer and a hard worker. He had an exceptionally large acquaintance among men and women. The social duties which devolved upon Sharp, though congenial, were heavy, and when he had in consequence to throw up his own personal engagements at short notice the situation became difficult, and he resigned in February 1889 and devoted himself entirely to music.

Sharp had in his pocket when he landed an introduction

9

to Arthur Boult, organist of St. Peter's Cathedral, Adelaide. He set to work to practise and before long was installed as assistant organist. He found congenial company among the music-loving members of the German colony, and in 1883 he was acting as Honorary Director of the Adelaide String Quartet Club, to which he appointed Herr Immanuel Gottfried Reimann as pianist. He early became known to all the musical people in Adelaide, including the Governors, first Sir W. C. F. Robinson (1883–9), and afterwards the Earl of Kintore. He conducted the Government House Choral Society and the Cathedral Choral Society, for whom he wrote some Nursery Rhymes that people liked; later on he took charge of the Adelaide Philharmonic Choir, who gave him a watch to keep time and a stick to beat it with in memory of them when he left finally in 1891.

He gained many private pupils for pianoforte, singing, theory, and composition; and in January 1889 he entered into partnership with Herr Reimann as joint Director of the Adelaide College of Music, Reimann contributing the capital and Sharp the connexion. He is described as 'a born leader in music'; within ten months of his joining the College the attendance was doubled, and his lectures and lessons are spoken of enthusiastically. An old pupil writes:

> In a short time he had sixty pupils. We all adored him; we were usually spoken of as 'the sixty love-sick maidens'. . . . I learned a great deal more from him than singing. . . . The change from a certain silly old German who made love to all his pupils was refreshing.

His stay in Australia was interrupted by two visits to England. The first was in 1886 after a serious attack of typhoid which left him paralysed in both legs. He found his parents in their new home, an old manor-house at Weston Turville. The doctors were not encouraging; but Sharp forced himself to take a daily walk in the drive, gradually increasing it in length, and cured himself. He wanted to stay in England and educate himself seriously in music, but could find no employment, so he returned with reluctance to Australia. And the second visit to England was from January to March 1891. During that short time, as before, he tried in vain to get his musical compositions published.

Soon after his second return to Adelaide (March 1891) the partnership between him and Herr Reimann was dissolved. The leading members of the Staff, Herr Vollmar and Herr Heinicke, threw in their lot with Herr Reimann, under whose sole direction the College was continued, becoming the Elder Conservatoire in 1898. Sharp was urged to stay on in the city and continue his musical profession, and an address containing over three hundred signatures, headed by that of the Bishop, expressed this desire of his friends, but he decided to return to England. He had no doubt that he could have made a career for himself in Adelaide, but he had 'not the heart to set to work and begin all over again'.

The letter which follows preserves the memory of the Adelaide days. The Duffields, Walter the father and Geoffrey the son (who organized the Solar Observatory), the Howards, and Guy Boothby were his great friends. Others were E. B. Grundy, a lawyer with whom he at one time shared rooms in Carrington Street, and Charles Marson, a clergyman, of whom we shall hear more.

W. Geoffrey Duffield to the Rt. Hon. H. A. L. Fisher, 17.8.25
(enclosing a donation to the Cecil Sharp House Fund)

Cecil Sharp was one of our oldest friends; we first knew him in Adelaide when he was a gay, debonair Judge's Associate—a role which those who knew him in later life in England will find it hard to realise that he had ever played. With Guy Boothby he wrote a comic opera[1] which as a boy I remember hearing. A few years ago I played over one of the airs from it and asked him to name the composer; he had forgotten his own child and ascribed it to Schumann. . . . He and I used to subscribe ourselves 'Brother

---

[1] This operetta, *Sylvia*, was performed at the Theatre Royal, Adelaide.

Musico'—I forget how it originated; I have never earned the title, unless playing wrong notes on the double-bass is a sufficient qualification.

The picture is filled in for us by a letter of Charles Marson's about 1890:

We had such a delightful evening at the Duffields: Sharp, Otto Fischer, and the D's, and the talk was of the merriest and the music of the best. A fierce argument about Carlyle and 'abstraction' carried us into metaphysic. Not a word of scandal all the evening. Fischer sang Schumann's 'Ich grolle nicht' and Sharp played one of his sonatas admirably; but he would not play 'anything great' as the piano was not good enough, he told our hostess, with such merry geniality that she could not be offended. . . . Cecil Sharp abhors Girton and Newnham and the 'mental loudness' they produce in girls. . . . He is a really good and enthusiastic man who is married to music and serves her with a knightly and unending service.

CHAPTER II

1892–1896

MUSIC AS A PROFESSION

La guerre ne vient-elle pas d'un manque d'union entre les hommes?
Et si tous les hommes apprenoient la musique, ne seroit-ce pas le
moyen de s'accorder ensemble, et de voir dans le monde la paix
universelle?—MOLIÈRE, *Bourgeois Gentilhomme*.

In January 1892 Sharp was back in England with no resources to speak of but with a considerable experience. For a few months he lived with his brother Lewen in Duke Street, Adelphi; in April he took rooms at 5 Langham Chambers (now Cavendish Mansions), Langham Street. It was there that his biographer first set eyes on him, in a roomy ground-floor studio, seated at a grand pianoforte under the skylight, harmonizing a song. Music talk began at once, and was incessant. One remembers chiefly a penetrating eye, a humorous curl of the lip, and a suavely modulated voice.[1]

[1] A recollection of Sharp's personal appearance at a later date is given by Mrs. May Elliot Hobbs:

'The first time I saw Cecil Sharp—in 1911—as he came into Mrs. Arthur Sidgwick's drawing-room, he gave me an impression which has never changed—the piercing blue eye, falcon-like, the strong nose, the firm set of the head on the shoulders, the superb carriage, which he retained even when more bent with increasing age. There was a controlled suppleness in the whole body, loosely knit without being wobbly, and this it was that made his dancing unique in its grace and ease. It might be summed up in two words—line and carriage.

'Two other pictures come before me. An early one of him seated at the piano in my room, pipe alternately in his mouth or on the music-stand, playing and singing shanties just collected in Somerset, the hands, with the slightly crooked little finger, looking the most unlikely "piano hands", and yet bringing out the value of every note, just as he wanted it; and every now and again he would turn his head towards us, seated round and on the floor, with that characteristic one-sided pursing of the mouth and twinkle in his eye which always heralded a joke.

'Another picture, much later, sitting rather crouched in his armchair by the fire, a brown Shetland shawl round his shoulders, the fine modelling of

13

To Mrs. Walter Howard.

Good Friday, 1892.

I spent this morning choosing wall-papers for my rooms. After settling on one that best suited my taste and my pocket I took it to my landlady, who after looking at it for a moment remarked, 'It's wonderfully ugly, isn't it?' A little abashed by this scathing criticism, I said, 'Well, it will look better with an apple-green frieze. This was too much for her, and I'm sure she thinks me mad. Afterwards she asked me to sign the agreement, and I was about to do so when I by chance discovered that she had made the rent £10 less than we had arranged. I pointed it out, but she did not seem to think much of it, because she said we both knew what it really ought to be. After that I warmed to her and forgave her remarks about the paper.

He was fond of society. In a letter about this time he remarks:

My tea-party went off very well. It was delightfully informal and friendly. I always introduce everybody to everybody else, and my muffins are *sans reproche*, which only happens in bachelor establishments.

He wanted this large room for his music lectures, in which he preached Wagner opera with as much fervour as most young musicians of his day, and with more knowledge than some of them; his voluble enthusiasm found willing hearers.

On his visits to his parents at Weston Turville he spent much time in playing the organ, and wrote anthems for the Church service and one for a friend's wedding. He had come home with the fixed intention of giving himself up to musical composition. His letters in this year (1892) are full of his hopes and fears.

The Musical went off very well on Saturday. Bispham sang my song *beautifully* and Shakespeare accompanied it ... before a critical company [including Fanny Davies and Leonard Borwick] ...

the head more apparent as the bones showed up in age—a real sculptor's head, the eyes still as compelling as ever, the whole frame becoming more and more but a shell for the still eager spirit, full of nervous energy, concentrated but never restless.'

... Miss M's criticism [of a sonata] was 'clever and beautiful, not adapted to the taste of the British public'. But I think people are wrong in thinking that the public are unable to appreciate anything but gutter garbage. ...

I think I may fairly claim a great success with Schott yesterday. He commended the sonata very highly, saying it was scholarly and yet full of melody.

Sharp wrote in all, as far as can be discovered, about a score of songs and a score of instrumental pieces between 1885 and 1900, when composition stopped with the suite of morris dances for strings, hautboy, and horn: the greater part of them were written after his return from Australia. They are modelled on Schumann, but they do not show that the gift of composing was his, or that he ever would by that means have revealed the artist that was in him. Some part-song arrangements of nursery-rhymes, a hymn, two pianoforte pieces, and two songs were published. His technique improved greatly as soon as he had, in the accompaniments of the folk-songs, a definite purpose in front of him. He had intended to take lessons in composition, to make up for lost time in Australia, but need forced him to give them instead in elementary harmony. His friend, Mrs. Walter Howard, shepherded pupils to him, beginning with herself and her sister-in-law.

To Mrs. Walter Howard.

17 March 1892.

I am still wandering round in search of work and building plans ceaselessly, as I am more than ever disposed to remain in England if I can make a living. I am sure that without doing so [i.e. living in England] I shall never improve much or satisfy in any way my ambition, but I am beginning to realise that it means a hard struggle.

He played the pianoforte at musical 'At Homes' and small concerts and often accompanied his friend, Duloup, a Dutch violinist. He writes in January 1893:

I am greedy for employment. Private pupils are so uncertain and they treat me so unceremoniously that I am anxious to get as much lecturing, etc. in schools as I possibly can. This is the only certain thing that I can see.

In addition to his lecturing he succeeded in getting the conductorship of various small choral societies. He writes (18.1.93) to Constance Birch:

I took my first practice of my Society at Bedford Park last night. It was fairly successful, but I shall soon get tired of these small Societies. I want something bigger. Everlasting glees become tiresome—they are so finicking.

And (26.1.93):

I am itching to get work which I know I am qualified to do, but people are so afraid of giving an unknown man a trial, and I am not a good hand at advertising myself.

Mr. C. J. Dale (father of Benjamin Dale, the composer), Chairman of the Finsbury Choral Association, was not afraid, and after Sharp had taken several practices and gone through protracted negotiations he was, in June 1893, appointed conductor. In his own words:

He [the Secretary] handed me a letter, an official announcement of my appointment, but they only offer me twenty guineas for the season, whereas the Secretary before told me £25. However, I expect they are anxious about finances—at any rate I said nothing.

In addition, he was appointed at Mr. Dale's invitation to the Staff of the Metropolitan College, Holloway, where he conducted the orchestra, lectured, and had private pupils. It seems that he made his choir work, and that they liked him for it. They did the standard Handel and Mendelssohn, the *Spectre's Bride*, and the *Damnation de Faust*, and he would comment with some directness on the several works. He showed a will of his own and no inclination to compromise; there was no uncertainty in his beat, and his rhythm was a strong point. He writes to Constance Birch (14.2.93):

They tell me I can be very caustic and that I don't encourage by flattery enough. I hate to be always smoothing people down to get

16

anything out of them, don't you? If I had the right sort under my stick, they would not want it.

He held the appointment for four years and the incident which led to his resignation in July 1897 is as follows.

Miss Muriel Foster wished to be released from her engagement to sing for the Finsbury Choral Association in the *Redemption* on March 25th, in order to accept one at the Albert Hall, which was held to be of importance to her career. Dr. (later Sir Hubert) Parry of the Royal College of Music, to which she belonged, held Sharp responsible for the refusal of her request, and before hearing the facts wrote him a violent letter. The Committee of the Association had in the meantime accepted responsibility, but Dr. Parry had not seen their letter. Their Chairman, Mr. Dale, asked him to withdraw his letter, but he refused. The Committee met, and, reflecting that Dr. Parry and two of his friends were on their Council, asked Sharp to let the matter drop. He thought it over and decided on May 22nd to resign instead. He published the letters, and the Committee, to save face, wrote another, which added nothing material. In a few years the Association broke up.

Any one who has read the voluminous *Life of Parry* by C. L. Graves knows that he was a man of generous impulses who would always rather cut a knot than untie it. Any one who knew Sharp knew a man of some steadfastness, to whom an engagement was sacrosanct, whether his own or another's. And any one who has served on a committee knows that the reason why 'corporations never die' is partly that they never truly live; because though they have, individually, sensitive feelings, they are never allowed to express them corporately. Meanwhile we may join in the eulogies of Miss Foster's behaviour under trying circumstances, and rejoice that the incident probably helped, rather than hindered, a distinguished career.

At the beginning of 1893 Sharp was appointed music-master at Ludgrove, a preparatory school—mainly for

17

Eton—and began with Mrs. Dunn (wife of Arthur Dunn, the head master[1]) and four boys as pupils. Sharp held the appointment until 1910. The number of pupils soon increased, and during the greater part of the eighteen years he taught either three or four days a week at the school, spending two or three nights away from home. Later on, when he lived at Hampstead, he used to cycle to New Barnet in all weathers, starting at 7 a.m., and it was a matter of pride to him that throughout the eighteen years he was never once late. Also he never lost his interest in the work or his temper with the boys, who were devoted to him. One of his pupils, chatting one day with Mr. Sharp on the cricket-field in his last term, said: 'You remember, sir, telling me my first term that you were a hundred? Well, I thought you were quite serious, and I believed it all these years.' Then, looking at him attentively, he added: 'Now I don't suppose for a moment you are a day older than seventy.' The Masters' Common Room liked him too: one says, 'Life together was such a jolly one'; another speaks of 'a breadth of outlook', which reminds us of Marson's 'not a word of scandal' on an earlier page. He liked to air his Radical views and 'pull the legs of the Tories', and his wild flights of rhetoric were (except once, when he voiced pro-Boer doctrines) taken in good part.

Early in January 1893 Sharp became engaged to Constance Dorothea Birch. The engagement brought him the greatest happiness. Something of what it meant to him is expressed in a letter to Constance in which he quotes his adored Wagner:

'The love of the strong for the strong is *Love*, for it is the free surrender to one who cannot compel us.' This expresses something of my meaning when I tell you I want you and myself each to preserve our individualities; for then is our love the true and voluntary

---

[1] After Mr. Dunn's death in 1902 the school was taken over by Mr. G. O. Smith in partnership with Messrs. W. J. Oakley and A. N. Brown.

18

surrender to each other without compulsion. Love which exacts
is no love worth the naming.

For a moment it looked as though Constance was unable
to breathe the air on these heights of idealism, and we find
Cecil holding out a hand to support her:

You are always 'wanting a sign', which is not a good thing. . . .
If you are continually cross-examining yourself . . . and are sifting
and analysing your many feelings and thoughts . . . which of their
very nature must of necessity be variable, you will for a certainty
sooner or later muddle yourself to such an extent that one moment
you can say 'Yes', and the next 'No', to your oft repeated questions.
Remember how by much thinking you can forget the face of your
dearest friend. It is just the same with feelings. Take their average;
don't analyse every passing phase. . . . Life must be taken *broadly*,
not minutely. The general trend of things is infinitely more important than their direction at any particular moment.

Then there was the question of religion. Of letters on
such a subject, intended for one eye alone, one hesitates
at printing more than a sentence or so. After words in the
strain of Faust's

> Wer darf ihn nennen?
> Und wer bekennen:
> Ich glaub' ihn?
> Wer empfinden
> Und sich unterwinden
> Zu sagen: ich glaub' ihn nicht?[1]

he goes on:

It is only in the way you put it and in the expressions you use
that I cannot quite agree. . . . I cannot conceive it possible that God
could have placed in me a mind and a conscience whose conclusions
—if honestly and industriously arrived at—it would be right of me
to ignore. This truth seems to me such a self-evident one that if
I did not believe it I should simply flounder and lose all my trust,
faith, and belief in this thing as in everything else. This is the main-
spring of my conduct in life; with its corollary, which is to train

[1] Who dare name Him? Who dare aver, 'I believe'? Who that has
feeling can presume to say, 'I believe not'?

myself to allow infinite latitude of variance in others without permitting myself to say, 'I am right and they are wrong.' All I will ever say is I *believe* I am right, and believe they are wrong.

This difficulty, as to how far their difference of view was an obstacle to marriage, was laid, as many other problems had been, before his friend Charles Marson, who at that time had a London slum-parish. Marson promised to write to Constance as a priest and not as Cecil's friend. He did not disclose to Cecil what his priestly advice would be, nor did Cecil inquire, but two days later he wrote to Constance:

I cannot write a note of music and I begin to fear that Marson was quite right, and that it is sheer happiness which has nipped the current of my thoughts.

On August 22nd, the marriage took place at Clevedon in Somerset, and is thus described by the Rev. C. L. Marson in a letter to his wife:

The event came off to-day. I rose up at 6.30, better of my diseases, and turned up at All Saints where the 'furniture' is very gorgeous, and the altar very decently draped. The old curate served, and after the Credo I whipped off the casula and went to the steps, blessed the happy pair and exhorted them, and so finished the mass and the signing. Then we drove all together to the 'Wilderness' and had a neat cold breakfast in the garden on a lawn amphitheatre hewn out of the rocks. Above us waved holm oaks and arbutuses, and round were beds of bright flowers, and pines, and overhead sailing white clouds—an ideal party some twenty strong. Then we chatted about, and pretty Evelyn told my fortune, and the father Sharp talked architecture. Then the bride came in neat grey and we drank their healths in champagne, and they drove away, and we walked off.

Their prospects were not dazzling. Sharp was reasonably sure of earning £350 a year and was hopeful of increasing this to £400, whilst his wife had about £100 a year of her own. Neither of them allowed finances to worry them. In discussing ways and means before their marriage, Cecil wrote:

20

Do not trouble your dear old head about the idea that working for money will injure my music. I am not likely to go money-grubbing mad. I think you would not like it any more than I should. There is that great comfort that we think and feel alike on all important things. I don't seem to have a shadow of fear that we shall ever quarrel over anything.

They never did quarrel, although they did not always think and feel alike. Mrs. Sharp's lot was not an easy one. Poverty, the ill health of herself and her family, and the depressions and enthusiasms of her husband—she bore whatever came her way without complaint, and if at times she was worried she did not let Cecil see it. Once when showing a case of jewellery to a friend she pointed to a gap where a bracelet had once lain, and said, 'That was measles'. Perhaps the greatest disappointment of her married life was that Cecil should have given up composing for the sake of folk-music. She was far from being unsympathetic towards his work, but regretted that it should be so all-engrossing: she accepted its value from Cecil's estimation rather than from her own conviction. She lived until January 1928, surviving her husband by three and a half years.

Their first child—Dorothea Margaret Iseult—was born in September 1894 at Clevedon, and shortly after her birth they took a house in Manor Gardens, Holloway, where they remained until 1896. Two years later came a son—Charles Tristan; and having thus paid his homage to Wagner, he called two more daughters Joan Audrey[1] and Susannah Angel Birch, respectively.

[1] To Joan on her twenty-first birthday:

July 31st 1919.
I thought this morning before I got up of this day twenty-one years ago. I have very vivid recollections of what you looked like when you made your appearance, which by the way was so badly timed that it robbed me of half my summer holiday. But in those days I was only collecting wild flowers, not songs and dances, so that time was not so important. You were a nice little thing from the beginning and went on steadily getting nicer as you grew older, and I hope it will be long before the process ceases!

Before Dorothea's birth Sharp and his wife lived in rooms in the neighbourhood of Langham Place, and there was a Box and Cox arrangement whereby his brother Lancelot took possession of the Langham Chambers studio at night-time and Cecil used it during the day for his lessons and musical lectures. There were also meetings to discuss philosophy, religion, politics, or art. Each form of new thought he tasted thoroughly; it possessed him while he was trying to understand it. For a year or two Christian Science held him, and for a short time spiritualism. He was a vegetarian for his health's sake, and though in words he chaffed other people with being 'carnivorous' as opposed to his own 'pure living', in deeds he was careful not to give trouble by his demands or discomfort by any implied criticism. The last thing he wished to do was to appear singular. He was at all times an ardent social reformer and a strong opponent of capital punishment. The following extracts written shortly before his marriage give some idea of his political views at that time:

To Constance Birch.
20.1.93.

The argument which never fails to rouse my ire is when people try to explain the seeming and indeed real injustice of present class distinctions and the misery resulting by calmly squatting on their haunches and muttering with a sham sigh, 'It is God's will'. When you corner people, this is their one resource, and I am sorry to say it is an argument that I have often heard from the lips of a sleek country parson when he has been preaching to the poor and miserable! We are utterly unlike all the lesser parts of creation in that we have wills, consciences, and abilities to order things, so are directly responsible if our laws produce suffering and injustice as they undoubtedly do. You may as well blame Providence for producing an epidemic of typhoid when it is through our carelessness that our drains are neglected.

5.3.93.

I don't feel *very* strongly about the question of Home Rule. . . . I always read the speeches of the Irish because they are orators, and

22

their remarks breathe human sympathy as well as logic—moreover, they are not puritanical and for ever protesting, which is the one thing I hate in the English and Scotch character. It is perhaps fine, but it is very ugly. The Irish have their faults, which, however, are too easily discernible to do much injury, and on the other hand they have art power, and are generous in their sympathies.

Sharp was probably at no time a keen Party man, although he supported the Liberals and afterwards the Labour party. He has described himself as a 'Conservative Socialist', and that will perhaps serve as well as any other label. Above all he disliked catchwords; he did his best to realize his concepts. He did not sympathize with the Women's Suffrage movement, but the definite opposition which he at one time felt and expressed was probably not so much to the principle of female suffrage as to the methods of the suffragettes. During the last years of his life he enjoyed political discussions with his son, who has formulated this general outline of his father's opinions.

The salient points of his political beliefs were, as well as I can remember: (1) that untrammelled private enterprise was leading us nowhere, and that collectivism in some form or other was essential; (2) that any form of collectivist government must also be democratic if it is to function properly; (3) that it was grossly unfair that there should be such a thing as a privileged class, and that it was of very doubtful utility in any case; (4) that the mob in the long run was nearly always right.

It was as a profession of this faith that he joined the Fabian Society in December 1900.

Sharp continued to read widely during his early married life and he amassed a large general library in addition to an extensive collection of music and books on music. He became immersed in Schopenhauer, was enthusiastic over Ibsen, and was a not uncritical admirer of Cardinal Newman.

Cardinal Manning was a pigmy by the side of Newman whom I reverence very much, despite his lack of balance between faith, or conscience—whichever you like to call it—and head. It is as bad, perhaps worse, for the conscience to rule the intelligence as vice versa.

In 1896 Sharp became Principal of the Hampstead Conservatoire, now turned into the Embassy Theatre. The owner was Mr. Arthur Blackwood, whom Sharp had met in Australia. He himself took no part in the teaching. He appointed Sharp on a salary of £100 a year and a house, for two and a half days' work a week, which in 1899 was increased to £150 and one-third profits. Sharp collected a first-rate Staff, including Edward D'Evry, Michael Hambourg, Medora Henson, Madame Fischer-Sobell, and Auguste Wilhelmj. He himself lectured, conducted, and took classes in theory and harmony, in addition to a few private pupils.

By 1904 the Principal and the owner were clearly no longer on good terms, the former complaining that his salary had been, and was then, in arrears. The more they investigated this matter the less they agreed. After a correspondence lasting over a year, in which there seems to have been some lack of generosity on one side and expressions of grievance on the other, Sharp resigned in July 1905. He received in December a letter of respect and thanks signed by Mr. Francis E. Colenso, the Chairman of a Committee representing those interested in the Conservatoire. This expressed 'a very prevailing sense of the admirable manner in which you have served the institution', with a list of the names of pupils, parents, professors, and other friends, and it was accompanied by a 'little memorial of the personal esteem and regard in which you are held'.

CHAPTER III

1899–1906

ENTER FOLK-SONG

What's midnight doubt before the dayspring's faith?

R. BROWNING.

THE close of the century (1899) was eventful, according to Sharp, for three things which had a great effect on his life. They were, as he shortly described them, 'asthma, Mattie Kay, and Headington'.

Asthma was a development of hay-fever, and he suffered from it for the rest of his life. At first the attacks came only at a certain period of the year, but gradually the disease became chronic, and except for a short time in America and in Switzerland he seldom knew what it was to draw a clear breath. It would not have been surprising if he had given up the fight and subsided into the life of an invalid; but he struggled on, a martyr though no saint. 'If I should be unfortunate enough to be ill for a long time before I die,' he once remarked, 'please announce my death as "after a long illness most impatiently borne".' Asthma was not his only trouble. We hear shortly after his marriage of severe attacks of fever with delirium, commonly supposed to be influenza, though said by one doctor to be 'something of a malarial nature with a tendency to congestion and pneumonia'. These attacks, usually followed by extreme weakness and exhaustion, recurred at frequent intervals over a period of a dozen years. In addition he suffered from a form of gout in the eyes, which caused irritation and great pain, and often blindness. Those who saw him at his work would not have suspected that he suffered so much, but one who lived with the family at that time speaks of his 'uncertain temper' caused by illness and says that 'when he was not in the mood there was but little talk at table'.

25

When Sharp was staying with some relations in Lancashire he heard at a concert in Walton-le-Dale an untrained contralto voice, and was sure of what he had found. It belonged to Mattie Kay, now Mrs. Algernon Lindo. So sure was he, that he acted immediately. Mattie Kay was living in surroundings in which a musical talent could hardly develop, and he at once made arrangements, with the help of friends, for her to come to London. He took her into his own home, among his children, and put her under Medora Henson for singing; she was given a scholarship at the Conservatoire. He had no ulterior motive in doing this; he merely thought it was a great pity that a voice of such quality, with such purity of diction and such an inexorable sense of rhythm, should miss the training which was its due. There is no sign of his having as yet thought of folk-song, in which she eventually made her name, and repaid him many times over by singing at his lectures from 1903 onwards for over ten years. The following letter, undated, but of that period, from the Hon. Neville Lytton to Sharp shows the effect of her song upon an audience; and this judgement stands by no means alone.

Miss Mattie Kay is a wonderful singer. I don't think I have ever heard a more perfect pronunciation. I suppose her coming from the North accounts to a certain extent for the beauty of her accent. But she pronounces some words in a way that I have never heard any one else pronounce them, notably the word 'milk' in 'It's dabbling in the dew makes the milkmaids fair'. English is nearly always sung abominably and said abominably by actors on the stage, especially in poetry. Miss Kay's English is very personal and very beautiful, and such miming as she does is natural and subtle and attractive.

Sharp and his family spent that Christmas (1899) with his wife's mother, who was then living at Sandfield Cottage, Headington, about a mile east of Oxford. On Boxing Day, as he was looking out of the window, upon the snow-

covered drive, a strange procession appeared: eight men
dressed in white, decorated with ribbons, with pads of
small latten-bells strapped to their shins, carrying coloured
sticks and white handkerchiefs; accompanying them was
a concertina-player and a man dressed as a 'Fool'. Six of
the men formed up in front of the house in two lines of
three; the concertina-player struck up an invigorating
tune, the like of which Sharp had never heard before; the
men jumped high into the air, then danced with springs
and capers, waving and swinging the handkerchiefs which
they held, one in each hand, while the bells marked the
rhythm of the step. The dance was the now well-known
morris dance, 'Laudnum Bunches', a title which decidedly
belies its character. Then, dropping their handkerchiefs
and each taking a stick, they went through the ritual
of Bean Setting. This was followed by 'Constant Billy'
('Cease your Funning' of the *Beggar's Opera*), 'Blue-eyed
Stranger', and 'Rigs o' Marlow'. Sharp watched and
listened spellbound. He felt that a new world of beauty
had been revealed to him. He had not been well; his
eyes had been giving him pain, and he was still wearing a
shade over them, but all his ills were forgotten in his excitement. He plied the men eagerly with questions. They
apologized for being out at Christmas; they knew that Whit-
sun was the proper time, but work was slack and they
thought there would be no harm in earning an honest penny.
The concertina-player was Mr. William Kimber, junior, a
young man of twenty-seven, whose fame as a dancer has
now spread all over England. Sharp noted the five tunes
from him next day, and later on many more.

In telling the story of the folk-music revival Sharp
always spoke of this Headington incident as the turning-
point of his life. The seed was there sown, but it was to
take time to germinate. In point of fact he made no
immediate use of his discovery; beyond harmonizing and
orchestrating the tunes he did not see what to do with

them. He had, indeed, been feeling for some time past at Hampstead, and still more at Ludgrove, where the question of what to give boys to sing faced him every day, that the ordinary musical education, based on music of German origin, did not supply all that English boys needed; but he had no inkling that he held in his hand the solution of the difficulty.

In his need he turned to the folk-song collections made by other people, to Chappell's *Popular Music of the Olden Time* and other sources (for he had as yet collected no folk-songs himself), and out of these compiled *A Book of British Song for Home and School*, which was published in 1902, and dedicated to Arthur Tempest Blakiston Dunn, head master of Ludgrove. Out of his seventy-eight songs (sixty-six English) there is a fair sprinkling of genuine folk-songs, some of them modal; but he harmonizes them as in a key, with only a hint here and there that he knows a better way. He calls them all 'traditional', as his predecessors had called them, in the sense of *volkstümlich* and *populaire*; but his claim that the songs 'being chiefly of folk-origin are of assured humanity', and his note that Chappell had 'worked mainly among books and had made no serious effort to gather together the innumerable song and dance tunes that are still to be heard in country places' mark the effect that the Headington experience had had on him.

The book was useful. This was the first time that folk-song had, so far as he knew, been used in a class-room, and it clearly achieved its purpose there. But he realized, as he worked at the songs, the difference between the book form, as modified in the editing, and the unmodified form as transcribed by recent collectors, such as Miss Lucy Broadwood; and he determined to hear for himself the actual singing of folk-song. How should he set about that? He bethought himself of Charles Marson in his rectory at Hambridge in Somerset, to whom, since he took an important part with Sharp in the collection of the songs and was in himself a very vital person, the reader must now be introduced.

It was at Adelaide about 1889 that Sharp first met Charles Latimer Marson, who was a year older than himself. Marson was curate of Glenelg, a watering-place five miles to the south, and afterwards of St. Oswald, in the capital. He was rather a thorn in the side of his colonial bishop, to whom it was possibly a relief when in 1892 he left Australia to take up a curacy in Soho. Sharp left Adelaide that same year; when subsequently the bishop had followed and was appointed to the See of Bath and Wells, Sharp, who met him somewhere at dinner, rather gleefully told him that Marson, who meanwhile had become perpetual curate of Hambridge, three miles north of Langport, was in his diocese.

The kind of thorn he was may be gathered from an incident or two. When the bishop came to Hambridge on his diocesan visitation, Marson, after placing him (on the warrant of Mark ii. 16, 17) next to the landlord of the public-house, presented to him after luncheon his report, in which he described his parish as 'forward at the public-house but backward at Mass'. The bishop said he had nothing to object to in the report except, possibly, some of the nomenclature. This 'nomenclature' puzzled the parishioners, and Marson explained it to them; to the caretakers of the church he said it meant the holes and corners which were not properly swept; to the organist, that the bishop had noticed that the choir was singing flat; and so on. Again at a diocesan conference Dr. Warre of Eton had been insisting with general approval on the need for gentlemen as ordinands. This atmosphere was rent asunder by Marson's speech.

The playing-fields of Eton have a large place in our history. It is there that most of our battles have been lost. But what the Church requires is bounders like Peter and Paul.

Major ——— then got up and protested strongly against these aspersions on H.M.'s forces, and hoped that his lordship would effectually rebuke such remarks from one of his minor clerics. The bishop with suitable gravity replied that he did not think Mr. Marson's remark likely to damage the reputation either of H.M.'s forces or of his old school; and Marson blandly added that such remarks should rather tend to their reform.

On one of the rare occasions when Sharp discussed religion, he said that he was converted from indifference to Christianity by finding a parson on a gate telling fairy-tales to children.[1] This can only have been Marson. His first book, *Faery Stories*, published at Adelaide and evidently written for Australian children, shows a fertile imagination like Kingsley's, but with a simpler and more poetic style. He was a voluminous writer on Christian Socialism. He wrote (1894) for Adrian Reid's *Vox Clamantium* (for which Tom Mann also wrote), showing how the early Fathers one after another inculcated communism. *Charity Organization and Jesus Christ* is a thorough-going plea for unquestioning, unstinted giving, and a protest against inquiry and discrimination. He proposes as a motto for the Society, George Herbert's

> Only a sweet and virtuous soul
> Like seasoned timber—*never gives.*

and says that 'its theories become in the hands of meaner men than Mr. Loch the gospel of the buttoned pocket'.

For the way he put these views in practice Marson was beloved by his parishioners; and the love he felt for them, and the knowledge he had of them, may be read in his *Village Silhouettes* (1914). In it he tells of John Moore, the village musician; of how he played for singers and dancers on his battered fiddle that had its back patched up with two metal plates; and how from being in the choir he was promoted in time to first fiddle, and took

---

[1] See p. 7.

part now and then in a chorus of Handel. One day the parson brought a dashing young fiddler to see him, and this young man rattled off Cherubini[1] at him till old John hid his face in his hands, and shook with confusion and fear—'Music of that sort . . .', he began, but could not go on. Presently he suggested that they should play some of his old music together—'but your fiddle is tuned too high; could you lower it?' The visitor protested that if he did it would take three weeks to get over the deadness that would ensue. Old John, on the other hand, wouldn't raise his from the pitch at which he had kept it 'for three score years and ten without any variableness'. So, regardless of the suffering they inflicted on themselves and others, they played the piece through a semitone out.

It was with this alert imagination, sincere conviction, and Christian charity that Sharp was in contact for seventeen years off and on, and it is clear that the friendship meant a great deal to him; for the motive force behind his labours for song and dance was the rooted feeling that in them, too, a musician might hope to blend imagination, sincerity, and charity.

Sharp went to Hambridge in September 1903. The first songs he collected filled a volume of the *Journal of the Folk-Song Society* (vol. ii, no. 6); they date from September 1903 to August 1904 and are, of course, without accompaniment. In that year, and the two following years (1904–6), the first three volumes of *Folk-Songs from Somerset*, the joint work of Marson and Sharp, appeared with accompaniment; from the remaining two volumes Marson's name was omitted, for the seventeen years' friendship came to an end in November 1906. The joint authorship of the book had proved trying to both in a number of ways; they had not been able to meet much, and corre-

[1] Cherubini wrote very little for the fiddle and nothing that John Moore was at all likely to have seen, or that was in the least suitable. Marson no doubt knew this: he was seldom wrong about a fact.

spondence had led to misunderstanding over other matters besides the book. The actual occasion of the severance was a well-intentioned but indiscreet move on Sharp's part. The breach was irreparable. Sharp to Marson (9.11.06): 'There have, probably, been mistakes on both sides: our tempers are too individual and autocratic for us to run smoothly in harness.' They decided to play the rest of the piece—the remaining seven years of Marson's life—'a semitone out'. Sharp went to the funeral at Hambridge early in 1914.

CHAPTER IV

1903

FOLK-SONG COLLECTING

I have read books enough and observed and conversed with enough
of eminent and splendidly cultivated minds, too, in my time; but I
assure you, I have heard higher sentiments from the lips of poor un-
educated men and women, when exerting the spirit of severe yet gentle
heroism under difficulties and afflictions, or speaking their simple
thoughts as to circumstances in the lot of friends and neighbours, than
I ever yet met with out of the pages of the Bible.—WALTER SCOTT.

IT was natural that Sharp should first look to Hambridge
as a possible hunting-ground for songs. Marson was
sceptical; however, as he afterwards confessed (in the
Preface of *Folk-Songs from Somerset*, 1st series):

The folk-song is like the duck-billed platypus in this particular,
you can live for years within a few yards of it and never suspect its
existence. . . . Eight years of constant residence in the small village
of Hambridge in Somerset had left him [the writer] in Stygian
ignorance of the wealth of art which that village contained. . . .
Only one song, and that by chance, had fallen on his untouched ears.

That song was 'The Seeds of Love', placed first in the
book, and the singer was his gardener, John England.

And it was 'The Seeds of Love' that was Sharp's introduction to the live folk-song. He was sitting in the garden
talking to Mattie Kay, and John England was singing
quietly to himself as he mowed the lawn. Sharp whipped
out his note-book, took down the tune, and afterwards
persuaded John to give him the words. He went off and
harmonized the song, and that same evening it was sung
at a choir supper by Mattie Kay, Sharp accompanying.
The audience was delighted; as one said, it was the first
time that the song had been put into evening-dress. John
was proud, but doubtful about the 'evening-dress'; there
had been no piano to *his* song.

33

Marson and Sharp noted on that occasion forty songs in and around Hambridge, over half that number coming from the sisters, Louie Hooper and Lucy White. These two alone provided eventually over a hundred songs for Sharp's note-books.

The Christmas holidays (1903–4) were divided between Hambridge and North Devon, where he stayed with the Rev. Alex. de Gex; and in the Easter holidays he explored the Mendips, going there on the invitation of Mr. William Kettlewell of Harptree Court. For the first three years his researches were practically confined to Somerset, with an occasional short excursion to Devon, and because of the large number of songs that were collected there it is often supposed that Somerset must have been a richer field than other counties. There is not much in that; he would probably have had equally good results in any other county. He was drawn to Somerset by his connexion with Marson and stuck to it because from its rural character it seemed to promise well; but variants of the same songs are to be found elsewhere.

About his collecting experiences he has written a good deal; a few instances must suffice here. The scene would be, perhaps, the village inn, midday, with a dozen men and women resting drowsily. His request for milk and biscuits would lead—or he would lead it—to a mild argument on the comparative merits of milk and cider. A woman entered with a basket of fruit and eggs. Where did they come from? Where was she going?

Presently—'I, too, am going to market, but to buy not to sell: the fact is I have a great fancy for the old-fashioned songs. Perhaps you can tell me of a singer I could get one or two from.' Silence! 'Or there may be some one in this room. . . . You (to an old man) look like a singer.' The old man didn't deny this, but said he hadn't 'tuned a zong' this many a long day, and he didn't suppose he could 'zay a zong right through, even if I gave him a quart of zider'.

I took the hint, ordered the cider, and returned to the assault. 'Did you ever hear sing "John Barleycorn"?' I asked. 'I've a'eered 'un, but I never used to zing he,' was the reply. I then turned round to the rest of the company and suggested that one of them could remember the song. They all knew the song, but no one would venture to sing it. I explained that I only wanted one verse, as I knew all the words. Then up spoke an old man, who until now had been silent. 'If it's only the tune you do want, I can sing you the first verse, and that, I *h*reckon, will be enough.' And then, without further pressing, he broke forth into song. He had an extraordinarily beautiful voice, rich and resonant, and he held on to the last note of the refrain with consummate art, swelling it to a fortissimo, and then allowing it gradually to die away into silence. I saw at once that I had captured a fine tune. I called upon the landlord to fill up his mug, while I prevailed upon the old man to sing the verse once again, in order that I might write it down in my pocket-book. Having done this I sang the verse myself that he might see whether I had written it down correctly—much to the amazement of the company, and their amusement, too, I expect. Once again I made him repeat the verse, partly for my own pleasure —it was glorious to listen to him—and partly that I might revise my manuscript. He told me that he was a coal-miner, that he had heard the song when he was a boy, fifty or sixty years ago; that it was sung by a tramp who was passing through his village; that it had pleased his fancy, and that he had never forgotten it. . . .

. . . As a rule the singers in country inns sing modern songs only, or rather, the songs that were popular in mid-Victorian days, e.g. 'Woodman, spare that tree', or 'The 'Oodpecker'. Indeed, as a matter of fact, but a very small percentage of my collection has been recovered from tavern singers. . . . Of course, in the out-of-the-way districts—on the heights of Mendip, for example—I often take singers whom I have found in the fields into public-houses; for their homes are far off and there is nowhere else to go. But the majority of the songs have been taken in cottages, in barns, by the roadside, or in the open fields.

I once took down two excellent songs from a 'bird-starver'. It was his business to guard a patch of mangold seeds from being eaten by birds, and this he did by hammering a tea-tray. He was quite prepared to sing, but his conscience would not allow him to neglect his duty. So we arranged that he should hammer his tray between each verse of his songs, and thus combine business with pleasure; and we accomplished this to our mutual satisfaction and to the amusement of passers-by.

On another occasion I recovered a good song from the proprietor of a cocoa-nut pitch at Cheddar Cliffs, when business was slack; and I have many times sat by the side of stone-breakers on the wayside and taken down songs—at the risk, too, of my eyesight, for the occupation and the song are very often inseparable.

One singer in Langport could only sing a song when she was ironing, while another woman in the same court sang best on washing-day! I remember an amusing incident which happened to me at the house of the latter. I was in her wash-house sitting on an inverted tub, note-book in hand, while my hostess officiated at the copper, singing the while. Several neighbours congregated at the door to watch the strange proceeding. In one of the intervals between the songs one of the women remarked, 'You be going to make a deal o' money out o' this, sir?' My embarrassment was relieved by the singer at the wash-tub, who came to my assistance and said, 'Oh! it's only 'is 'obby.' 'Ah! well,' commented the first speaker, 'we do all 'ave our vailin's.'

A woman who had a great reputation as a singer lived in a mean street, which was inhabited—so he was told— by 'bad people'. She was out when he first called upon her, but was said to be at the public-house round the corner. As he approached the public-house he saw a group of women standing outside and chatting. 'Is Mrs. Overd here?' he asked. 'That's my name,' an elderly woman replied, 'and what do you want of me?' Sharp explained that he was hunting for old songs and hoped that she would sing him some; whereupon without any warning she flung her arms around his waist and danced him round and round with the utmost vigour, shouting, 'Lor, girls, here's my beau come at last.'[1] In the middle of this terpsichorean display Sharp heard a shocked exclamation,

[1] A quotation from 'Sweet Kitty', one of her own songs:
'He rode round her six times, but never did know,
Though she smiled in his face and said: There goes my Beau.'

36

'But surely that is Mr. Sharp,' and looking round he saw the vicar, with whom he was staying, and the vicar's daughter, both gazing with horror on the scene. When asked what he did, Sharp said: 'Oh, I shouted to them to go away—and they went.'

More than once it happened that Sharp would be sitting quietly with an old couple listening with enjoyment when the peaceful atmosphere would be disturbed by the noisy entrance of the grandchildren, who would be shocked to find their grandparents singing their silly old songs to the gentleman, and would endeavour to reinstate the family reputation by turning on the gramophone with the latest musical-hall records; songs of which one old man said: 'Can't make no idea to it, no more than that chair; 'tis a gabble of noise with no meaning to it.'

Sometimes he suffered even worse than gramophone records. Hear him, of an old gypsy woman of eighty-three:

I called on Lucy one day . . . and found her hale and hearty, upright as a dart, and looking anything but her reputed age. This, of course, I told her; whereat she looked pleased and replied, 'I be old but of fair complexion,' using the last word in its Elizabethan and wider sense. A compliment is a good foundation to build upon, and we were soon chatting away in a most friendly fashion. 'And thee be vond of the music, do 'ee?' she said, and before I could stop her, she had impulsively jumped up and set a-going a small musical box that was fixed in a clock that stood on the mantel shelf. 'There now!' she said proudly as the instrument started on the first lap of the only tune it could play, 'The Blue Bells of Scotland'. I feigned admiration, but at the end of the twentieth repetition or so mildly suggested that we might stop the music and proceed with the singing. My heart sank when she informed me, 'You can't stop he,' and intimated that we should have to wait until it had exhausted itself, and that that would take a full fifteen minutes! But she said, 'Thee won't hearken to it when I do zing,' and forthwith started off singing at the top of her voice. The song was a good one, but I couldn't take it down; the Blue Bells in a different

37

key broke in at every pause. It was distracting. I caught up the box, wrapped it in a shawl, and deposited it in the next room. This was of no avail; the Scottish National Anthem pierced the woollen shawl as though it were of gossamer, while the lath and plaster partition, which separated the two rooms, seemed to give it added resonance. I felt I should go mad. Even Lucy began to show signs of weariness, for she presently suggested that we should take it upstairs and muffle it in her bed. Upstairs, accordingly, we crept, the old gypsy-woman leading the way up the ladder with the clock still playing its nauseating tune with unbroken energy. To bed it went, shawl and all, and pillow and bolster piled on the top. This put the musical box thoroughly on its mettle; for when we got downstairs the whole room was full of its music. And there we waited—there was nothing for it—until the fifteen minutes were up; a *mauvais quart d'heure*, if ever there was one! Even Lucy seemed depressed, for, with deep melancholy in her voice, she confided to me that she had bought it only a few days ago off a pedlar; adding wearily that if I cared to have it she would let it go at a reduction! . . . Then at last we set to work and I noted down several interesting songs. . . .

And then as I got up to go away the old gypsy offered to tell my fortune; I produced the customary piece of silver and off she went. I had crossed the water twice . . . I had an enemy; he was short and dark and cunning and was plotting to do me great harm, etc. etc. I eventually tore myself away, and as I shook hands at the door of her cottage she put her face close to mine, looking me deep in the eyes, and whispered, 'When you are in trouble, you do think of the old gypsy-woman; she can help you, for she's a *seventh* daughter!'

The Rev. W. Warren, at one time curate of Bridgwater, used to give hospitality to Sharp and often accompany him on his visits. He writes:

In his dealing with the old folk, Mr. Sharp exercised the most extraordinary tact and patience. . . . He had to try various tricks in the first place to catch them out into an acknowledgment that they knew anything about the songs. I have heard men who turned out to have an endless store most determinedly declare that they had never sung such a thing or ever heard any one do so. Mr. Sharp's constant practice with such men was to involve them in general conversation and then to ask them whether they had ever heard certain words, which he would repeat, perhaps wrongly; if they were any good this would be too much for them and they would hasten to correct him according to their version. The cat would then be out of the bag, and they would have to acknowledge that they had at least heard one song. Soon their suspicion would be carried away by their intense love of the song and his genuine sympathy with that love. I can remember a man in the Bridgwater workhouse, who was reported to be a singer, receiving us with the utmost coldness, but ending by placing a fatherly hand upon Mr. Sharp's thigh as he taught his pupil at his knee and addressing him as 'my dear'. And when we rose to take leave, he clung to Mr. Sharp's hand and shed tears, so great had been his pleasure in finding one who would listen to the songs he so loved, and actually take them down on paper.

Often he would overcome suspicion with the humour and ready wit of which he had a great store, and when, after many a joke and much laughter, he had convinced them that he was a jolly good fellow, they would open out their hearts to him.

During these days, he suffered terribly from gout in the eyes, and I have known him roll on the floor in pain, but he never let this stand in the way of his pursuit, and perhaps he owed his sympathetic manner to a large extent to this fact that he suffered so much himself.

Another incident has remained in the memory of one who heard Sharp tell it in a lecture over twenty years ago.

Cecil Sharp had heard that a song which he had not hitherto recorded was known in an out-of-the-way corner of England. Accordingly he rushed off to secure it. On arriving at the place he was told there was only one person who knew it and this was an aged woman. On arriving at her cottage he found she had gone out to work in the fields. After much difficulty he discovered her, engaged in gathering stones off the land. The day was bleak and there was a cutting wind; when the old woman heard Cecil Sharp's enquiry, she replied that she knew the song. 'Shall I sing it to you?', she said; and raising her old weather-worn face to his, taking the lapels of his coat in her hands, and closing her eyes, she sang 'The Lark in the Morn' in her quavering yet beautiful voice, while he rapidly made notes. When the song was finished, she gazed into his eyes in a sort of ecstasy, and, in perfect detachment from herself, exclaimed, 'Isn't it lovely!'

And in a letter to Sharp dictated by a Somerset singer we read:

I sometimes get an old line or refrain come into my head, and I think that's one of Granny's old songs, I wonder if Mr. Sharp has that; but it goes so quickly, and I have no one now to jot it down, I forget them again. I often feel thankful that you were led, Sir, to save some of the dear old ditties.

'Forty years agone,' said one, 'I'd a-zung 'un out o' sight.' But the songs had for the most part to be dug out of the recesses of their memories. 'When you come to me all to once I can't come at it,' said another, and the only way was to leave him 'to bide and stud'.

Sharp has often said that the peasant mind is as good as any one else's, but it moves more slowly, and he knew well how to adapt his pace to theirs. Though naturally of quick action and of conversational disposition, he would be content to sit in silence for long stretches of time puffing at his pipe and waiting for the clearing of the throat which indicates that the song is about to begin.

He gives instances of wonderful memories. There were the two sisters, Mrs. Louie Hooper and Mrs. Lucy White, from whom he noted over a hundred songs, and who would have given him three times as many had he wished to include composed songs. And an old man of eighty-two, who was appealed to for a Robin Hood ballad, was able to recall the tune and the complete ten verses of the song, which he had learned as a child of ten, although he had not sung it for over forty years.

The persistence, the accuracy, and the care with which Sharp noted the songs are shown by the two following letters. The first (21.7.07) is to his wife, from Minehead Vicarage, where he was staying with his friend, the

Rev. F. M. Etherington, 'as delightful a companion as man could have, witty and serious and most sympathetic'.

Yesterday after taking down many songs from old Parish, we went on to Simonsbath where I wrote to you. We had decided to make our way over the moor to Withypool and were just wheeling our cycles up the hill when Etherington gave a penny to a very dirty but picturesque little child who took it and ran to a small cart that was under a tree down a little lane, and gave it to his father—evidently a gypsy. So I went up to him and chatted, and broached the question of songs. No! *he* didn't sing but his wife did, but she was in a house close by trying to sell some crockery. We waited, gave him baccy and played with a second child, a baby tied up in the cart. It was a peaceful little scene, and he showed us his stove and the contrivances for making a tent in which they camped out every night—only using his van during the winter. Presently out came the wife, Betsy Holland, aged 26, a bright, dark-eyed woman. The baby cooed with delight directly she appeared. We attacked her about the songs which she had learned from her grandmother. A little persuasion and she sat down on a stone, gave her baby the breast, and then began a murder song[1] that was just fascinating. Talk of folk-singing! It was the finest and most characteristic bit of singing I had ever heard. Fiendishly difficult to take down, both words and music, but we eventually managed it! I cannot give you any idea what it was all like, but it was one of the most wonderful adventures I have ever had. I photo'ed the baby and her, and she is mad to have the picture and told me they were making their way down to Cornwall via Bideford and Barnstaple. They will be at Bideford on Saturday, and I shall, I know, find it hard to keep away!

He evidently found it impossible, for four days later he wrote from Meshaw Rectory to Mr. Etherington as follows:

Well! I got to Barnstaple yesterday at four and then biked slowly on to Bideford keeping my eyes open, but seeing nothing of our draggle-taggles. Then I searched the waste places round Bideford till dusk, but could find them not, nor could I hear news of them

[1] James McDonald (*Folk-Songs from Somerset,* 4th series).

from police, or other people, nor from the post-office where I enquired. To bed, therefore, rather despondent in an expensive and uncomfortable hostelry. . . . Then I made a plan of campaign and put it into execution this morning. I searched from 9 till noon, by which time I had got nearly five miles from Bideford. I then decided to give up chase, examined the map and took the road to Barnstaple, thinking perhaps they were still on the road. Directly I started, I found that the waste lands I had been examining extended along the road I was taking—a fact which I had not realized before. So I continued the search and there I found them!!!!

Tent up, three children (there was one asleep in the cart when we met them) rolling about in the grass, Betsy superintending the cooking over a large kettle, Henry eating a large dumpling with a pocket-knife. They received me quite quietly, both saying they were quite sure I would turn up! I stayed nearly an hour with them and they were perfectly delightful. She sang me three other songs which I noted down, but none comparable with the Simonsbath song. That she sang again to me, and I found I had noted it accurately, as I think it *can* be done in ordinary notation. I added a few lines in the words which she had left out when dictating to you. They said that 'They went off in a Scilly gold' meant, 'They went off in disguise'.

I enjoyed my visit to them immensely. . . .. They were very keen I should go and see her grandmother, aged 90, who still sings like a lark. They gave me a vague address in the neighbourhood of Honiton, 'Stafford Cottages'. Her name is Rebecca Holland. Rebecca may give me a different cadence to that tune: I have an idea it might end on A, not C, in which case it would be more regular; but I am not certain.

Rebecca was run to earth six weeks later, and although she had nearly forgotten the song she was able to sing enough to satisfy Sharp that it was cast in the Lydian mode—the only example of that mode he had found in English folk-song.[1]

[1] This song (F.S.f.S. No. 103) needs a note. Mr. Etherington says that in the Scilly Isles an annual mumming ceremony takes place in which one of the main features is the *disguising* of the participants by means of the

Another adventure with gypsies occurred one Christmas morning. He was noting songs by phonograph from a woman in a caravan, when suddenly she stopped singing and, turning deathly white, announced that she heard her husband approaching, and as he was of a jealous disposition she was afraid he would kill Mr. Sharp. Sharp did not want to be killed, and there was nothing for it but to present a bold face. Opening the caravan door, he shouted to the man: 'A happy Christmas to you. Stop a moment and listen. I've got your wife's voice in a box.' The man listened to the record of his wife's song and was so amazed and delighted that he forgot to kill him, and, instead, they became great friends.

In December 1922, Sharp wrote to a friend:

It has been a great rush this Christmas and I have croaked and wheezed in the streets buying Christmas presents for all and sundry. There are so many folk-singers and -dancers I should like to send presents to, but I can only pick out one or two, which is rather sad. Of course, I don't rob them as I should if I bought their old tables and chairs—but still I feel under a great obligation to them.

His obligations were fully paid, not only through the pleasure that he gave by his appreciation of the songs, but by his genuine friendship for the singers. The Rev. Dr. Allen Brockington, who was a great friend of Sharp's, writes (*London Mercury*, April 1928):

---

interchange of men's and women's clothing, and that this is called 'The Goose Dance'. Is 'goose' connected with (*a*) 'disguise', or (*b*) with 'guiser', a name used elsewhere in England for mummers' plays and for sword-dances? And (*c*) is 'gold' some corruption of this, or some independent Romany word?

As this is the only song yet recorded which is quite definitely in the Lydian mode, it is worth mention that the melody is almost certainly not English. With a tonic C and an F $\sharp$ it emphasizes strongly the notes E and A, and so corresponds exactly with the well-known Indian Lydian, 'Hamīr-Kaliān'. Sharp also records that it was 'fiendishly difficult to take down', a thing he has not said of any other song; and it seems likely that this was due to slides and graces that were almost certainly put into it. It has often been remarked that Hungarian gypsy music bears the same sort of relation to Indian that Romany does to Hindostani.

Cecil Sharp believed in the beauty of human life, and he sought for and found the best qualities of our nature in the humblest peasants. One may, perhaps, say that he was truly great in this power of *recognition*, and, though he approached men and women of what we conveniently call the lower orders because he might collect from them characteristic songs, he was intensely alive to the glory of their human relationships and impressed and even awed by their high qualities. I remember when we were collecting folk-shanties from Mr. John Short of Watchet he asked Mr. Short about his wife. The sailor led us to a bedroom, where lay a sweet-faced smiling old lady, crippled and twisted by rheumatism. Cecil questioned her, and she told him that John did everything for her, cleaning the house, cooking the food, carrying her from her bed to the parlour—that he was her sole attendant. Cecil said to Mr. Short, when we were once more out of the lady's presence and preparing to resume singing, 'Mr. Short, you are a very fine singer, but your greatest achievement is in the next room.'

Sharp was equally quick to recognize the qualities of the artist. To Mrs. Stanton of Armscote, who gave him much assistance in collecting, he comments thus on the death of a singer who was, as he described himself, 'as good a whistler as ever cocked a lip':

I was glad to have your letter despite its sad news. Poor old Tom. I was afraid his days were numbered, but I hoped he would last through the winter. He left quite a mark in my mind; there was something about him which raised him from his fellows and singled him out. A pathetic figure of one who was himself his only enemy. His very recklessness endeared him to me. Well, I fancy he got a great deal out of life, more perhaps than many of us who live in a very different environment. He had the waywardness of the musician and a patience which enabled him to bear unruffled a querulous and slatternly wife—no mean performance. I have been harmonising 'Nelson's Praise'[1] quite lately, so I have poor Tom in mind. What a gorgeous tune it is, and I can always hear his voice in it.

There are many evidences, too, of the affection the

---

[1] *English Folk-Songs, Selected Edition*, vol. ii, no. 38.

singers bore him. The first of the two letters quoted below (dated Hambridge, 12.10.31) is addressed to the present writer:

Sir—I was looking down the paper when I seen Cecil Sharp's name. And you wanted to know if any one knew him. Now I must say I Louie Hooper and my sister Lucy White both of this place knew him quite well and spent many a happy hour singing to him at the Vicarage Hambridge with Father Marson his friend. He took our photos and put them in the first book of Somerset Folk Songs[1]. . . . He gave me a nice concertina. I would play it. And Mrs. Sharp gave me and my sister a new blouse each. I went to Ilminster Fair with him to hear the old people sing, and I remember quite well there was an eclipse of the sun the same day and he smoked a piece of glass for me to look and see it through. And he had a nice concert at Langport and gave us a nice tea. . . . I and my sister used to go to the Vicarage and he used to pay us very well. And we used to have our supper together. Mrs. Sharp was there sometimes. The last time I seen him was when Father Marson was buried. That was in March the same year as the War broke out. I am 72 years of age. . . . He came to my house one Christmas time and took the photo of my dinner Christmas Day, and when I went to Langport to a lantern lecture that he gave I seen my Christmas dinner come through on the slide. . . . He gave me a book of songs after he had mine and he said exchange was no robbery. And he wrote it in the book. . . . I liked him very much, he was a very kind gentleman. . . . He also gave the old men tobacco that used to sing to him. I often think of the days. It was a happy time. I often say I should like for some one to have the concertina in memory of him. He used to like to hear me play it. Now I hope you will be able to understand this letter that I have sent.

From Yours faithfully .
Louisa Hooper.

The reference to the eclipse of the sun fixes the date of Ilminster Fair as August 30th, 1905.

The second letter was written to Sharp himself by the son of an old morris-dancer. It runs:

I now take the pleasure in writing a few lines to you in answer

[1] Unfortunately, not so; but one of them is here on a later page.

to your kind and welcome letter and father thanks you so much for the tobacco you sent him. He was so pleased with it. Dear Sir, father is very ill and has been for a long time. He has been under the doctor's hands. He has been in bed for a long time but he is just getting a little better. He tells me again to thank you for the tobacco and pipes. Father would have wrote before only he has been waiting to get you a little present. Then he had his downfall of being ill and he could not get it, but he says he will get you something as soon as he is able to get to work again. We all wish you a merry Christmas and a happy New Year when it comes.

It says much for the courtesy of the people that never once throughout his visits to their cottage doors was he asked what his business was. And their kindliness and generosity is exemplified by an old lady who was rather deaf and had not understood Sharp's preliminary inquiry about a certain song, but had only heard his final appeal for help. Her response was, 'Well, we're poor folk, but if a penny will be any good to you, you are welcome.'

CHAPTER V

1903–1906

PROPAGANDA

Be not like the empiric ant which merely collects nor like the cobweb-weaving theorists who do but spin webs from their own intestines; but imitate the bees which both collect and fashion.

HEADINGTON, Sharp's first introduction to folk-music, *A Book of British Song*, his first attempt to embody it in his practical work, and Hambridge, his first actual contact with the living song, mark three principal moments of his entry upon his life's work. On November 26th, 1903, at Hampstead, he gave the first of his many lectures. His illustrations were songs from Somerset, beginning, of course, with 'The Seeds of Love', and his suite of morris dance tunes, beginning with 'Laudnum Bunches' played by the Hampstead Conservatoire orchestra; Mattie Kay, Helène de Sérène, Walter Ford, and Leonhard Sickert sang;[1] Edward d'Evry and himself accompanied. This got into the papers, especially the *Morning Post*, where he had a friend in T. Lennox Gilmour,[2] who was second leader-writer. 'The Fates', says Mr. Gilmour, 'who presided over my birth, unkindly denied me the gift of music, but they gave me some sense of historic values and a certain capacity to respond to contagious enthusiasm. And was there ever a more attractive enthusiast than Cecil Sharp! His sincerity was crystal clear; his egotism was not for himself but for the cause.'

The two had a talk early next year (1904) about this cause and what could be done for it. Mr. Gilmour invited Sharp next day to come and see him, and when he arrived

---

[1] Another singer, of whom Sharp thought highly, and of whose help he was glad to make use, was Campbell McInnes, who could do for these songs what only an artist can.

[2] Lord Rosebery's private secretary and all the time a practising barrister.

made him sit down and listen. He read him his 'interview' of the day before, while Sharp bubbled with laughter as he recognized in the formal statement his own arguments and asides. In allusion, no doubt, to this moment Sharp wrote (22.4.06) that a statue ought to be erected 'To one who himself unable to distinguish between "God Save the King" and "Pop goes the Weasel" yet gave his life to the advancement of Music'.

The gist of the interview was that the county councils might ultimately be approached, but as this would take time, and the collecting of the songs was urgent, there should be some *ad hoc* organization to appeal for funds, unless, perhaps, some philanthropist would provide them. Letters followed. An *ad hoc* organization! wrote Mr. T. L. Southgate; but haven't we got the Musical Association, to which belong professors, heads of music schools, prominent musicians, and notable amateurs, &c.? Then there is the Folk-Song Society, only its publications do not appear to have met with any distinct measure of success. But, rejoins Sharp, 'these professors, &c.' are just the people who know little and care less about the subject. In the titles of the papers read before the Musical Association since 1874 there is not a single allusion to English folk-music. As for the Folk-Song Society, it has published 109 folk-songs in six years, its Honorary Secretary is ill, and there have been no meetings for two years. It is moribund. The Folk-Song Society protested next day that it was alive, but impecunious; and the persistent Mr. Southgate pressed upon Sharp his suggestion about a sub-committee of the Musical Association. Others turned it over in imagination to the Folk-Lore Society; others, again, said that the songs were not worth collecting.

When they had all said their say Sharp presented his ultimatum on February 2nd, 1904:

All your correspondents agree that if the old songs which are still being sung by the peasantry of England are to be preserved for the benefit of future generations, they must be collected without delay. This general admission inspires the hope that at last some determined effort will really be made to complete a collection of English folk-song. If the members of the Musical Association or the Folk-Lore Society wish to join the movement by all means let them do so. There is an immense amount of work to be done, far more indeed than most people imagine.

Mr. Perceval Graves, Mr. Frank Kidson, and the committee of the Folk-Song Society have, naturally enough, done their best to present the past achievements of the Society in the most favourable light, but they cannot blink the fact that, except for the printing and private circulation of a hundred songs or so, the Society has done absolutely nothing to further the object for which it was founded more than five years ago.

So far as I am aware no attempt has been made to systematise the private efforts of individual collectors; no appeal for public support has been issued, nor has any effort been made to popularise the movement. Unless, therefore, the Society is disposed to put its house in order, reorganise its forces, and become an effective instrument, its continued existence is a menace rather than an aid to the cause it nominally espouses. In saying this I realize that the Society numbers amongst its members many of the best known and most distinguished collectors of folk song, and that it would be difficult to suggest a stronger committee so far as the names of its members are concerned.

Nevertheless, great names on a committee are not always an advantage, for they are often attached to those who lead busy lives, and can give but little time to honorary work. However, whatever may be the cause of its shortcomings and of its past sorry record, the Folk-Song Society should surely see that it must now either wake up, clean its slate, and start again on new and efficient lines, or else retire from the scene altogether, so that the field may be occupied by a more effective organization. I feel that I can speak more freely as I am myself a member of the Society. In proof of the interest that is being aroused by the action taken by your journal will you allow me in conclusion to quote from a letter I have just received from the Rev. S. Baring-Gould, the well-known collector and editor of Cornish and Devonshire songs: 'I am so grateful that at last the public is being roused to the fact that we have a body of fine traditional music. It is full late now to collect; all my old men are dead, but one.'

On February 8th, 'An Outsider' (possibly the leader-writer mentioned just now) suggested a meeting of the Folk-Song Society to which others, not members, should be admitted, and the Society be reconstructed on a broader basis. The Society's answer to this broad hint was to put Sharp on the Committee and to appoint Miss Lucy Broadwood as Honorary Secretary.

The first volume of *Folk-Songs from Somerset* was, as has been mentioned, published in December 1904. This was followed by four more volumes, the last published in 1909. These five volumes contain 117 folk-songs (of which 7 have a second version), 4 carols, and 2 shanties; total 130. Sharp was entirely responsible for the music, including the settings for pianoforte, of the whole book; Marson for the preface and texts of the first three volumes only. In the preface to the first volume the editors explain that

the collection is presented as nearly as possible as it was taken down from the lips of the singers; in the tunes with exact fidelity. We have not tried to reproduce by spelling the Somerset dialect, because such attempts are useless to those who know, and merely misleading to the ignorant. Anything like a peculiar use, archaisms, and rare words, we have carefully kept. In a few instances the sentiment of the song has been softened, because the conventions of our less delicate and more dishonest time demand such treatment, but indication has been given, and we plead compulsion and not desire in these alterations. We have corrected obvious slips of grammar, and reluctantly changed the weak perfects into strong ones.

It is unfortunate that the words of the folk-songs which have come down to us are not, generally speaking, on the same artistic level as the tunes, although there are notable exceptions, for example, 'O Waly, Waly', 'Searching for Lambs', and 'Scarborough Fair'.[1]

[1] *English Folk-Songs, Selected Edition,* vol. i, nos. 23 and 32, and vol. ii, no. 22.

Thirty years ago the charge was made that the musical editor of *Folk-Songs from Somerset* invented the tunes. He repelled it with the remark that to be able to do that would put a man at the head of all the melodists of the world. Another charge was, and is, that the editors bowdlerized the words. The words and tunes in Sharp's autograph are in the Library of Clare College, Cambridge. When this is compared with the printed copy it will be seen that some alteration was inevitable. There are two cases: (1) the sense is often obscure, or completely unintelligible, and (2) the sentiment is sometimes outspoken, or actually obscene. When the sentiment was of that nature, it was Sharp's opinion that the song was of individual, not communal, origin, and that this individual was often the ballad-maker[1] who hawked the songs about round the country. This view gains a little support from the fact that in the Appalachians where the broadsides did not exist, sentiment of that kind is not known in the songs. The obscurity hardly needs explanation; as the editors say: 'People remember short tunes more faithfully than long sets of words.' And it may be added that sometimes, not being themselves singers, they 'tell the poetry', caring only for the story and oblivious of rhyme or diction. Also, the folk have no sense of history—there would be nothing improbable to them in St. George meeting Bonaparte in the same ballad; and a known place is readily substituted for one unknown—'He sailed East, he sailed West, Until he came unto Torquay' (Turkey).

Sharp's principle was not to 'improve'; he restricted himself to slight verbal alterations when words and tunes did not fit, to the correction of grammatical errors, and to the collation of different versions of the same text when the single text was incomplete and unintelligible. He recorded in his published notes the changes that he had made.

[1] He was to be seen with his long printed sheets, and to be heard crooning rather than singing, in Bermondsey, thirty years ago.

Marson set out with the same conscientious purpose of
keeping as close as possible to the original oral texts, but
occasionally his poetic mind was too much for him. Here
and there his literary lines are as incongruous as hot-house
orchids in a bunch of wild primroses, e.g. 'Dabbling in
the Dew', which was not re-written, but written, and expressions such as 'hapless grave' in 'The Drowned Lover'.
In later editions, Sharp in most cases either reverted to the
original words or made a closer adaptation.

The first volume of *Folk-Songs from Somerset* is 'dedicated by permission to Her Royal Highness the Princess
of Wales'—now Her Majesty Queen Mary.

During the years 1904–7 Sharp had the honour of
giving musical instruction to the royal children at Marl-
borough House. He was asked to discover what musical
talents they possessed, and to develop them in respiration,
good carriage, diction, and discipline. The class consisted
of Their Royal Highnesses The Prince of Wales, Prince
Albert, Princess Mary, and nine other children, and later,
Prince Henry. It was held twice a week during the summer, and the lesson lasted for three-quarters of an hour.
This covered notation (on the blackboard), rhythm by
clapping, pitch (scale solfeggi), instruction in breathing
and enunciation, and the singing of rounds, national
songs, and folk-songs. In his annual report for 1905
Sharp writes

that both Prince Edward and Prince Albert have keen ears for a
tune will be apparent if reference is made to the appended list
of fifty songs[1] which they are now able to sing. The speed with
which they will fasten upon and learn a new tune has continually
surprised me and I consider that Prince Edward and Prince Albert
are both possessed of a musical instinct and ability far above the
average.

[1] The list includes some twenty folk-songs, and the rest are national
songs.

The following letters reached him, thanking him for the gift of folk-songs:

York Cottage,
12th November 1905

Dear Mr. Sharp,

Thank you very much for the book of songs you were kind enough to send me. I shall be glad to learn some of them when we go back to London. I can play the first page of the book you got for me. I like it very much.

With kind remembrances I remain

your little friend
MARY

York Cottage,
February 2nd 1907

Dear Mr. Sharp,

Thank you so much for the nice singing books you sent us. It is very kind of you. We learnt two new carols at Christmas. David had learnt them at Osborne. We shall have to learn some of the songs out of it. We are coming up at the beginning of March. Please give my respects to Mrs. Sharp.

We remain

yours very sincerely
ALBERT
HENRY

In July 1905 Sharp having resigned his position as Director of Studies at the Hampstead Conservatoire—a post which he had held for nine years—moved to 183 Adelaide Road, where he remained until 1911. His only certain source of income was now derived from his teaching at Ludgrove; but although less was coming in, he had more time to give to the absorbing work of folk-song, and his activities in that direction increased.

In 1905 he collaborated with the Rev. S. Baring-Gould and undertook the musical editorship of the fifth volume of *Songs of the West* (Methuen), a volume of 121 songs collected in Devon and Cornwall by the Rev. S. Baring-Gould, the Rev. H. Fleetwood Sheppard, who died in

1901, and the Rev. F. W. Bussell. Sharp is responsible for about two-thirds of the accompaniments.

Sabine Baring-Gould, born 1834 of an old Devonshire family, became rector of Lew Trenchard in North Devon in 1881. The *Songs of the West* represent only one corner of an alert mind; his books have an exceptionally wide range of subject. A friend of the family writes:

In his song-collecting I think he used to get the tunes along with the words, but said he was much hampered by not being more of a musician. Mr. Sharp said that after he had altered or added to the original words, as often happened, because they were 'outway rude' or fragmentary, he was apt to forget that his alterations were not part of the real song.

It was a funny household at Lew. They were an amusing family: I only knew Daisy, Veronica, Barbara, Cicely, Diana, Joan, Felicitas, John and Julian; but there were lots more than that—twenty altogether, they said. 'All regular English girls,' said Mr. Sharp, 'and each one prettier than the other.' He was wrapt up in his books, and sometimes forgot the names of his children; they were wrapt up in 'Papa' and did not always trouble to learn the names of his books. If the girls could not get to a meet in any other way, they would ride the cart-horses; and it was said in the county that nothing kills a Baring-Gould. A horse that kicked their dogcart to pieces was objected to by them only because they said they could not take Papa out with it again. The lake at Lew, with precipitous, rocky sides, was the place where the elder children used to amuse themselves setting the younger ones adrift in tin baths. None of them could swim. 'And Papa used to sit in his study and say he knew we should all be drowned.' Another game was to run about on the roof and jump across spaces from one roof to another.

I think he was a very kind squire. I have stayed there for one of his village dance evenings, and he walked about and talked to them all, and saw to it that they all had cider afterwards. There is a plaster ceiling in the ball-room at Lew, made by one of his villagers: he was ill and depressed, and Mr. Baring-Gould started him on this work to give him an interest and cheer him up, which he succeeded in doing: the man was an excellent workman and soon got keen on his job.

He did not care only for old things: in his church he had a good
new carving as well as old. He set an artistic daughter to paint the
panels of the screen with Saints of whom no one but himself had ever
heard. The Service was perfectly plain; no music except a hymn,
and as a contrast a sort of plain-song Creed which he sang himself.

The following year (1906) the collaboration between
Sharp and Baring-Gould resulted in the publication of
English Folk-Songs for Schools (J. Curwen & Sons). The
songs are drawn from Sharp's and Baring-Gould's collections, and the Introduction explains that 'this collection
has been made to meet the requirements of the Board of
Education, and is composed of melodies strictly pertaining
to the people, to which words have been set as closely
adhering to the original as was possible considering the
purpose of the book'. Sharp was not very happy about the
texts in this volume, although he had given his approval
to them. He felt, rightly or wrongly, that the all-impor-
tant thing was to get the songs with their beautiful melodies
introduced into the schools, and if a slight bowdlerization
of the words would assist that object, then the end justified
the means.

In 1908, when the general educational value of folk-
songs was not quite such a new idea, he published with
Messrs. Novello & Co. the first book of folk-songs in
their 'School Series'. Ultimately eleven volumes, com-
prising 114 songs collected and arranged by Sharp, were
published in this series, and here he presented the words
in a form which approximated very much more closely
to the originals, though not without some opposition. The
publisher took exception to such phrases as 'to my oor,
bag boor' in 'Midsummer Fair'; and in 'Green Broom',
to 'He'd marry this lady in bloom' and 'he swore he'd set
fire to his room'. The education authorities, he said, 'will
prefer the "poetical" moral lyric and its "made" tune'.
Sharp, after yielding on one or two points, replied:

Your criticisms strike at the very root of the whole question of the suitability or otherwise of the folk-song for school uses. It is not a question of theory or argument so much as one of feeling and temperament. . . . Hence, it is peculiarly difficult to explain this view and therefore also to reply to your objections. I cannot, for instance, rebut in so many words your dislike to 'I'm seventeen' with its 'rue dum day', etc. except by asking you to watch the expression of school children when they sing it, and by referring you to school teachers who have taught it, and to experts like Mr. Edward Burrows, H.M.I., who have recommended it.

And the publisher having said his say gracefully bowed to Sharp's decision.

In concentrating, as for the moment we have to, on Sharp's collecting and publishing of folk-songs we must remember, as he always did, that he was not the first in the field, and we may add that he was not the last; the men who give their names to a movement seldom are either. It will be convenient, therefore, to pause here and review other labours.

The texts of traditional songs and ballads are to be found in broadside collections of as early a date as the second half of the seventeenth century (e.g. those of Wood, Rawlinson, Douce, and Pepys), and a few got into early eighteenth-century printed collections of songs. But the first comprehensive collection was that of Percy's *Reliques* (1765), which, though it has been severely criticized on account of its literary embellishments, yet served its purpose in arousing enthusiasm for popular ballads. Bishop Percy's collection was followed by many others during the next fifty years, e.g. those of Ritson in England, and Herd, Scott, and Jamieson in Scotland. In these collections interest centred solely in the texts, and the tunes which should have accompanied them were ignored. A few traditional tunes are recorded in early eighteenth-century musical collections, but Johnson's *Scots Musical Museum* (1787–1803) is the first publication to contain any considerable number of traditional tunes, though which of these are taken from traditional sources is uncertain. In the third decade of the nineteenth century a number of collections appeared—mostly Scottish—and those of Kinloch and Motherwell (both 1827) contain several airs said to have been recovered from tradition. However, the first publication which is devoted exclusively to songs, with tunes, noted direct from the lips of the peasants is that entitled *Sussex Songs*, by the Rev. John Broadwood (uncle of Miss Lucy Broadwood), privately printed in 1843.[1] This has sixteen tunes. Some dozen publications of a similar nature appeared between the years 1877 and 1904 (see Appendix of *English Folk-Song: Some Conclusions*), accounting for, in all, between eight and nine hundred tunes. There were also the two great storehouses: of tunes, William Chappell's *Popular Music of the Olden Time* (1855–9); and of texts (with only 55 tunes), Francis J. Child's *English and Scottish Popular Ballad* (1882–98). But in both cases the material is from printed sources.

[1] This was reprinted in 1899 with additional songs collected by Miss Lucy Broadwood.

CHAPTER VI

1906–1907

DEFINITIONS

To such a mood I had come, by what charm I know not
where on thatt upland path I was pacing alone;
and yet was nothing new to me, only all was vivid
and significant that had been dormant or dead:
as if in a museum the fossils on their shelves
should come to life suddenly, or a winter rose-bed
burst into crowded holiday of scent and bloom.

ROBERT BRIDGES, *Testament of Beauty.*

IT was all very well to collect, arrange, publish, and
lecture upon these songs, but what Sharp wanted now
was to get them into the schools. He knew quite well
that a song is very little, and a folk-song nothing at all,
until you sing it yourself, and sing it as a bubbling over
of the spirit that is in you. He had no fear that it would
not stand wear, or that it would repel by its difficulty, and
it was therefore the very thing for those who were beginning either music or life. Accordingly when the Board of
Education issued early in 1906 their *Suggestions for the
Consideration of Teachers* recommending 'National or Folk-
Songs' as being 'the expression in the idiom of the people
of their joys and sorrows, their unaffected patriotism', &c.,
he was at once on the alert. He complained in the *Morning
Post* of April 19th and the *Daily Chronicle* of May 22nd
(1906) that the list of songs they proposed did not give
'logical' expression to these views. Of the fifty songs
seventeen are ordinary art-songs, like 'Tom Bowling';
twenty-six are founded on folk-tunes of bygone days, like
'The Vicar of Bray'; and seven are true folk-songs. He
feared that the confusion between 'national' and folk-songs
would have disastrous results.

Schoolmasters, in the belief that they are teaching folk-songs, will
give the children the songs suggested in the Blue-book. The results

which folk-song enthusiasts have confidently predicted will not, of course, follow. The experiment will be voted a failure, and folk-songs, without a trial, will be branded as unfit for school use and excluded for ever from the schoolroom.

Sir Charles Stanford answered in the *Daily Chronicle* (23.5.06), hotly defending the action of the Board:

Archaeologists who have personally dug up an antique are apt to glorify it at the expense of those which have been dug up by their predecessors. This is the key to Mr. Cecil Sharp's reckless and unjustifiable attack upon the list of songs issued by the Board of Education. It issued a list of songs which are folk-songs, are songs of the people, and are songs of and for the nation, but which in his eyes have the disadvantage of having stood the test of a long life in the public ear; and if he wished his more recent discoveries of songs to reach the schools also, there is no better way than to begin with a list of those which have long been acknowledged as the backbone of national music.

Sir Charles was in fact advocating just such a book as Sharp had written four years before in *A Book of British Song*. That had included authenticated and dated songs (Savile's 'Here's a Health unto his Majesty', 1667, Leveridge's 'Roast Beef of Old England', 1790, Davy's 'Bay of Biscay', 1805, &c.) with many anonymous and undated, all described as 'traditional'. To Sharp, the distinction between the two senses of ' tradition' had now become definite. He replied the next day:

Sir Charles has mistaken my contention. I agree, of course, that 'Tom Bowling' is none the less 'a people's song, because we know Dibdin to have written it'. But I deny, not that it is a people's song, but that it is a folk-song; that is, a song made by the people, as well as sung by them. The distinction is not academic; nor is it archaeological. It is intrinsic, for it distinguishes between two kinds of music that are fundamentally different from one another. And to this even Sir Charles Stanford must agree, unless he is prepared to place 'Tom Bowling' and 'Heart of Oak' in the same category as 'The Golden Vanity' and 'The Seeds of Love', or to couple 'Sir Patrick Spens' with Tennyson's 'Revenge'.

The mere knowledge of the name of the composer has nothing whatever to do with the matter. I should never mistake 'Tom Bowling' for a folk-song even if the name of its author were unknown. Its every phrase proclaims the individual composer and the period in which it was written; it lacks all the distinctive characteristics of the folk-song.

I am sorry that Sir Charles Stanford should credit me with believing that 'folk-songs grew like trees in the fields, and national songs came out of human brains'. 'Brains created both', no doubt; but while the national song is the product of the individual, the folk-song has been evolved by the brains of countless generations of folk-singers and composers. The one is individual, the other communal and racial. They differ not only in the manner of their birth, but in the finished product.

Among the correspondence which ensued was a letter from Dr. Vaughan Williams, who supported Sharp's views, and, 'as a collector in a small way', was delighted 'to see the distinction between the genuine folk-tune and the "composed song" so clearly stated'.

A month later Sharp wrote again in the same paper, explaining folk-song to be folk-made song (the view, in fact, that he puts forward in *Folk-Song: Some Conclusions*, see p. 107). He adds (28.6.06) as his underlying motive:

> One reason why we have in England no national school of music is because we have so unaccountably neglected our folk-music. . . . Little or no effort to repair this deficiency is made . . . at the musical colleges. . . . Our younger musicians are now studying English folk-music, and . . . their compositions already reflect the new and inspiring influence; but how much better it would have been if . . . they had absorbed it in their young days.

Suggestions for the Consideration of Teachers was followed up later in the year by another Memorandum entitled *Music in Secondary Schools*, with which Sharp dealt just as firmly, giving instances of the way in which the misuse of the term 'folk' led to the confusion and deception which he anticipates. He continued:

The writer, in the attempt to clear up this confusion, has set us some more terminological puzzles. He has discarded the use of the word 'folk-song' altogether, and he now describes his list of songs under the heading of 'traditional songs'. And this is how he defines that expression: '*Traditional song is a term used here to cover the whole range of national, folk-song, carols, and ballads, whether made by peasants and crystallised by musicians, or made by musicians and crystallised by peasants, or wholly peasants' work, or wholly musicians' work, anonymous or otherwise; all those which have obtained wide national acceptance, and which have stood the test of surviving three or more generations.*' I presume this is not a joke, but I confess I find it difficult to take it seriously. How can a musician 'crystallise' a folk-song, or a peasant 'crystallise' the work of a musician? And why should 'The Bay of Biscay' or 'Where the Bee Sucks' be dubbed traditional, simply because they have 'obtained wide national acceptance, etc.'? To stretch the meaning of words in this way is to defeat the purpose of language. If 'traditional' means anything at all, it means that which has been handed down from generation to generation by word of mouth and not by printed or written document. But under this amazing definition Schubert's 'Erlkönig' must be accounted a 'traditional' song, and 'Paradise Lost' 'traditional' poetry. (*Morning Post*, 21.12.06.)

Most of those who had collected, or made a serious study of folk-song, were in general agreement with Sharp's views, but few were willing to support him in his uncompromising condemnation of the Board's action. The Folk-Song Society actually blessed the *Suggestions*. Their Annual Report said:

The Board of Education has for the first time recorded the importance of our National and Folk Songs in the musical training of children, and urges earnestly that such songs shall be taught throughout the country. This scheme, if consistently carried out, must become a powerful means towards cultivating a healthy musical taste, and certainly claims the support of all who believe in the enormous influence exercised by folk-music upon composers of all nations.

Sharp was not present at the meeting that passed this. When he saw the report, he protested to Miss Broadwood, Honorary Secretary of the Society, that he was hereby committed to an opinion upon a subject of great importance with which he was unable to agree. Miss Broadwood replied that in her opinion Mr. Sharp was not compromised, for they were all united as to the general scheme and nothing had been said about the offending 'List'. Sharp maintained, however, that if the paragraph were allowed to remain in its present form it would be cited against him in the public contest which he was waging, and the incident would be regarded merely as a squabble about something upon which the experts disagreed. At this point Miss Broadwood reminded Mr. Sharp that when individual members of the Society had expressed their disapproval of the lack of moderation in his attacks on the Board—and in this connexion we may mention that he had received a severe rebuke from the President of the Society himself—he had affirmed that he was carrying on the controversy as an independent individual and that the Society was not in any way involved. The logic of it was against him, but he did not allow himself to be persuaded. He forwarded an amendment to the General Meeting of the Society proposing certain alterations in the paragraph. This amendment was later withdrawn in favour of another, moved by Dr. Vaughan Williams, proposing that the reference to the action of the Education Department be referred back to the committee for reconsideration. This was not carried.

The whole thing reads to us, perhaps, like a tilting at windmills. He may seem to some now, as to many then, to have been fighting for a mere verbal definition, which he had himself ignored four years earlier. But the full extent of what he was fighting for was only now dawning on him. He was convinced, now, that such a song as 'Barbara Allen'—in a mode, multiform, anonymous—was different in *quality* from 'Tom Bowling'—in a key, uniform, of definite authorship; and he believed that on the strength of this quality the former would, and the latter would not, win its way permanently to the heart of a singer. It was for the recognition of this that he was fighting. The Folk-Song Society and other collectors were aware of this difference of quality, but, since the promulgation of folk-songs did not lie within their scope, there was no need for them to take action upon it. And now, when one man proclaimed that action was necessary, he seemed to be opposing their view, when he was really carrying it out to its logical conclusion; also, since he was only one collector among many, and a particularly successful collector, he seemed to be aiming merely at self-advertisement. It is significant that in later years when folk-song and folk-dance had become generally accepted as normal activities, Sharp rarely took part in any press controversy. 'Once you have gained your point it does more harm than good to keep on rubbing it in,' was his advice to others and to himself.

On the strength of the fifteen hundred songs[1] he had

[1] Between September 1903 and September 1907 Sharp collected 1,500 tunes in about 330 days (an average of thirty tunes a week), his only available time being in his school holidays. The details are as follows:

Date			Days	Tunes
1903 Sept.	.	.	9?	42
Dec.–Jan.	.	.	14	81
1904 April	.	.	10	90
July–Sept.	.	.	49	221
Dec.	.	.	21	57
1905 April	.	.	6	21
Aug.–Sept.	.	.	45	157
Dec.–Jan.	.	.	32	146
1906 April	.	.	21	111
May–June	.	.	4	15
Aug.–Sept.	.	.	41	191
1907 Jan.	.	.	14	85
March–April	.	.	23	125
July–Sept.	.	.	45	143
			334	1,485
				16 (by correspondence)
				1,501

63

collected, and as a result of this controversy with the Folk-Song Society, a book about the length of what is in your hand, called *English Folk-Song: Some Conclusions*, appeared in October 1907. 'I felt', he said, 'the book *must* be written, and I went straight home from the meeting and wore out three fountain pens.' Failing to find a publisher he published it himself, with Barnicott & Pearce of Taunton as printers. It was written in ill-health—some of it had to be dictated owing to blindness caused by gout in the eyes; but it expressed his considered opinion.

Its eleven chapters are thus apportioned: four to definitions, origins, and general characteristics; three to modes, scales, and rhythms; one to folk-poetry; one to the singers and their songs; and two to the antiquity, decline, and future of folk-song.

Analysis. All forms of mental activity proceed from the development by education of qualities that are natural and inborn. We shall, therefore, best gauge the musical potentialities of a nation by the utterances of those who are least affected by extraneous influences. Folk-music is created by the common people, art-music is composed by the educated. 'Common' means 'unlettered' (not 'illiterate'), and the common people were once more numerous and more homogeneous than they are now. Was it the man or the community that invented the *words* of a song? Sir Walter Scott said, the man; the brothers Grimm said, the community; Böhme (*Altdeutsches Liederbuch*, 1877, pp. xxii, xxiii) said, 'one (nameless) man sings a song (words and tune) and others sing it after him *changing what they do not like.*' It is these italicized words that constitute the difference between communal and individual authorship. The individual composer, a namable man, invents and criticizes, and his last draft may be very unlike his first. Communal invention is analogous: a nameless author and a succession of nameless singers, who criticize by the way they perform the song, correspond to the composer's successive drafts, and the final result may be very different from the original.

This joint authorship, or communal creation, is made possible by two things. It is open to any one to sing a melody, but not every one can play a sonata and no one man can play a symphony; and, sonata and symphony are fixed by notation, but the song is not. But if the song can thus be altered, may it not be spoilt as often as improved? It may. But the poor song dies out, nobody wants to sing it; the successes remain. The song is, in fact, evolved. Evolution has the three stages of persistence, variation, and selection. The folk-singer's well-known and remarkable memory makes for persistence, his fancy for variation, and the community selects. The process may be compared to the behaviour of a flight of starlings. The flock 'persists' in its unanimous course, individuals dart out from that and 'vary' it, and the flock 'selects' which, if any, individual it will follow. The flock of starlings is looking for a suitable place to roost in; the singing community is looking for a song which shall satisfy its understanding and its sense of beauty.

The chapter on the Modes is written to show two things: (*a*) that a melody which is in a mode need not be, and is not in folk-song, old in spirit (like the Church tones), though it may happen to be old in time; and (*b*) that if harmonization is employed, it ought to confine itself to the mode of the song. That on English Folk-scales sums up a large practical experience, and contains the pith of the book; it is concerned chiefly with the identification of the tonic, a knotty point, and with the sense in which modal melodies modulate. That on Rhythms and melodic figures gives a probable explanation of some apparent irregularities.

The singer and his song are dying out, and what is to happen now? It is not too late; some thousands of songs are on record, and we might sing them and know them.

When every English child does so as a matter of course, then, from whatever class the musician of the future may spring, he will speak in the national musical idiom. He will not write English music by going to English folk-song for his themes, though that would be all in the right direction. We must wait till the younger generation has absorbed folk-song. The publication by Bishop Percy in 1765 of forty-five ballads killed at a blow the cold formalism of the preceding age, as Wordsworth and Sir Walter Scott bore witness. Is it unreasonable to suppose that the present collecting and publishing of English folk-song will lead to a similar revival in music?

'What *is* the national musical idiom?' asked Mr. Ernest Newman five years later (see the *English Review* for May, July, and August, 1912). The answer is given in Sharp's book (p. 130): 'No school of music has yet arisen and flourished in Europe that has not primarily been concerned with the expression of national aspirations.' And Dr. Dyson (see Appendix A) echoes this, when he points out that cosmopolitan music is at all times the coming into vogue of the music of one or other nation.

'It is not much of a book,' Sharp wrote to Miss Gilchrist with his fourth fountain-pen, 'but it contains something that should be said; and although I realise that I have said it all very clumsily, yet on the whole I think it should be said so rather than not at all.' Two satisfactory tributes reached him. Professor F. B. Gummere, whose *Popular Ballad* was published at about the same time as Sharp's *Some Conclusions*, wrote:

It is the sort of work that you have done which really counts. It is an unspeakable comfort to have a man who knows folk-song at first hand write such words about it as you have written.

And Gavin Greig (author of *Folk-Songs of the North-East of Scotland* and, posthumously with Alexander Keith, of

Last Leaves of Traditional Ballads collected in Aberdeen-shire, Buchan Club, 1925) addressed Sharp as

the greatest dynamic in the folk-song world. You have been doing a magnificent work. Some of the older school would theorise without first-hand material and the discipline that comes from collecting it, while some of your younger enthusiasts do nothing but collect and cannot see the wood for the trees. What we chiefly want is workers who both collect and can generalize.

With these two letters in his pocket from fellow-workers in the same field it did not much matter to him that some of the press—for instance *The Times Literary Supplement* of January 23rd, 1908—twitted him with being a 'late-comer' in the field of folk-song, asked what he could know of England when he had examined only Somerset (suppressing the fact that he had found more there than any one anywhere), accused him of confusing modes and tones (when he had carefully distinguished them), and cavilled at his examples instead of refuting his argument. The book is not perfect—the pages on harmonization were written when he had not long begun to think about the matter—but it was considerably in advance of anything that had appeared at that date.

CHAPTER VII

1905–1909

THE MORRIS DANCE

Sicker this morrowe, ne lenger agoe,
I saw a shole of shepeheardes outgoe,
With singing, and shouting and iolly chere:
Before them yode a lusty Tabrere
That to the many a Horne pype playd,
Whereto they dauncen eche one with his mayd.
To see those folkes make such iousance,
Made my heart after the pype to daunce.

ED. SPENSER, *Shepherd's Calendar.*

THOSE Headington dances—we have to keep on reverting to them—made an immediate appeal to Sharp. In his College days he had been what would be called a 'dancing man' and he had enjoyed the Alhambra ballet, but all this was no more than pleasurable entertainment. He admired Ruth St. Denis and the early Russian ballet, when they came, as much as any one, but that was later. The Headington Morris was his first intimation that dancing was an art comparable with music. These dances astonished and moved him, but they were outside a musician's province. The songs were in his own line and he attacked them with vigour, as we have seen. He no doubt realized that the dances were saying the same thing only in other words, but he did not know what to do with them and for the moment he was completely absorbed in the songs. His friend, Mr. Warren, had drawn his attention once to the country dance, but Sharp had put it aside, thinking of it perhaps as a debased form of the quadrille of his youth, but more probably because he grudged to the dance the time which might have been spent on the song; he was never good at dividing his attention.

Now, in September 1905, a request came to him for songs suitable for a club of working-girls, mostly seam-

stresses. This was the Esperance Club in Cumberland
Market, St. Pancras. It was under the care of Miss Mary
Neal, with Mr. Herbert MacIlwaine[1] as choir-master; the
girls' amusements were singing and dancing. Miss Neal
describes her visit to Sharp in a pamphlet, *Set to Music*:

We had performed year after year some school cantata which our
friends had been kind enough to say they enjoyed, and which had
kept the girls happy during the long winter evenings. But a chance
article in the *Morning Post* . . . on English folk-songs set us on
a new track. I went to see Mr. Cecil Sharp to ask his advice as
to whether these songs would be suitable for a Working Girls'
Club. In ten minutes we were deep in the subject of Folk Song,
and I was told that I should be surprised at the way in which
English boys and girls would understand and appreciate their own
Folk music. 'They will learn it', said Mr. Sharp, 'by a sort of
spiritual sixth sense.' . . . I went away having made up my mind
to the experiment, although I confess that the music looked to my
inexperience very difficult. In a fortnight I wrote to Mr. Sharp
telling him that I could only express the result of the first few
lessons by saying that the Club had gone mad, that they were perfectly intoxicated with the music.

The Esperance Club (first under that name, then as
the 'Association for the Revival and Practice of Folk-
Music', and later as the 'Guild of Morris Dancers') will
occupy us now for a chapter or two. Miss Neal was a
philanthropist in the best sense; she planned quickly and
worked with energy, and she had the Irishwoman's warm
heart. She was not a musician, and did not herself dance;
but she had a gift for organization. She sympathized with
the Women's Suffrage movement, but took no active part
in it; she is now a Sussex magistrate and exerts herself to
uphold the cause of Labour. Having found the songs,

[1] Herbert C. MacIlwaine, son of Canon MacIlwaine of Belfast Cathe-
dral, after some years on an Australian cattle-station, wrote *Fate the
Fiddler*, *The Undersong*, and other novels. He was musical director of the
Esperance Club (1901–8), where he was followed by Mr. Clive Carey.
He died in middle age, October 1st, 1916.

Miss Neal's next object was to find dances that would go with them. Sharp told her of the morris dances and of William Kimber, and in a short time she had gone down to Oxford to interview Mr. Kimber, and had arranged for him and another dancer to come and teach her girls. In two evenings they had learned enough to be able to give a performance at their Christmas party of dances, songs, and singing-games, the latter collected by Mrs. (now Lady) Gomme; and, at Laurence Housman's suggestion, the public heard and saw them at the Small Queen's Hall in the following April, when Sharp lectured.

In July 1907 Sharp published, in collaboration with Herbert MacIlwaine, *The Morris Book*, Part 1, and the accompanying music for the dance was issued in two sets with pianoforte arrangements by Cecil Sharp. *The Morris Book*[1] is dedicated to 'our friends and pupils, the members of the Esperance Girls' Club', and the reason of its publication is given in the Introduction, of which the literary style seems to be that of MacIlwaine rather than of Sharp. It is not, we are told,

primarily for the information of the archaeologist and scholar, but to help those who may be disposed to restore a vigorous and native custom to its lapsed pre-eminence.

The authors give credit to Miss Mary Neal, who 'not only made the venture possible in the beginning, but with her powers of organization gave it a reach and strength that neither of us could have given'. Again, in 1910, Sharp wrote in the *Morning Post*:

Without the help of the Esperance Club these tunes would probably still be hidden away in my note-books; so that I owe no small debt to the Club, an obligation which I am glad once again to acknowledge.

The historical account of the dances, supporting faint-

---

[1] It should be recorded that Miss Lucy Broadwood advised Sharp not to publish until he had collected more; the book contains eleven dances, and refers to two dozen of which he had as yet only the tunes.

heartedly the theory that the morris is Moorish in origin
and was brought to England in the reign of Edward III,
does not show signs of deep research, and it was revised
and re-written by Sharp in a second edition published in
1912. In this later edition extensive alterations were also
made in the technical description of the dances in view of
the wider experience gained,[1] and three dances from Bid-
ford, now thought to rest on insecure authority, were
discarded, though full credit was given to Mr. d'Arcy de
Ferrars for his revival of them in 1886. The remaining
eight dances in the first edition were noted from Mr.
William Kimber, Junior, who had played the concertina
at Headington when Sharp first saw the morris in
December 1899. The Headington 'side' had been disbanded in 1887, and revived again in 1899 at the instigation of Percy Manning, whose scholarly researches have
contributed much valuable information on the subject.
The 'revived' side included four dancers from the old
team. Mr. William Kimber had not danced with the old
team, but his father, who had danced as far back as 1847,
had been foreman of the 'side', and with his fiddle and
concertina had often understudied the regular fiddler.

It was from his father that Kimber had learned the
tunes and most of the dance movements, and it was no
doubt from him that he got the love of the thing. The
following account of a visit to his father is taken from a
letter which William Kimber wrote to Sharp in February
1915, sending him at the same time an old drinking-cup:

He was in the best humour I have ever seen him. We had talked
some time about one thing and another, and all at once (I wish you
had been there) he says, 'I think I have got something you can
have that you can turn into a bob or two.' Of course I wondered
what it was going to be. He went to the same old place where he

[1] In the first edition the notation was based partly on the dancing of the
Esperance Club girls. This process was manifestly unsatisfactory, and in
the second edition the dances were noted directly from William Kimber
and other traditional dancers.

had taken out the old peeling-horn and brought out this cup. This is his version:

'You see this! Well this is one of the oldest relics of Headington Morris and Wheatley. This cup belonged to old Mr. Hall of Noke, him that used to play the whittle and dub for us to dance. It was made from the horns of some animal out of Holton Park. When old Hall finished, this cup was left at the pub at Wheatley, and the old Benefit Club took care of it till it was broken up. Then one of the Wheatley men knowing that I should prize it brought it to me. I remember drinking out of it before I knew your mother—that's over fifty years ago. Old Tom Carter wanted it, so did Joe Trafford, but I kept it. But you can have it now, we shall never see such times again.'

I wish you had been there to have seen him holding this cup and talking to it just as if it were human and very dear indeed to him. I told him where I was going to send it, and he said, 'Perhaps I may tell him that cup's history some day when we meet.' I asked him its age and as near as he can say, according to old Mr. Hall's version, it is 110 to 150 years. I think you are entitled to all this old stuff, but if it is no good let me have it back.

Kimber has been described as 'a bricklayer by trade and a dancer by profession', but above all he is an artist, and that no doubt made the bond of friendship between him and Sharp—a friendship which continued unsullied for twenty years.

Shortly before *The Morris Book* was published Kimber wrote to Sharp as follows:

Last week I heard a piano playing opposite where we are working, and I listened, and to my astonishment it was playing 'Country Gardens'. I could not work. I had to lay my trowel down and listen. My mates said, 'What's up, Merry' (my nickname)? Of course they did not know the tune. I said, 'Wonder where they got that from.'

One man said, 'It was "Vicar of Bray"', but, as I told him, there was a lot of difference in 'Country Gardens' and 'Vicar of Bray' —as much as chalk and cheese. . . .

Well the young lady kept on playing for ten minutes, so I just gave them a turn on the planks, up close to the chimney, for we were just preparing to build the chimney-stack. . . .

I had a good mind to ask her where she got it from but another thought struck me. I wondered if the book was out, so I thought that by writing I should know for certain.

His frequent letters to Sharp always drew sympathy and often opened a helping hand.

I was delighted to hear from you and to hear of your splendid luck in the matter of pigs. May they thrive and grow up handsome and profitable pigs,

Sharp writes at one time; and at another, when the luck had not been so good,

I am indeed sorry to hear that you are in the wars again. Things do seem to have gone awry with you of late. Never mind, cheer up and perhaps some day the clouds will roll by. I am quite sure that if a man sticks to his job through bad as well as fair weather somehow or other things come right. But he's got to stick to it. Let him grumble if it lets off steam. I often do this! In the meanwhile I send you a small present in the hope that it will help things a little.

At another time (27.1.10) Sharp writes:

The next Parliament will be interesting but I hope the Irish will help us to polish off the Lords or else we are done. The election has been bad, but it might have been worse. You must get hold of the rustics in the small villages about you and knock some sense into their noddles!

The correspondence, which is a big one, is, however, mainly concerned with their mutual interest in the dancing. The philosophy of folk-dancing has perhaps never been better expressed than by Kimber, when in a letter to Sharp dated April 1st, 1921, he inquires how the dancing is progressing and adds,

I was reading the other day how they are going to modify classic dancing. I thought to myself, 'Ours doesn't want any modifying at all—they are now what they were and always will be.'

And that same year he writes bemoaning the fact that he is spending such a quiet Christmas time:

Not a single step of any sort. I was only thinking the other morning as I passed Sandfield Cottage and looked at that room

73

where you and I had our first tune, it doesn't seem all that time ago. Yet it's too true, a great many things have happened since then. And the old saying of bricklayers crossed my mind, 'And you, old boy, have at last wound up your line'—which makes a fellow just a bit down. As I always said, when I could not have a dance, I hope it would soon be all over; for if ever one loved a certain thing in this world, the one thing I loved was the Morris.

After their success at the Small Queen's Hall in April 1906 the members of the Esperance Club continued to give performances of the morris dances both in London and the provinces, and Sharp, although he had no official connexion with the Club, often co-operated by lecturing at the performances. In order to satisfy the demand for instruction in the dances the Club girls were sent out as teachers, and by 1908 two girls were teaching whole-time, one part-time, and eight others were doing evening-work. The chief teacher was Miss Florrie Warren, an exuberant and vital dancer; and the authors of *The Morris Book* acknowledge the help that she gave them in noting the dances.

On November 14th, 1907, Miss Neal called an informal Conference at the Goupil Gallery 'to talk over plans for putting at the service of all who wish for it, this great possession of English folk-music in which it has been our good fortune to be the means of reviving active interest', and in her preliminary leaflet she states that

the practice of folk-music, which began just two years ago in the Esperance Club, has already from such small beginnings, spread all over England. . . . It has gone far beyond the Club in which it began, and it is quite beyond the handful of people who inaugurated it to meet the demand now made upon them, for information and for help, from villages and towns all over the country.

At the meeting, which had received the blessing of *Punch* (13.11.07), Mr. Neville Lytton took the Chair.[1]

[1] Present: Lady Constance Lytton, Lady Gomme, Mrs. Pethick Lawrence, Mr. E. Burrows (H.M. Inspector of Schools for Sussex), Miss Neal, Mr. Sharp, and others.

Sharp, who had his doubts about the Society which it was proposed to form, urged that collecting (a matter for experts) should not be one of its objects. It was resolved that a Society be formed for the development and practice of folk-music, and that a provisional committee, which included him, be appointed to draw up rules. In this committee Sharp moved that the Society should be thoroughly representative of all those who knew anything about the subject, and that the rules should provide for the periodic retirement of the Executive in rotation, a proposal which aroused opposition. The Committee did not report to another meeting; but a Society, with which Sharp was not associated, was afterwards formed under the title of the 'Association for the Revival and Practice of Folk Music' under the presidency of the Earl of Lytton with Mr. Neville Lytton as Chairman, and Miss Neal and Mr. MacIlwaine (and later Miss Neal alone) as Honorary Secretaries.

There appears to have been some misconception in the minds of the public concerning the scope and purpose of the Association, for Miss Neal found it necessary to write in the *Saturday Review* of April 11th, 1908, in reply to a letter from Mr. John F. Runciman:

We do not propose in any way to do the work of collecting folk music, which, as he [Mr. Runciman] points out, is being done so admirably by experts such as Mr. Cecil Sharp. What we propose to do is to facilitate the use and practice of folk music by the younger generation, and it is because we have already done this so successfully in connection with the Esperance Working Girls' Club, which has carried these dances all over England, that we have found it necessary to form an association for carrying on the work. . . . The dances which we are already teaching . . . were collected by Mr. Cecil Sharp, who in collaboration with Mr. MacIlwaine had already published two volumes of the dance tunes, also a handbook of instructions, and they are both at present engaged in bringing out another volume.

The volume referred to was *The Morris Book*, Part 2, published the following year (July 1909), together with two sets of music. It contained five more set dances and four solo jigs from Headington, and two processional dances from Derbyshire. This book, like the first, was re-written; the second edition was published three years after the death of Mr. MacIlwaine.

For some time past Sharp had been dissatisfied with the standard of the dancing and teaching of the Esperance Club girls, and this no doubt is the reason of the warning note which is sounded in the last paragraph of the Introduction to the 1909 edition:

In our Morris Book, Part 1, we said in describing the Morris that it was '. . . essentially a manifestation of vigour rather than of grace'. This, and other similar remarks of ours in the description of the dance, while they are strictly correct, have in some instances been given a somewhat too liberal interpretation. Here and there we have noticed a tendency to be over-strenuous, to adopt, upon occasion, even a hoydenish manner of execution. These are utterly alien to the true spirit of the dance; for although it is characterized by forcefulness, strength, and even a certain abandonment, it is at the same time and always an exposition of high spirits under perfect control.

or, in the concise words of a morris dancer, 'Plenty of brisk but no excitement'.

During 1908, although there had been a certain amount of friction due to difference in outlook, Miss Neal and Sharp co-operated on several occasions, the most important of which was an entertainment at Stationers' Hall, organized by the Worshipful Company of Musicians, at which Cecil Sharp lectured, Mattie Kay sang, and the Esperance girls danced. But at the beginning of 1909 Sharp is in a state of irritation, for he feels that the revival of the dances is getting artistically on to wrong lines. He writes in January to Mr. Neville Lytton,

I am sorry to find myself in antagonism with your Association to which, as you know, I have hitherto wished nothing but success.

However, two months later Sharp writes to Miss Neal:

I shall always be glad to come down and hear your Club members sing any new song that they are adding to their repertoire, and give you any hints about traditional *tempi* and so forth. My great desire is that at the outset these songs and dances shall be introduced to the present generation in the purest form possible—the next generation will have to take care of itself. When tradition plays such a great part as it does in folk-music the printed note and word may often be misunderstood, and the prevention of that is one of my chief interests. I hope therefore that you will not hesitate to call upon me if you are in any difficulty.

And after Cecil Sharp and Mr. Burrows had judged folk-song and dance competitions at Stratford-on-Avon, Miss Neal wrote to Sharp (May 5th, 1909) telling him that during his talk to the children she was vividly re-minded of the early days in which they worked together, and that she regretted the misunderstandings which had arisen. Later in that month, too, she suggested that he might like to use local teams which had been taught by the Esperance girls to illustrate his lectures, and soon after-wards she asked him to attend a rehearsal at the Club and run through a few of the things they were performing at Oxford.

Both desired, and the friends of both, Mr. Lytton and Mr. Burrows, desired that there should be co-operation. But Sharp felt that Miss Neal approached the dances from a philanthropic rather than an artistic point of view, and that her interest lay in her Club rather than in the move-ment in the broad sense in which he conceived it. Mean-time the need for a body of teachers was pressing, since the Board of Education in its revised syllabus of Physical Education (1909) officially recognized the morris dances. This was an important step which Sharp had used all his influence to bring about. Mr. E. A. G. Holmes was then Chief Inspector to the Board. One who is in a position to know describes him as 'an educationist of the first order, a poet, and a man of broad sympathies'. Mr. Burrows arranged a meeting between him and Sharp, and Sharp made the most of his opportunity. Mr. Holmes was described as being favourably impressed by his view and outlook.

It had not originally been Sharp's intention to play an active part in the teaching of the dances, but he had underrated the difficulties and dangers of popularization. He now realized that satisfactory results would not be obtained unless first-hand instruction were given by himself and he had direct control over his teachers. In the Physical Training Department of the South-Western Polytechnic (now the Chelsea Physical Training College) he found an organization which met his requirements, and in September 1909 a School of Morris Dancing was established in connexion with the College, with Sharp as Director. Its object was:

(*a*) to form classes in morris dancing;

(*b*) to train, examine, and grant certificates to teachers of morris dancing;

(*c*) to keep a register of certificated teachers, lecturers, &c., and to give advice and disseminate information respecting folk-dances, folk-songs, children's singing-games, &c.

And a leaflet explained that the authoritative pronouncement made by the Board of Education 'has made imperative the establishment of a Training School for folkdancing' to prevent 'the dances being practised in ways not sanctioned by tradition'. This leaflet emphasized the insufficiency of book-knowledge:

No notation can tell the student how to hit the just mean between freedom and reserve, forcefulness and grace, abandonment and dignity.

The school was 'to conserve the Morris in its purity and to teach it accurately'.

The Head Mistress of the College was Miss Dorette Wilkie, a woman of imagination and broad outlook. She at once perceived the practical value of Sharp's gospel. Not only did her readiness to co-operate with him make the School possible, but throughout their association her encouragement and sympathy were of real help.

Miss Wilkie gave Sharp a free hand, and before the School opened he gave personal instruction, assisted by occasional visits from Kimber, to the College students and members of the staff, so that he was already provided with a competent body of teachers. He was also able to draw upon the students to illustrate his lectures, and of those who then danced and taught for him Miss M. W. Sinclair and Miss Kennedy (Mrs. Kennedy North) are still actively concerned in the progress of the folk-dance movement.

It should be admitted that Sharp's first venture into the dance was open to the criticism, which was in fact made, that the dancing was wooden and without grace. It may be added that that criticism is frequently made in other matters when the teaching has not yet had time to be absorbed, and that it was made repeatedly by Sharp himself in after years of his pupils.

CHAPTER VIII

1910–1912

THE VALLEY OF DECISION

Οὐ καλὸν ὦ φίλε πάντα λόγον ποτὶ τέκτονα φοιτᾶν,
μηδ᾽ ἐπὶ πάντ᾽ ἄλλω χρέος ἰσχέμεν· ἀλλὰ καὶ αὐτὸς
τεχνᾶσθαι σύριγγα· πέλει δέ τοι εὐμαρὲς ἔργον.[1]

BION, *Frag.*

THE year 1910 was spent in assiduous collecting, teaching, adjudicating, and lecturing (with demonstrations by the Chelsea Physical Training College students). Owing to pressure of work Sharp was persuaded by his wife to resign his post at Ludgrove (which he had held for eighteen years) at the end of the summer term. It says much for his faith in the movement and for Mrs. Sharp's self-sacrificing devotion to her husband that this step was taken when the Ludgrove teaching was his only regular source of income. Apart from that he had only royalties and lecture fees to depend on, and many lectures were given gratis;[2] these in 1910 brought in an income of £536 (£373 in royalties and £161 in lecture fees)—not a vast sum on which to bring up four children. It may be mentioned here that throughout his life Sharp never sought a change of work. As he wrote later to his daughter Joan:

On principle I do not believe in change. In this matter I have always allowed events to dictate to me rather than attempt to control them myself. I can think of but few cases in my own life when I have deliberately forced a change—perhaps it might have been better if I had. But . . . it seems to me that normally change waits on development; I mean that as one gains experience in one's work

[1] You want a pipe made? Well then, try my plan:
Don't hand it over to another man
To make; make it yourself. You'll find you can.

[2] Mrs. Lindo wishes it to be stated that her fee was always paid after these lectures, even if it left nothing, or less than that, for him.

extension of opportunity is natural—and pretty sure to offer itself—
and then being natural the change is of the best kind.

Miss Neal was equally busy at this time. Her *Esperance Morris Book* came out in April, and she gave a successful exhibition of the morris at Kensington (May 5th).
These activities and the inclusion of the morris dance
by the Board of Education (see p. 77) in its syllabus of
Physical Training kept the whole question, and the differences of view, in the public eye. A snowstorm of letters in
the *Morning Post* about this time added a little public
acrimony to a dispute which, as long as it could be
private, both principals had to their credit kept within
bounds.

The Association for the Revival and Practice of Folk
Music was superseded by the Esperance Morris Guild;
and this emphasized what had always been in fact the
close connexion between the Club and the general dance
propaganda. Sharp, to prevent misunderstanding, wrote
to the *Morning Post* (April 1st, 1910) disclaiming any
connexion with the Guild:

Any Society which really succeeds in reviving English traditional
dancing ought to have the support of all those interested in the subject. It is, however, obvious that if our folk-dances are to be revived
amongst the lettered classes it is of supreme importance that they
should be accurately taught by accredited instructors and that only
those dances should be disseminated which are the survivals of
genuine and unbroken tradition. And these, of course, are questions
for the expert.

Miss Neal, on the other hand, maintained that

it behoves those of us to whom has been entrusted the guidance and
the helping of this movement for the renewal of beauty in life to
tread reverently, and to see to it that the blighting touch of the
pedant and the expert is not laid upon it. As the folk-music and
dance and drama are communal in their origin and the work of no
one individual, and have come from the heart of the unlettered
folk, so the handing on of them and the development should also

be left in the hands of the simple-minded and of those musically unlettered and ignorant of all technique. (*Vanity Fair*, 14.4.10.)

And in an interview in the *Morning Post* of May 5th, 1910, she said:

This is not a personal matter between Mr. Sharp and myself, nor of any difference between the Morris Guild, for which I am responsible, and any institution in which Mr. Sharp is interested. It is merely an example of a deeply rooted, age-long controversy which is always going on. It may be described as the difference between the form and the life, the bookman and the workman, between the pedant and those in touch with actual life itself. I am not characterising Mr. Sharp as a pedant or anything else, but only speaking of the principle. In the first instance Mr. Sharp worked very amicably with the Esperance Club, but I have always expected what has happened. Where we join issue is in our definition of the word 'expert'. I recognise no expert in morris dancing but those who have been directly taught by the traditional dancer. In this sense, therefore, the teachers sent out by the Esperance Club are expert teachers. I gather that Mr. Sharp defines an expert in a totally different sense, the chief qualifications in his view being a thorough knowledge of the technique of music and dancing. Certainly it is necessary to be possessed of technique and experience in collecting folk-songs, but, in my opinion, any average person of intelligence can collect a morris dance, and, having seen a traditional dancer, is quite able to say whether the dance has been handed on in a correct form. To me it seems as unreasonable to talk about an expert in morris dances as to talk about an expert in making people happy.

Sharp's reply was to criticize the exposition of morris dances as given by the Esperance Club and to point out the difficulties by which the collector is beset and the need for expert knowledge, in order to 'appraise the traditional value of the revived dance, to detect the faked dance, or to exercise a wise discrimination with regard to corrupt dances'.

As activities increased so did the causes of offence on either side. The public, while distressed in a general way that people should have to quarrel about a pastime which was intended to give pleasure, were inclined to take Miss Neal's view, especially as they saw her delivering the goods; and a sentence by the music critic of *Vanity Fair* expressed this:

I do not care two straws whether the steps are traditional or not; if we can save the soul of the morris dance, the body is of little account;

a sentence which blandly ignored the fact that both parties relied on tradition. Some of them, who were aware that there was a point at issue, but were not sure what it was, pinned their faith to dogmas about the 'straight' and 'bent' knee, and made party cries of these.

In 1910 the Summer School of the Morris Guild was an attractive incident in the Stratford-on-Avon Shakespeare Festival. Mr. (now Sir Archibald) Flower was the Chairman of the Board of Governors, and Mr. (now Sir Frank) Benson, when he was not busy with the theatre, considered with him this question of folk-dance. Both were struck by the organization of the Guild and its effective result. At the same time they were aware that the inaccuracy with which it had been charged might sully the reputation of their festival. They tried the compromise of having a definition of the morris step drawn up and signed both by Miss Neal and by Sharp; but this, of course, fell through.

Miss Neal now decided to strengthen her position. Only a few months earlier she had denied that there was any expert in morris dancing but the traditional dancer himself. She went in October to Headington to see and talk with other members of the morris side from which William Kimber had come, and to get some tunes (which were afterwards harmonized by Mr. G. Toye); she was accompanied by Mr. Clive Carey, Mr. F. Toye, and a typist. The inquiry was directed to finding out (1) whether it ought to be straight or bent leg—on this the evidence was conflicting; (2) whether Kimber was a 'traditional' dancer —and her information seemed to show[1] that he was not the leader, but a member of a traditional team (which was disbanded soon after he entered it), that he had been taught by traditional men, and that his father was a dancer; and (3) small details about various dances. The object of the expedition, as it was explained to Sharp when the typewritten notes were handed to him, was to show that since Kimber's 'tradition' could be questioned, Mr. Sharp's knowledge of the morris, as obtained from him, was not the knowledge of an expert. Sharp's comment was:

Taking your notes as they stand, there is nothing in them which in my opinion throws any doubt upon Kimber's authenticity, or (except a few points which I believe to be not strictly accurate) which conflicts in any way with what I have written or said in public.

and Kimber's,

Please keep up your spirits. I will stick to you like a leech, and would like to stand in any hall in London and face the biggest audience so as to explain the truth.

The notes were then sent to the Governors at Stratford. Nothing happened in consequence.

With Mr. Flower, as Chairman of the Governors, lay the decision as to whether Miss Neal should be invited to bring her dancing to Stratford, or Sharp his. He found himself between Mr. Lee Mathews, who was strongly in favour of Sharp, and Mr. Benson, who almost as strongly supported Miss Neal. He thought the best way would be to invite Sharp to meet them both. We have only Sharp's account of the meeting.

They were all very friendly to me and I enjoyed myself very much, although I knew the ordeal was of vital importance and had not closed my eyes for two nights. I talked incessantly—they made me and wanted me to; and I am quite sure, whether they agreed or

[1] The actual facts are given on p. 71.

not, that I really interested them, simply because they had never before realized in the least what the folk-movement means.

As the result of this meeting, Flower asked for a short statement of Sharp's views. It was:

The question is this: Is the morris dance to be transferred to the classes in its traditional form, or is it to be arbitrarily changed to suit the caprice of Miss Neal or of any other responsible or irresponsible person? On this point, there can, as far as I am concerned, be no compromise.

At the beginning of 1911 Sharp talked of throwing up everything and emigrating to Australia. He was in poor health, for his asthma was getting steadily worse; his eldest daughter, Dorothea, was seriously ill; the family was in straitened circumstances; and, worst of all, he felt that his work of reviving the dances was severely handicapped by the misconceptions and misunderstandings which had arisen concerning them. Prospects gradually brightened. In May the family moved to Uxbridge on Dorothea's account, where she slowly recovered her health. Sharp had a fine, large room for his study and enjoyed digging in the garden when he was at home, but he found the constant journeys to and from town an effort.

In July he was told he had been awarded a Civil List Pension of £100 a year in consideration of his services in the collection and preservation of English folk-songs. This was a welcome addition to the family income, which was then £500 a year, including his wife's patrimony, and the recognition heartened him. A friend who was instrumental in getting the pension wrote to Sharp:

I wish you could have seen the document we sent to the Prime Minister—it was the most remarkable collection of distinguished names I have ever seen—about 30 in all—and I am certain more would have signed if they had been asked, only we were advised that with such a list we need go no further. . . . You have admirers in all sorts of unexpected quarters.

85

This was all the more gratifying seeing that the professed musicians as a body ignored him; and, even in the article on Folk-Song in the 1910 edition, Grove's *Dictionary of Music* had no mention of his name.[1]

Meanwhile Sharp went on with his propaganda and continued to give, all over the country, lectures illustrated by the students of the Chelsea Physical Training College. In June, at the Festival of Empire held at Crystal Palace, he gave a series of lectures, and organized demonstrations of dances and singing games. In these the Physical Training College students took part, as well as children from the Oratory School, brought by Father Kerr. Miss Neal conceived the idea that Sharp had exceeded his rights in making use of the Chelsea students for his own private advantage, and threatened to have a question asked about it in Parliament. This was not asked; if it had been, not much would have come of it, as he had not received money for the lectures.

Miss Neal spent the early part of 1911 lecturing in America. She found on her return to England that she no longer had the whole-hearted support of the Governors of the Shakespeare Memorial Theatre; she therefore resigned her position as Honorary Secretary of the Summer School, pending a Conference which the Governors proposed to call, to discuss the diverse views on folk-dancing. In June

[1] When in 1918 Sharp was asked if he would allow his biography to appear in the American supplement, he replied:

'It is nice of you to wish to include my name, but I do not quite see what I have to do with the American volume, seeing that I am an English musician and am merely temporarily a visitor here. If my name and work were worthy of mention in the *Dictionary*, the proper place would, of course, have been in the English volumes. As, however, the editor thought fit to omit my name I do not feel particularly inclined to allow it to appear in the supplementary American volume. The only part of my work which might, perhaps, be mentioned in your part of the publication is that which I have done in the way of folk-song collecting and publishing in America and that, it seems to me, could be mentioned under the heading of folk-song or folk-dance.'

Sharp's programme was substituted for Miss Neal's. He describes the opportunity as 'a grand one and I mean to make the most of it'. In discussing with Mr. Flower the appointment of a teaching Staff, which included Mattie Kay, Miss Walsh (Mrs. Kettlewell), Miss Maud and Miss Helen Karpeles (Mrs. Douglas Kennedy), and students of the Chelsea Physical Training College, he writes:

I believe that if we can get the teaching properly done and organised the thing will succeed; otherwise it is foredoomed. . . . The less talk in the papers the better. There are scores of people who want the substance and not the shadow and who are ready to go to plenty of trouble to get it.

The School was held in August. Apart from the weekly demonstration of dances in the Theatre Gardens, activities took place in the seclusion of the Council Schools or in the 'Parish Parlour'. For about five hours each day sixty or seventy people met for folk-songs,[1] dance-classes, and lectures; and to stress the social side, a country-dance party was held at the end of each week. The School was repeated for one week during the Christmas holidays. Among the students was George Butterworth, who said of it that it was one of the few occasions when he felt he had lived in a really musical atmosphere.

About this time some members of the Chelsea Poly-technic classes, Miss Maud and Miss Helen Karpeles,

[1] It was of such a gathering that W. D. Howells wrote in his *The Seen and Unseen at Stratford-on-Avon* (Harper, New York, 1914):

'. . . One of the ballads was so modern as to be in celebration of the *Shannon's* victory over the *Chesapeake* in the War of 1812, when the American ship went out from Boston to fight the British, and somehow got beaten. It had a derisive refrain of "Yankee Doodle Dandy O", and whether or not the lecturer divined our presence, and imagined our pain from this gibe, it is certain that the next time he gave the ballad to be sung, he adventurously excused it on the ground that it possibly celebrated the only British victory of the war. Nothing could have been handsomer than that, and it was the true Shakespearian spirit of Stratford where fourteen thousand Americans come every year to claim our half of Shakespeare's glory.'

87

Miss Maggie Müller, and Miss Peggy Walsh, began to get up folk-dance meetings with friends, whom they taught, and eventually, as the Folk-Dance Club, they gave a performance for a charity in the Portman Rooms, Baker Street, at which Sharp lectured and Mattie Kay sang. The advantage of their being an organization independent of the Chelsea Polytechnic was obvious, and now that it had come about in a natural way Sharp threw his aegis over it, and the Club became the nucleus of the English Folk Dance Society.

At a meeting on December 6th, 1911, at St. Andrew's Hall, Newman Street (Mr. T. Lennox Gilmour in the Chair), Cecil Sharp moved

that a Society, to be called The English Folk Dance Society, be established, having its headquarters in London, with the object of preserving and promoting the practice of English folk-dances in their true traditional form.

He emphasized the artistic character of the movement and the importance of a high standard of execution, and summarized its objects thus:

The instruction of members and others in folk-dancing; the training of teachers, and the granting of certificates of proficiency; the holding of dance meetings for members at which dancing shall be general, and of meetings at which papers shall be read and discussed; the publication of literature dealing with folk-dancing and kindred subjects; the foundation, organisation, and artistic control of local branches in London, the Provinces and elsewhere; the supplying of teachers and providing of lectures and displays to schools, colleges and other institutions; the technical and artistic supervision of the Vacation Schools of Folk-Song and Dance at Stratford-on-Avon, organised by the Governors of the Shakespeare Memorial Theatre.

A committee[1] was appointed. A guarantee of £113 was

[1] Lady Gomme, Mrs. Arthur Sidgwick, Miss Maud Karpeles, Mr. A. D. Flower, Mr. Hercy Denman, Dr. R. Vaughan Williams, Mr. Cecil Sharp, Mr. Perceval Lucas, Mr. G. J. Wilkinson, and Miss Helen Karpeles (Hon. Secretary). Subsequently the names of Mr. George

promised, but was not called upon. Mr. Wilfred Mark Webb (of the Selborne Society) offered the Society temporary accommodation at his offices in Bloomsbury Square, and this was accepted for a period of six months.

The Stratford-on-Avon Summer School of 1912, again directed by Sharp, was held under the auspices of the English Folk Dance Society, and on August 13th a Conference was convened by the Governors of the Shakespeare Memorial Theatre. The issue to be debated was what it had always been, whether the dance, especially morris, should be taught to a standard of accuracy affording artistic delight, or should be cultivated mainly for enjoyment with such accuracy as would then be obtainable.

With Mr. Flower in the Chair, the speakers included Dr. (Sir Arthur) Somervell, Mr. Selby Bigge (Secretary to the Board of Education), Mr. Frank Benson, Dr. Vaughan Williams, Mrs. Mary Davis, Lady Margesson, Miss Neal, and Mr. Sharp. The Chairman opened the meeting by saying that he hoped the Conference would assist the Governors to find points of agreement on the three following questions: (1) Was it wise to establish the School of folk-dancing? (2) If so, what standards should be set? (3) Had Stratford special opportunities for encouraging such a School? He added that it might be said that the proper way to learn the dances was to go straight to the 'folk' who danced them, but that was not practicable; and the only plan was to secure instruction from experts who had collected and studied the dances and to bring students and experts together in one centre. He asked whether it was possible to establish a standard that would be generally acceptable, for the Governors were anxious that their foundations should be secure.

Sharp said that the subject attracted ethnologists, educationists, and philanthropists; that the most important

Butterworth and Miss Wilkie were added; Captain Kettlewell was appointed Honorary Treasurer, and Miss Walsh (Mrs. Kettlewell) Secretary.

aspect was the artistic, and that they had to understand that they were first collectors and then disseminators, and that they were in the position of trustees in a task requiring at every stage the help of all those who were imbued with the idea that the things that were being passed on were arts. Once folk-song and -dance were established as arts and were practised by the whole nation and not by a part of the community, the main difficulties would be overcome.

Mr. Benson, in pointing out the danger that existed of over-emphasizing the art side at the expense of the unconscious joy side, voiced the opinions of many of Sharp's critics. Their way, according to him, lay 'between the Scylla of academic perfection and the Charybdis of the untutored joy of the savage'. Miss Neal had been working in wildernesses of bricks and mortar and had brought joy and gladness to many hearts. He hoped that the Conference might result in drawing the two leaders more closely together.

The Rev. Francis Hodgson proposed that a National Board of Folk-Song and Dance should be formed with Mr. Sharp and Miss Neal on the directorate, and Miss Neal replied that she was prepared to assist in putting some such scheme in action. Dr. Vaughan Williams held the view, shortly, that 'every art, however simple, if it is to be of value, must be founded on something natural in the human being; therefore if we keep the traditional side pure, we may be quite sure that we are not departing from anything natural in the human being . . . and we are teaching something which is spontaneous and which is sincere.'

All the cards were now on the table and the issue was clear. It was too late to talk picturesquely of the Symplegades: the choice was between a definite Morris Guild and an equally definite Folk-Dance Society. The Morris Guild was, indeed, not aiming at 'the untutored joy of the savage'; but who knew that it would not run through the country like a prairie fire, and in a few years there

would be nothing left of the dance? The English Folk
Dance Society offered no unconscious joy, only conscious
work, and that joy which would infallibly come from it. Its
friends called this offer 'accuracy', its enemies 'pedantry'.
But those were *words*; the *thing* was simple:—Is this dance
—the morris, for the moment, but with the country and
the sword looming behind that—now rehabilitated by a
scholar and accepted at last by all who take part in it as
their birthright, worth the effort to establish it firmly; or
is it a plaything to be discarded when we are tired of it?

The Conference cleared the air to some extent by
accepting the Chairman's summing up in favour of accuracy, but apart from this nothing came of it, and Miss
Neal and Mr. Sharp continued to work independently
through their own organizations. The Esperance Club
continued its activities until 1914, but during the War
these lapsed and were not afterwards revived.

As to 'pedantry', there is some evidence as to how
Sharp felt about it. He writes to a fellow-collector:

> I think it is very easy to be too touchy about the vulgarisation of
> things like folk-songs which one loves. A lover of Beethoven's
> music must feel the same if ever he thought of the way his favourite
> composer's music is being rendered in Crouch End, Hornsey, etc.
> If anything good is to be made popular, many things will happen
> which will shock the sensitive feelings of the elect. This is inevit-
> able and must be accepted. I accept it in this case because I believe
> so sincerely in the innate beauty and purity of folk-music that I am
> sure it cannot really be contaminated, but that it must and will
> always do good wherever it finds a resting-place.

And when, later on, after the dance was established, an
enthusiastic dancer asked him in horrified tones whether
he realized how much bad teaching of it existed in the
——shire schools, he was sympathetic but unmoved. He
merely asked her if she was aware how much bad teaching
of Shakespeare and of arithmetic there was in these same
schools. But to his own staff he showed the other side of

91

the picture. He pointed out to them that the scraping and scratching of a street-fiddler could do no harm to music, because no one, however unmusical, would be likely to mistake that for the sort of thing that was to be heard in the Queen's Hall; but in the absence of a generally accepted standard of folk-dancing any shortcomings on the part of his Staff would be attributed not to themselves but to the art which they were presenting. It was never in Sharp's mind to discard all but the best. The important thing to him was the establishment and recognition of a standard, not the uniform conformity to that standard.

The temptations to get side-tracked were many. Some thought folk-dance an opportunity for dress-reform; some for obtaining or maintaining health; some thought it an antidote to communism, as keeping the proletariat content, others a step towards communism as bringing them together in a common purpose. Against all these Sharp was on his guard, but perhaps most of all he feared the philanthropist. Early in 1910 he wrote to a friend:

Enthusiasm that is uninformed seems to me to be capable of working more harm in the world than anything else. The fact is, philanthropy and art have nothing in common, and to unite them spells disaster.

Sharp's aim was 'to transmit two elaborate forms of artistic expression [the song and the dance] from one class of the nation to the rest of the community'—nothing less would satisfy him; and this aim rested on the faith that these arts, 'although surviving amongst only a small section of the community, belong to and express the ideals and aspirations of the entire nation'.

It you want a thing done, do it yourself. The net result of this seven years' war was that he had to learn to do his own organizing. When he turned to this he was not found wanting, as we shall see. His wife was not always in sympathy with this preoccupation with folk-music; she thought he ought to have been, and could have been, a composer, or failing that, would have made a great prime minister. We shall honour her faith and still more the works with which she supported it; but incidentally her remark pays tribute to what she felt to be his powers of organization. Seven years of opposition taught him what government should be. To the arguments for the cause in which he believed, which had been based on knowledge and feeling, he was to add the stronger argument of work done.

[1] Rule will show the man.

CHAPTER IX

1910–1914

FOLK-DANCE COLLECTING

Daucing (bright Lady) then began to be,
When the first seedes whereof the world did spring,
The Fire, Ayre, Earth, and Water did agree,
By Loues perswasion, Natures mighty King,
To leaue their first disordred combating;
And in a daunce such measure to obserue,
As all the world their motion should preserue.

Since when they still are carried in a round,
And changing come one in anothers place;
Yet doe they neyther mingle nor confound,
But euery one doth keepe the bounded space
Wherein the Daunce doth bid it turne or trace:
This wondrous myracle did Loue deuise,
For Daucing is Loues proper exercise.

SIR JOHN DAVIES (1569–1626).

WE must now look a little more closely into the three dances — morris, country, and sword. The folk-dance revival started with the Headington morris. Morris dances from other villages were soon added; by 1907 there were country dances, and three years later sword dances. For collecting Sharp had no cut-and-dried plan; he went to any place where he had news of a dancer, or thought he was likely to find one, but since this news came usually from a neighbouring village he tended to have centres, just as for folk-song he had Somerset and Devon, leaving Wiltshire and Cornwall to any other man of abounding energy with short holidays and short purse, with a fund of patience and a sense of humour. Thus he found morris from Stow-on-the-Wold, where he happened to spend the summer holidays of 1908, and from there spread his net gradually over Warwick, Gloucester, and Oxford, where the morris chiefly persisted—such places as Bampton, Eynsham, Leafield, Sherborne, Longborough,

94

Ilmington, and Adderbury, also Bledington and Bucknell, where George Butterworth continued his work, and Badby (Northants), which Butterworth found for himself. The sword belongs, of course, to the north, and he found the long-sword in Yorkshire (Kirkby Malzeard, Haxby, Escrick, Handsworth, &c.), and the rapper (short-sword) in Northumberland and Durham (Earsdon, Winlaton, Beadnell, and others). The country dance, like the folk-song, is not peculiar to any one locality, and he collected examples of this from a few scattered places where it had survived.

To Bampton he bicycled (20 miles) daily from Stow. It is the only village in England where there has been no break in the morris tradition, and the annual Whit-Monday is an institution, though the dance of the present day differs in important particulars from the dance of the older men which Sharp noted. It is there that William Wells, from whom he got the tunes and most of the dances, still fiddles (with the middle six inches of his bow), though now almost blind.

Bampton, Headington, and Eynsham were the only villages in which Sharp saw a complete team; elsewhere the dances had to be obtained from single individuals, many of them long past their prime, who could do no more than indicate the movements. His best chance of getting the dances was to find the man, if he was still alive, who had acted as foreman, i.e. had danced as No. 1. Sharp would ask him to take his old place and he himself would stand at his side as No. 2, and the rest of the team had to be imagined. Then while he hummed the tune they would together go through the movements of the dance, Sharp watching and imitating as best he could while he jotted down a few pencil notes. In all cases the first thing was to note and learn the tune, so as to hum it over to the dancer, for no morris man can reproduce the move-

95

ments unless he has the tune in mind. Even then he will be unable to analyse or explain what he is doing. He cannot dissociate his movements from the tune; and it is a continual surprise to him that it does not similarly connote the dance to others. The playing, too, is an instinctive business. Sharp once presented a bow to Charlie Benfield of Bledington, an old fiddler whose own bow had been broken some years previously, since when he had been unable to play his fiddle. The old man tuned up and played over a few tunes, but the result did not please him. Thoughtfully he examined and fingered his new bow, and said: 'It looks all right, and it seems a nice bow, but somehow it won't keep time with the other hand.'

The Morris Book, Part 3, was published in 1910, and Part 4 in 1911. In the Preface of Part 4 Sharp regrets that pressure of work has prevented Mr. MacIlwaine from taking any part in the compilation of the new volume. He would have left his name on the title-page, but to this Mr. MacIlwaine would not agree, and Sharp was compelled with reluctance to respect his wishes.

For *The Morris Book*, Part 5 (1914), Sharp found another collaborator in George Butterworth. Butterworth also took his share of arranging the tunes for pianoforte. He undertook the task without serious apprehension, and arranged the tunes to his own satisfaction as a musician, but then discovered that his settings were entirely unsuitable as dance-accompaniments, and that the only satisfactory solution was to scrap them and imitate Sharp's methods. This he did with such success that Sharp himself could not after a little while remember which were his own arrangements and which were Butterworth's.

In the year 1910 Sharp published in collaboration with Lady Gomme the first of five series of children's Singing Games. His note-books show that all the games in this publication are versions collected by himself, so that there would have been nothing to prevent him, had he wished, from publishing an independent collection. He did not do so because Lady Gomme was, as is well known, the authority on English children's games, and he did not wish to trespass on her domain.

In the same year he published *The Country Dance Book*, Part 1, which consists of eighteen traditional dances collected in Derby, Devon, Somerset, Surrey, and Warwick. They are all 'longways for as many as will', practically the only type of country dance which has lingered on into the twentieth century.

The moment has now come for the reader to take off his hat to John Playford, a very great man. Sharp wrote of him:

> There are many ways by which men may become great and win the honour of posterity. Some achieve greatness through the possession of unusual intellectual or inventive faculties; others, like John Playford, without any special natural gifts, by patient work performing a greatly needed service for their own generation and doing it well and truly. This to plain people like ourselves is no small comfort.[1]

John Playford's *Dancing Master*[2] is the book at which Sharp worked for months in the British Museum, deciphering the dances. In 1911 he published a description of thirty of these (in *The Country Dance Book*, Part 2). *The Dancing Master*, called in the first edition *The English Dancing Master*, went through seventeen editions (1650–1728), which have all become rare. During the three parts of a century covered by this book the dances appeared in altered forms; some dropped out and others were constantly added. Of the earlier editions John Playford was not only publisher, but probably took a large share in the editing of the dances. He is not easy to decipher: the

---

[1] From a lecture given at Aldeburgh Vacation School, August 1923.

[2] Two other of his books were *An Introduction to the Skill of Music*, 1654 (twenty editions, to one of which Purcell contributed), and *The Whole Book of Psalms*, 1677 (twenty editions), the storehouse of the old English hymn-tune.

directions are laconic (they are, of course, such as could be 'called' quickly) and the misprints numerous. The book is addressed to those who knew the dance already and would not need explanation; Sharp could arrive at a tentative definition of 'to side', for instance, only after a deal of correlation of texts.

Although Playford was the first to give us a technical description, the dance was known at least a century earlier. In *Misogonus*, *c.* 1560, two Playford dances, 'Putney Ferry' and 'The Shaking of the Sheets', are mentioned. Unlike the morris and sword the country dance is a social and non-spectacular dance, and it does not appear to have been the exclusive possession of any one class of society. The Earl of Worcester in 1602 writes to the Earl of Shrewsbury: 'We all frolic here at Court; much dancing in the Privy Chamber of country dances before the Queen's Majesty, who is extremely pleased therewith'; and Pepys describes the performance of a country dance at the Court of King Charles in 1662, where it took its place amongst the Branles, Corantos, and other French dances.[1] At the beginning of the eighteenth century, and perhaps earlier, the English country dance travelled abroad, was danced at many European Courts, and enhanced our reputation as 'the dancing English'.[2] During the eighteenth century the dance held its sway together with the Minuet, which occupied the first part of the programme at the Assembly Rooms.

[1] A quotation from Selden's *Table Talk*, 1689, may also be given:
'In our Court in Queen Elizabeth's time gravity and state were kept up. In King James's time things went pretty well, but in King Charles's time there has been nothing but Trenchmore and the Cushion Dance, omnium gatherum, tolly-polly, hoite come toite.'

[2] In 1717 Lady Mary Wortley Montagu writes from Vienna:
'The Ball always concludes with English Country Dances to the number of thirty or forty couples, and so ill danced that there is little pleasure in them. They know but half-a-dozen and they have danced them over and over these fifty years. I would fain have taught them some new ones, but I found it would be some months' labour to make them comprehend them.'

Many of the tunes in the Playford collection are not pure folk-dances, although they may be said to rest on a traditional basis. Some of the tunes—particularly those in the later editions—are popular composed tunes of the day, which were pressed into the service of the dance, or may even have been written expressly for it. The country dance, as Sharp has pointed out, ordinarily consisted of figures arbitrarily chosen to fit a given tune, and only in certain instances did a particular combination of figures become stereotyped and achieve universal acceptance. The older dances in the collection had probably been danced for many generations in the same way to the same tune, but there is no doubt that others owe a great deal to the creative efforts of John Playford and his assistants. This conscious manipulation of traditional material by those who were immersed in the spirit of the dance brought forth some beautiful results, but the creative development was not sustained. During the eighteenth century, under the influence of the dancing-master, whose opportunity came with the rise of the middle class,[1] the dance became formal and sophisticated. Its fashion moved towards the 'longways' form,[2] which lent itself more easily to decorous treatment; the 'rounds', 'square eights', and other forms gradually disappeared. In the early nineteenth century the 'longways' dance itself was displaced from popular favour by the waltz and quadrille, since when it has survived only in a few English villages and in certain rural districts of America.

In his choice of dances—he published 158 in four

[1] 'Even the wives and daughters of low tradesmen, who like shove-nosed sharks prey upon the blubber of those uncouth whales of fortune, are infected with the same rage of displaying their importance and the slightest indisposition serves them for a pretext to insist upon being conveyed to Bath where they may hobble Country Dances and Cotillions among lordlings, squires, counsellors and clergy.'—Smollett's *Humphry Clinker* (1771).

[2] Out of 104 dances in the first edition 38 are longways; whilst in the last edition there are 914 out of 918.

volumes[1]—Sharp was guided by aesthetic considerations and by the practical problem of accurate deciphering, but he gave preference to the earlier versions of the dance in which the traditional element was strongest. The question is sometimes asked why he should have paid so much attention to the 'Playford' dances, seeing that they were not of pure folk-origin. It seems all the more surprising when we reflect that he gave such a firm ruling about 'traditional' song. But he was an artist and not an antiquarian; the dances were the direct outcome of an unbroken tradition, *and* they were beautiful. 'That was ample reason for our Punch.'

In July 1910 Sharp saw his first sword dance, that is, the team dance of northern England in which five, six, or eight men take part, not the Scottish solo dance. The dance is one of great complexity, demanding strength, skill, and, above all, fine team-work. A false movement on the part of any one performer will throw the whole into confusion, for the dancers are linked together in a ring by their swords, each holding the hilt of his own sword in one hand and the point of his neighbour's in the other. Without breaking this link they perform the most elaborate evolutions, twisting under the swords, jumping over them, turning the ring inside out, breaking it up into smaller rings, and so on. The climax of the dance is invariably brought about by the plaiting of the swords into a star of five, six, or eight points, according to the number of dancers. The plaited swords are then held aloft by the leader, and afterwards placed, as a rule, round the neck of one of the dancers or of an extra character. At a word from the leader each dancer releases his sword by drawing it towards him; whereupon the victim suffers a mimic

---

[1] *The Country Dance Book,* Part 2 (1911); Part 3 (1914) and Part 4 (1916), both in collaboration with George Butterworth; and Part 6 (1922).

decapitation and, falling down, feigns death, from which he is afterwards miraculously brought to life. The dance is known in various forms throughout Europe and is held to be the survival of a pagan fertility rite, possibly the dramatic representation of the cyclic death of the old year and the re-birth of the new.

The sword dancers of Kirkby Malzeard, Yorks., had in 1886 performed at the Ripon Millenary Pageant, and it was from Mr. d'Arcy de Ferrars, the Master of the Pageant, that Sharp had heard of the dancers. When he first interviewed them they said that they had not performed the dance for some time, and that they were doubtful whether they could put it together again. Sharp asked them to think about it, and to practise, and said he would come back in a week's time, which he did. The men told him that they had at first despaired of remembering it, but at their last practice it had all suddenly come right. Sharp noted the dance, and at a later visit verified it. Those who have seen a sword dance will realize the difficulties that were involved. Sharp said:

When first I saw the dance performed it looked to be one continuous movement. It was not until I had seen it repeated that I realised it to be really compounded of a series of distinct and separate figures, like beads on a string.

On Tuesday evenings Sharp used to hold what he called an 'experimental class' at the Chelsea Polytechnic, where he tested any dance that he had just collected, or had deciphered from 'Playford'. The Kirkby Malzeard Sword Dance was, however, collected during the holidays, and so the experimenting had to be done within the family circle. It was only on the days when the charwoman came that a complete team could be got together; and when finally the dance was performed in public there was no more appreciative or critical member of the audience than that charwoman. This dance, together with the Grenoside (Yorks.) and two forms of the rapper, were published in 1911 in *Sword Dances of Northern England*, Part 1.

During the next two years Sharp gave much time to the collection of the sword dances of Yorkshire, Northumberland, and Durham; and as a preliminary he sent a reply post-card to the incumbent of every parish in these counties. *Sword Dances of Northern England*, Part 2, was published in 1912, and Part 3 in 1913. In all fourteen dances were published.

The third volume contains, as does the first, an introduction dealing with the origin and significance of the sword dance, and also the text of a version of the folk-play which was formerly associated with the dance. This used to be performed at Ampleforth, a village about eighteen miles north of York, but had been discontinued about twenty years previously. A visit to Ampleforth brought to light only one man who knew the play, and he could remember only a few lines; but Sharp was told of an older man who had left the village and would probably remember more, since he used to dance, and at times play the part of the Clown. His name was said to be George Wright, and his present address, 'No. 4, Darlington'. That seemed vague, but Sharp, knowing the habits of our people, casually took up a china ornament on the mantelpiece and found it stuffed with old letters, among them being one with the old man's address, 'No. 4 The Bank, Darlington'. Calling there next afternoon he was told by a young woman that she had just put grandfather to bed with a poultice to keep him comfortable, but she would get him up if the gentleman wished. Glad to be got up, the old man described the dance and gradually remembered many lines of the play he used to act fifty years before.

This is only one of the many instances of 'detective' work which Sharp had to undertake to find a singer or a dancer. He would often spend a whole day toiling along on his bicycle—this was before motor-transport was common, and anyhow he could not have afforded to travel that way—to trace a dancer or a singer of whom he had heard, to find him in the end, perhaps, only a few miles from where he had started. 'Well,' he said one day after arriving home tired out, wet, cold, and hungry, 'I am not likely to have many competitors at this job.'

His love of prompt action was nowhere more marked than in collecting; and if his morning correspondence contained any likely clue, he would be off with his bicycle by the next train. His promptness was sometimes justi-fied: the old man who gave him the Escrick sword dance died just two days later—not, Sharp was relieved to hear, as the result of his exertions.

In many cases he got his information of the sword dances, as of the morris, from one single survivor of the team. One man can give little idea of the sword dance by his individual movements, but fortunately the dance is not the purely instinctive business with the Northerner that it is with the Southerner, and the sword dancer would usually be able, with the help of china dogs, &c., to explain the intricate movements clearly enough for Sharp to recon-struct the whole.

In the promulgation of the dances Sharp was, as we have seen, handicapped by the absence of a scientific and generally accepted system of dance-notation. The most notable systems of the past are to be seen in Arbeau's *Orchésographie* (1588) and Feuillet's *Chorégraphie* (1701). The latter, which is said to have been invented by Beau-champs, dancing-master at the Court of Louis XIV, is an elaborate system of symbols and diagrams, which owing to its complexity is of little practical use. On the other hand Arbeau's notation is, so far as it goes, clear and explicit. Sharp studied them both. In particular he got from Arbeau the idea of indicating the timing of the steps by showing on which notes of the accompanying melody they fall. In Sharp's Morris Dance Books the movements are shown by printing under the melody a line of abbreviated symbols for the steps and a lower line for the track, whilst the hand-movements are placed above the melody. The system which he evolved with the help of Herbert MacIlwaine proved not only serviceable at the moment but capable of extension for the description of the many forms of morris dance which he afterwards collected. In the sword and country dances, which unlike the morris have no great variety of steps, the figures are made clear by a description of the relative tracks of the dancers and, in the case of the sword dance, by defining the position of the swords. From 1911 onwards Sharp submitted all the drafts of his dance-books to Dr. E. Phillips Barker, and acknowledged more than once the assistance which he got from his clear and analytical mind.

Sharp has been criticized (see p. 70 n.) for publishing his dance investigations at too early a stage, and, as we remember, some of the dances in his first Morris Book were discarded in the second edition as being of doubtful authenticity. In all later publications he selected and discriminated with great care. To what extent he used his powers of selection both of songs and dances may be seen from the following figures, which include his final collections and publications (excluding the tunes transcribed from 'Playford').

		Published		
	with accompaniment	*without accompaniment*[1]	*Unpublished*	*Collected*
English {Song	291	209[2]	2,313	2,813
{Dance	148	0	334	482
Appalachian Song	62[3]	909[4]	711	1,682
Total .	501	1,118	3,358	4,977

[1] These numbers do not include tunes which were also published with accompaniment. [2] Including 41 posthumously.
[3] Sharp had intended to add to these, probably another 50.
[4] 596 of these posthumously.

It will therefore be seen that from a total collection of nearly five thousand tunes, Sharp published, in all forms, just over sixteen hundred. Of actual dances (movements and figures) he noted over two hundred, and published (excluding 158 dances from Playford) one hundred and fifty.

CHAPTER X

1912–1914

ORGANIZATION

Totter dantse is meer van doen
Dan het draeghen van ros schoen.[1]
Old Dutch Saying.

WE must now follow the fortunes of the English Folk Dance Society for the first three years. By 1914 the membership of the central society numbered nearly five hundred, and twenty-one provincial branches had been formed. Lectures and demonstrations had been given all over England, in Paris, and in Brussels; numerous classes had been organized in London and the provinces, besides the annual Summer and Christmas Schools at Stratford-on-Avon; examinations had been introduced, and 169 certificates of proficiency granted.

The direction of the Society was a whole-time job, but not a lucrative one, for Sharp received no honorarium, and whereas he was able to earn a little by his lectures on folk-song, he insisted on all fees for folk-dance lectures being paid to the Society. During 1913 his earnings amounted to about £500 (£400 from royalties and £100 from lecture fees). In 1914 he accepted after much persuasion a present of eighty guineas subscribed by some members of the Society, and in expressing his gratitude, wrote:

It is nice to feel that there are so many kind people in the world, and that I am now able to contribute something more to the needs of those who are dependent upon me. After all it is they who have suffered from my restricted income far more than I.

It is significant of Sharp's absorption in the work he was doing, that in the organization of the Society it had

[1] It takes more than a pair of red shoes to make a dancer.

not occurred to him to create the office of Director, and that he had intended to take no more prominent position than that of an ordinary member of Committee. It was only after some persuasion from his fellow committee members that he agreed to accept the post of Honorary Director. Whatever his position, he would, as a matter of fact, have had things his own way on the committee because no one could miss his clearness of vision or run counter to his intensity of purpose. But in any difference of opinion he never allowed his arguments to override other people's objections, and in any important step he postponed action, whenever possible, until the committee was unanimously behind him.

There was nothing pretentious in Sharp's leadership. His address was simple and unaffected. 'Like all big men who work with single-mindedness he had no fireworks or grand ceremonial in his make-up' (Mr. Plunket Greene). In whatever company he found himself he was at his ease and made others feel so. Many would agree with the old morris dancer who spoke of him as 'an understanding gentleman'. The shy, or the taciturn, or the dull, opened out to him. He got the best out of people, because he detected their latent possibilities. An example is given in correspondence to the writer:

He came to Reading to judge a Folk Dancing Festival. There was one class for Women's Institute teams in which my own Institute entered. It was not a good team; they had only had a very few lessons, were none of them under forty (to put it kindly!), and were all busy working-women; but they had so thoroughly enjoyed their classes that it would have appeared too discouraging not to let them enter. The teams against them were composed of quite young women, for the most part light of foot and prettily dressed. My own old ladies were in thick serge skirts and full blouses! When it came to giving the awards and criticisms of the teams I trembled for what might come, but Cecil Sharp, with his wonderful charm and courteousness, said: 'I should like especially to congratulate this team. I understand it is composed entirely of—a little hesitation here as I think he nearly said "grandmothers"—married ladies. I can only hope that their husbands were here to enjoy watching them as much as, obviously, they enjoyed dancing. They have learned to appreciate one of the greatest charms of folk-dancing, namely, that it was not intended only for the young, but for the recreation of the workers of the world, as it has the power like nothing else of taking their minds off the daily drudgery which must fall to their lot. The dancing of this team showed that in this respect it had completely fulfilled its purpose.' If my team had been awarded the first prize, it could not have been more delighted, and many of the onlookers who were inclined to make fun, rather maliciously, were completely silenced. For an act of graceful tact, I think this cannot be beaten, and I have always felt grateful to Cecil Sharp for his charming handling of a trifling situation.

Mr. Arthur Batchelor, too, a sympathetic and discerning friend, has written of Sharp:

It was that delightful gift of sympathy and understanding, combined with his obvious sincerity, which gave him the *entrée* straight into the hearts of the shyest of peasants or the silliest of patricians. I have been privileged like Mr. E. V. Lucas in *London Lavender* to accompany him 'collecting', and have marvelled at the ease with which he managed and made a personal friend of the most secretive and intractable possessor of a folk-song. I have also been amazed at his masterly handling of that incredibly foolish type, the well-meaning 'county' Lady Bountiful with undigested views of her own on what she called 'olde Worlde' dances. In half-an-hour and without relaxing an inch of what he very rightly regarded as essential he had that lady in the palm of his hand, and converted one who, artistically, was a public danger, into an enthusiastic and valuable ally. These were the qualities which gave him such influence on both sides of the Atlantic.

Sharp was conscientious over the details of the organization. He took as much pains over the drafting of a circular as he had taken over the notes of a tune and the steps of a dance. He would carry round the swords and sticks to each classroom himself, or have a personal word for each charwoman. No doubt he might have delegated this; but with the swords he carried good humour, and good temper is a part even of scrubbing floors. Besides, the start of a new movement is not the time to leave anything to chance.

When congratulations and compliments flowed in after a successful demonstration of dances, he put them aside with 'Oh, no! one feels there is so much more to do'. He seized even the smallest opportunity of enlisting people's sympathy. He believed in answering letters carefully and promptly, whether to a learned professor or a village schoolmistress. 'You never know what may come of it,' he would say. In the early days of their acquaintance Dr. Phillips Barker writes:

I begin to regard you as a shining example of what one often hears: that if you want questions answered or business done promptly and completely you must apply to the busy man. I ask you questions, which might conceivably, had you been an idle person with plenty of time, have been answered on a postcard or on one side of letter-paper; you reply by treating the subject fully in a long, interesting, and informing letter.[1]

He could attend to detail, but he kept his sense of proportion. Mr. Granville Barker spoke once of his 're-markable prescience', and illustrated it by his attitude to mechanical music:

Had he been the dilettante which people often think that such enthusiasts are, he would doubtless have said that folk-dances without an old fiddler in a smock frock and a top hat on a village green were impossible. Instead of that he immediately took advantage of the gramophone, had records of the music made, and used them to spread it far more widely than he could otherwise have hoped to do. He saw at once that the question was merely whether the machine was to be the master of the man or the man of the machine. He saw, too, that if one had the root of music in one, machine-made music could do no harm at all, though if one had not, it very well might.

It was, indeed, difficult to uproot the 'Merrie England'

[1] The left-hand corner of the envelope was always marked C♯ — a habit he adopted in Australia, in order to distinguish between private and official letters. (Hence the cover of this book.)

idea of the dances and to convince people that they were not just 'quaint' and 'old world'. In order to stress the modernity of the country dance, Sharp once had a lecture (one of a series given at the Small Queen's Hall in 1913) illustrated by men and women in evening-dress.

It has been said that he had a genius for compromise, which probably means that he took the line of least resistance where unessentials were concerned and stuck out for essentials. If, for instance, he was conventional in his habits, well dressed, and neat and orderly in appearance, it was because it was less trouble to behave in an orthodox than in a Bohemian fashion. In sanctioning women's morris he bowed to the inevitable. Two things influenced him: firstly, the morris had to be taught and he was dependent on women-teachers; and secondly, women's morris, though a translation rather than a representation of the traditional dance, could be an expressive thing in itself. At other times, he could hold a line of his own; for instance, of a proposal to form a folk-song choir, he writes:

26.2.15.

Of course, *we* can have nothing officially to do with it if they go beyond English songs, or at any rate, Scotch, Welsh, or Irish, and that would be rather a stretcher. I was very keen about concentrating ourselves on English things, and that is why we are The *English* Folk Dance Society. You see no one of us knows what are genuine of the foreign ones; then there is the difficulty about translations and if we dabble in them it is likely to have a weakening effect on our own stuff. We have our hands full in running the English folk-songs and -dances and it would, I think, be a fatal error to take on something of which we have no authoritative knowledge whatever. . . . Privately anything may be done, but officially you must be very wary.

Sharp could, no doubt, had he wished, have made a 'boom' in folk-dancing, for here was something novel and decidedly attractive; but that was not his idea. As he wrote to Mr. Hercy Denman in 1911:

Real and genuine interest has been aroused and the need is not to excite more but to guide it into right channels. The time for 'popularising' methods has gone by. Morris dances are not pink pills or any other quack medicine. They are art-products, and as such should be dispensed by artists and trained teachers.

He realized that the size of the movement was limited by its teaching powers, and the educational work had to go on side by side with the propaganda. Incidentally it may be noted that he insisted on a living wage for his teachers.

Although a red-hot enthusiast, Sharp did not make the mistake of forcing the songs or the dances down people's throats. When Mr. Batchelor asked advice and assistance in introducing folk-tunes as marches into the Army during the early days of the War, Sharp wrote:

I find it very difficult to decide what action to take. I rather fancy the best way is to leave it to those who know these tunes to introduce them as opportunity offers and just when the spirit moves them. This I feel is a better plan than attempting to force them upon people. There are so many now who are really saturated with the tunes and have fallen victim to their attractiveness that it must after all be merely a question of time before they obtain a pretty wide currency. This is not to say that enthusiasts like yourself should not do all in their power to jog things along.

His tactics were to a certain extent Fabian, and he accepted certain conditions as insuperable barriers. For instance, although he lectured on song and dance (with illustrations) in nearly every boys' public school in England, he made no serious endeavour to get the dances generally taught in the schools, knowing that the curriculum would not allow of it; but he hoped that they would be introduced gradually when and as individual members of the staff became keen on the subject. In the meantime he felt that the main value of arousing interest in the public schools was to pave the way for a later period when the men would come across the dances at the university, &c. Actually, at Dr. Rendall's instigation, Sharp taught the Kirkby

Malzeard Sword Dance to six athletes of the Sixth Book at Winchester, and it was danced with enthusiasm for a time.

Tentatives like these were the hammer strokes while the weapon lay upon the anvil. It was now to take its plunge, and undergo the process of hardening. In December 1912 the Society made its first appearance on a London stage at the Savoy Theatre, lent for a matinée performance by Miss Lillah McCarthy and Mr. Granville Barker. Sharp made his apologies in a programme note:

The theatre is not, perhaps, the ideal place for an exhibition of folk-dances. . . . Nevertheless, it is the only place in which the dances can be advantageously seen by a large number of people. It is not contended that a succession of dances, however beautiful each individually may be, necessarily constitutes a spectacle of a high order. The aim of The English Folk Dance Society is, rather, by setting a high standard of performance to exhibit the dances in such a manner that others may be encouraged to learn and practise them, not with a view of giving public entertainments, but for the sake of the dances themselves. Indeed, it is hoped that a few years hence an exhibition such as this will be as unnecessary and uncalled for as, at the present time, would be a public demonstration of waltzes, polkas, and other drawing-room dances.

The men dancers at the Savoy Theatre were George Butterworth, Douglas Kennedy, Perceval Lucas, J. Paterson, George Wilkinson, and Claude Wright. This 'side' made its first public appearance at the Society's inaugural 'At Home' at the Suffolk Street Galleries on February 27th, 1912, and from that time onwards they were, with the frequent addition of R. J. E. Tiddy, Sharp's invariable exponents of the dance until the outbreak of war in 1914. Although engaged in other work they were always ready to give their services and there were few week-ends when they were not illustrating a lecture of Sharp's in some part of the country.

We may here break off for a moment for a few thumbnail sketches of some of these dancers. Douglas Kennedy is well known to folk-dancers of the present day as Director of the English Folk Dance and Song Society, but Lucas, Wilkinson, Butterworth, and Tiddy, to whom Sharp was also looking to carry on his work, were all killed during the British offensive (in the Battle of the Somme) of August 1916. Their loss to Sharp personally and to the folk-dance movement generally was a great one. Perceval Lucas was a younger brother of E. V. Lucas, and like him, a writer of charm. He edited the first two numbers of the *Journal of the English Folk Dance Society*. He was a delightful companion and he brought to the dancing, as to everything else he did, a gaiety and freshness of outlook which was very stimulating to his fellow-dancers. Sharp has said of him that he was the first man who really understood what the folk-dance revival meant. George Jerrard Wilkinson, a professional musician, succeeded Sharp at Ludgrove. He was a beautiful dancer—neat and finished in his movements; as a teacher, his sense of form and the clarity of his exposition did much to develop the technique of the dancing.

Reginald John Elliot Tiddy was twenty years younger than Sharp. He went to Tonbridge and University College, Oxford; he was elected to a prize Fellowship there in 1902, and three years later to one at Trinity, where he lectured on classics. English literature was his real subject, and a 'great work' he projected at the age of twenty-five was to have been on Anglo-Saxon. Sprung from the folk—his father was a yeoman and his mother a farmer's daughter—he turned instinctively to folk-poetry, and to this end he read and knew every scrap of song or play he could lay hands on, down to the Elizabethans and beyond. The dance was much more than his hobby: nothing made him more deeply happy than to be teaching it to and learning it from the villagers of Ascott-under-Wychwood, near Woodstock. They were all his friends: he talked their dialect with them, not at them. To his Oxford friends he quite as easily talked *their* 'dialect', and his genial cynicism and unaffected wit made him everywhere at home. Into his dancing eyewitnesses say that he put a world of quiet fun; once at one of Sharp's lectures, after months of absence, he wept as he heard the old tunes. That absence was those months of training for the War. It was a weary business. In eighteen months it came to an end. It had not been useless: he had won his men; he was both a leader and a friend. The 24th Oxfordshires went out in May 1916. On August 10th Tiddy was killed instantaneously by a shell.

Some brilliant essays introduce his collection of *Mummers' Plays* (Clarendon Press, 1923). Sharp read them in October 1923 and called them

quite wonderful—by far the best contribution that has yet been made to the subject, as, in my opinion, it is the first written by one who really knew and had felt what he was writing about. . . . Nothing can compensate us for his loss and that of George Butterworth. I felt when the dreadful news came that I didn't want to carry on any more, and I still have the same feeling. . . . I found the memoir entrancing and very difficult to read with dry eyes.

Ralph Honeybone was Tiddy's pupil at Ascott and his batman at the Front. They were such good friends that they had some difficulty in remembering to call each other, in public, 'Honeybone' and 'Sir'. The survivor wrote, 'he was more than a brother to me'. When monetary help was to be given him after the War, Sharp, whom they intended not to ask, heard of it, and wrote:

I expect I can afford it quite as well as any of you: besides, if £20 meant nothing to me, there would be no fun in giving it! That's what rich people can't understand.

George Sainton Kaye Butterworth, born (12.7.85) in London, fell at Pozières near Albert (10.8.16). He called himself a Cockney, but belonged in spirit to Yorkshire. He spent his boyhood at York and went to Aysgarth, to Eton (as a scholar), and to Trinity, Oxford. He had carried a note-book about at Eton to jot down musical ideas, and it became clear to him after Oxford that music in some form must be his life's work, and music meant, for him, composition. But in what form? He tried teaching (at Radley) and criticism (on *The Times*), but found neither congenial. He spent a year at the Royal College of Music in order to fit himself for a musical post. He then found occupation in collecting and arranging folksong and -dance (see p. 96), but this did not solve the problem of a livelihood. The War came, and there was no need to inquire farther. He enlisted in the Duke of Cornwall's Light Infantry in August and was given a commission in November.

A colleague at Radley wrote of him: 'He had strength of character, opinions and the courage of them, a rugged directness of manner coupled with a gift of keen criticism and an absence of heroics. Few men can have been worse at making an acquaintance or better at keeping a friend.'

The music he left behind is small in quantity but great in merit. He put his heart into it, and did not easily satisfy himself; it is fresh, therefore, and original, wayward but convincing; of the open air. Good judges think highly of it.

One would like to speak of the work of many others who, like Mrs. Arthur Sidgwick and Mrs. Bruce Swanwick, gave so much time and thought to the welfare of the Society; but it would be impossible to make a complete list. Mention must, however, be made of the Society's first president. It would not have been in keeping with the character of the Society if this office had been filled by a mere figure-head, and this Sharp realized when he asked Lady Mary Trefusis, whom he had known in Australia as Lady Mary Lygon, to be President. She accepted in 1912. She was the eldest daughter of the sixth Earl Beauchamp, and, until her death in 1927, Woman of the Bedchamber to Queen Mary. In Cornwall, where she married Colonel Trefusis, she threw herself into Diocesan work, and sat on the committee which issued the valuable pamphlet, *Music in Worship* (1922). She edited for her brother, a member of the Roxburghe Club, the musical works of Henry VIII (1912). In 1920 she organized the Cornwall Branch of the English Folk Dance Society, and the first big open-air folk-dance festival was held at St. Austell (1921), when over a thousand took part. She brought success to everything she touched because she cared, and because others, seeing this, were ashamed of not caring enough. She had a clear head; at Sharp's death, when it was not certain how matters would be with his, and her, Society, she made every necessary inquiry, then acted unobtrusively, and the thing was done, and done right. She was a first-rate player of the dances, and quite tireless; she would often play at a country dance party for a whole evening.

In spite of his preoccupations with the English Folk Dance Society, Sharp managed to give a certain amount of time to collecting, and during the three years, 1912–14, he added another 350 tunes to his collection, bringing the total to 3,070.

In 1912 he published *English Folk Carols*, a volume of twenty-one carols. It is dedicated to R. Vaughan Williams, who said of it:

It is a fine book. I've always loved carols. I remember the time when, if I said 'carol', I could not get a spark out of you—now as usual you have gone ahead and left me in the lurch.

In 1914 three books appeared almost simultaneously: *Songs of Sea Labour* (shanties) by F. T. Bullen (words) and W. F. Arnold (music), and Sharp's *English Folk Chanteys* were published, and W. B. Whall's *Ships, Sea-Songs and Shanties* reached its third edition. They contain 42, 60, and 50 shanties respectively. Whall and Bullen were sailors and had been shantymen, and they wrote down the tunes as they remembered them and as much of the words as they could print. Sharp took down 150 variants from sailors in various ports, especially from Mr. John Short of Watchet. He admitted that he had no technical or practical knowledge of nautical matters, but approached the subject from its aesthetic side. Whall's book is attractive with its many illustrations and particulars of ships, and such shanties as there are seem genuine; in Bullen's book the music is not always as trustworthy as in Sharp's.

Folk-song, carol, shanty; and now about their accompaniment. That has always been a knotty point. The first question is why there should be any at all, seeing that the original singers did without it, and even, as we saw with the 'Seeds of Love', thought it a drawback, or were unable to recognize the tune when harmonized. The answer is that the accompaniment is not for them, but for us who cannot hear with their ears; the folk-song is so simple that we, lovers of the complex, can hardly get hold of it without that. But it is also necessary to represent the atmosphere, and the way the folk-singer set points in relief or left them in abeyance; how necessary, we become aware when we examine collections of these tunes without accompaniments (Miss Densmore's books, *The Journal of the Folk-Song Society*, &c.).

Granted that there is to be an accompaniment, of what kind shall it be? 'The folk-song is for all time,' said Stanford; and he argued from that that each generation must make its own account with it, and set it according to the best musicianship of the day. 'The folk-song is for all time,' said Sharp, and therefore of no one time, and it is the language of to-day (1907), with its copious modulation, that we must especially avoid. Perhaps the two views are not so far apart as they seem at first blush. Irish song, which Stanford was setting, has for generations been accompanied by the harp, and that admitted of simple modulations, which are all that he uses; the song itself, too, is not always strictly in one mode, and much the same may be said of Welsh. German song, also, to Brahms's settings of which Sharp raised objection, has had its melodic points generalized by the harmony which has been 'in the air' for centuries. The Scottish harp is not powerful and the English have had none; their modes are consequently purer, and modulation at once destroys them.

Sharp resolved therefore to keep his accompaniment in one mode throughout and to avoid chromatic chords. He did not at first grasp how to do this, and we see him wrestling with the songs in the first Somerset book, 'The Seeds of Love' and 'The Sweet Primeroses', to wit. He subsequently altered these and others for the better. It is of interest to compare his two settings of 'The Seeds of Love' (*Folk-Songs from Somerset*, No. 1, and *English Folk-Songs, Selected Edition*, No. 17) and of 'The Sprig of Thyme' (*Somerset*, No. 110, and *Folk-Songs from Dorset*, No. 5), and these again with Vaughan Williams's setting of a distant cousin of the same tune ('The Seeds of Love', No. 11, of *Folk-Songs from Sussex*, with violin *ad lib.*).

Chromatics is one thing—as when Vaughan Williams tells the poet of 'Come all you worthy Christians' (*Folk-Songs from Sussex*, No. 9) what sort of man he must be if he goes about the world saying that 'the only thing that doth remain is enjoying our misery'; modern sophistication is another. Sharp was asked if he would allow the songs he had collected to be treated in this modern way; and he declined to do so. Not only had he the right to do this, as any collector has, but there was nothing ungracious in exercising the right. 'The law', said Sharp, 'protects the product of the man's brain, not the thing upon which he exercises it.' His correspondent was not satisfied with this, but it is hard to see why; there was nothing to prevent his going to a village to hear and write down the song, and then nobody could have objected to his making what use he pleased of the product of his brain. It is true that this would have involved time and money as well as wits, and he seems to have assumed that any collector to whom he applied should give him at least the two first. The incident is worth mentioning only because it is so often said that 'the collector claims copyright in the song'; and if that were true it would seem outrageous that a song which belongs to the nation, if to any one, should be held to belong exclusively to one member of it. But it is not true. All that the collector claims, and has, is the right in the copy that he himself has made.

As a matter of fact, Sharp but rarely used his right of veto in the arrangement of folk-tunes collected by himself, and certainly never when it was intended to treat the tune as a theme for composition. He was broadminded enough to be able to appreciate methods other than his own. 'I do not always like his way of harmonizing,' he wrote after studying a book of folk-songs,[1] 'but it is always musicianly —and the rest is a matter of taste.' Again, he made a point of meeting Mr. Howard Brockway—hitherto a stranger to him—for fear some remarks he had made about his accompaniments might have annoyed him. He told Mr. Brockway frankly that he had criticized his settings of Kentucky songs as being too sophisticated, but he wished him to know that he admired his musicianship, which, he said, far surpassed his own.

Sharp was never happier than when harmonizing tunes at the piano.

To Mr. Etherington.   14.10.06.

I get right inside these beautiful melodies when I try to translate them into harmony, and the further you dive into them the more seductive and glorious they appear.

His settings have been blamed as being commonplace,

---

[1] *Songs from the Hills of Vermont*, collected by Edith B. Sturgis, music arranged by Robert Hughes.

amateurish, halting, and devoid of workmanship, but praise has not been lacking. One wrote (7.6.14):

You have evolved gradually a charming style of accompaniment, poetical and sunny, suggesting more than it states, and the 'drawing' is strong,

thinking, perhaps, of 'My Bonny Boy', 'The Cuckoo', 'Nelson's Praise', and others. And four months earlier a similar appreciation came from Mr. Bernard Shaw:

Many of your accompaniments are both ingenious and exquisite; but that accomplishment is not really so rare nowadays as your power of finding out the strength of a melody and giving it its value in a simple and sure way without rich, thick modern chords—you know what I mean unless you are a deplorably modest man.

In 1906 Vaughan Williams wrote (in the *Morning Post*):

Those who study Mr. Sharp's accompaniments will realise how rich in suggestion the folk-song may be to a well equipped and sympathetic musician.

His later view is given in full in Appendix B.

People have found Sharp's accompaniments difficult to play. The truth is that all songs are difficult to play for one who is not a singer, and every dance for a non-dancer. When the players did not satisfy him he could only turn them away, sparing, or not sparing, their feelings, and play for them to hear, and profit, if they could. He could be delightfully peremptory about it all: he made one feel that there was only one way, and that he possessed it. But then he did possess it. The actual quality of his playing was well described as having 'the sound of the pipe or twanged string in it, never a touch of anything merely soft'.

When in 1913 Sharp developed neuritis in his right elbow and was for a time unable to play the piano, the effect on the dancers was immediately noticeable, for there was then, and still is, no one who could lift them off the floor as he did.

It was to save his arm that Maud Karpeles offered herself as his amanuensis, and gradually she was able to relieve him of a good deal of secretarial and clerical work.

In February 1914 Sharp arranged the music and dances for Granville Barker's production of *A Midsummer-Night's Dream* at the Savoy Theatre. In his Preface to the copy of the music he rejects three ways in which it might be done—(1) to take contemporary settings (but none are extant for that play), (2) to write in the Elizabethan style (which would be a fake), and (3) to write in the style of to-day (and go probably, as Mendelssohn has gone, out of fashion)—in favour of a fourth, folk-music, 'mating the drama which is for all time with the music which is for all time'. This is probably not the best logic, since 'for all time' is used in two different senses; but taking him to mean that folk-music is for no one time more than any other, his solution meets the objections of archaism and anachronism. It is obvious that in any of the four methods the proof of the pudding will be in the eating. For the Bergomask dance he took a genuine folk-dance (The Wyresdale Dance) for three men, and the rest were composed by him in the folk-style. An incidental interest in arranging the dances lay in their approximation to an eventual folk-ballet 'like the Russian'. He spoke of the venture as 'the most exciting time of my life', and Mr. Granville Barker wrote that 'workers know each other by instinct and thank each other by what they do'. Sharp worked with him again, similarly, on 'The Dynasts'.

CHAPTER XI

1914–1918

AMERICA

After all not to create only, or found only,
But to bring perhaps from afar what is already founded,
To give it our own identity, average, limitless, free,
To fill the gross the torpid bulk with vital religious fire,
Not to repel or destroy so much as to accept, fuse, rehabilitate,
To obey as well as command, to follow more than lead,
These also are the lessons of our New World;
While how little the New after all, how much the Old, Old World!

WALT WHITMAN.

IN August 1914 Sharp was directing the English Folk Dance Society's Summer School at Stratford-on-Avon. In spite of a few cancellations the School ran its normal course and the men's demonstration team remained intact until the end of the month, when its members dispersed, never to dance together again.

Sharp quickly realized the magnitude of the war, and some of his younger friends who found it difficult to know where their duty lay were grateful to him for his advice. His son Charles, without any advice, added three months to his age and, though first refused on account of short-sight, eventually got into the Middlesex Regiment as a Private. Later on he had a commission in the Grenadier Guards. Cecil Sharp himself at fifty-four was too old for active service, and there was no kind of war-work for which he was suited. Folk-dance and folk-song activities, except for a few classes, were in abeyance. He found himself accordingly without any vital occupation and with but little prospect of being able to provide for his family.

At the end of the year Granville Barker asked him to help with his New York production of *A Midsummer-Night's Dream*. He accepted the invitation, hoping that, in addition, he would get some lecture engagements which would relieve the financial situation. He sailed in the *Lusitania* and arrived in New York just before Christmas. At that time it was still the fashion to speak with contempt of the 'skyscraper', but Sharp was enchanted by the beauty of New York. He would often after the day's work leave his hotel—the Algonquin in West 44th Street—for the pleasure of wandering alone in the Grand Central Station and the neighbouring streets.

He found the new life exciting and stimulating, but on the whole he was not very happy. On Christmas Day, a day or two after his arrival, he writes:

Twenty or thirty years ago I could have stood this startling change better than I can now. My outlook is so different from that of every one here that I feel out of everything. At the present moment nothing would please me more than to know that I was returning to England by the next boat. Very likely I shall get used to things by degrees and get on better, but I feel very lonely at the moment.

He was nervous and anxious about his prospects, and at one time felt inclined to give up all idea of lecturing and to return home as soon as his work at the theatre was done. He resisted this temptation, determined to try his luck, and cabled for Mattie Kay to join him.

Of his first lecture, at the Colony Club, New York, he writes:

To Maud Karpeles.   18.1.15.

I have got through my first lecture—a terrible ordeal. I am afraid I did very badly indeed. I was not nervous, but the audience consisted of a social crowd, 90% of which didn't care a hang for the subject, and I was sensitive enough to realise this and it choked me off after my first few sentences. . . . I am afraid I have ruined my chances here of becoming a popular lecturer—at any rate, of getting private drawing-room lectures which would pay me best.

And in the same letter:

There is really an enormous lot of work to be done here in

popularising the subject, but it would take ages to do it—in fact, it would be doing over again all that I have done in England, and this I have neither the time to do nor the inclination to attempt. It all convinces me that I am not cut out to make money—I haven't the right temperament for that sort of thing. So I must be philosophic and resigned to my lot, and to dying a poor man! After all, the work I have done is far more important than a mere means of making a living, and I know it has some permanent value which will last long after I have disappeared from the scene; so that my own individual comfort is of small moment.

Two public lectures, given at the Plaza Hotel some days later, went better. At the second of these he shows country dances for two couples, in which he danced himself.

The two lectures went rippingly. Mattie Kay sang a couple of songs, I lectured, played a lot of Morris tunes, showed slides, played the pipe and tabor, and finally danced four country dances, or rather five, as 'Merry Conceit' was encored! The people were really most enthusiastic and every one remained to the end, i.e. for over two hours.

During the first six weeks most of his time was occupied with the theatre. Whilst the rehearsing of *A Midsummer-Night's Dream* was still in progress, Granville Barker produced Anatole France's *The Man who married a Dumb Wife*. For this Sharp arranged some songs, street-cries, and dances, introducing the tune of Dargason, a happy choice, for the Blind Man's Song and Final Dance. During the rehearsals of *A Midsummer-Night's Dream* we find him full of fears. The dancers do not fulfil his expectations; the conductor is unsatisfactory, and although it is proposed to make a change he is afraid the new one will be no better.

To Maud Karpeles.

29.1.15.

The most annoying part of it all is that Cecil Forsyth, who is over here, has offered to conduct for me, and of course that would be an ideal arrangement, but he is not a member of this infernal [Musicians'] Union and if he were to conduct, every member of the band would promptly walk out of the theatre, followed in all probability by all the scene-shifters and attendants at the theatre. And he can only become a member of the Union by paying $25 and then only if he is elected and has previously spent six months in the country. ... They won't even let *me* conduct my own music except for one performance! How music can flourish in a country such as this I do not know.

But the first performance belied his fears and after a few weeks he writes:

To Maud Karpeles.   28.3.15.

It [the dance in Act II, Sc. ii] went just splendidly, better than I have ever known it go before. It delighted me beyond measure and I know it is beautiful. Indeed it seems to me quite perfect— I don't mind saying this to you—and I am quite certain I shall never do anything half so beautiful again. How I came to do it I really can't imagine. It is the only thing that I can call 'inspired' that I have done. ...

But I am not really fond of the theatre—still less of theatrical life and theatrical people. I think I must be too serious an artist, but I can't help disliking the slap-dash way in which theatre people work and the way they leave so much to the chance or inspiration of the moment; the way they will cut down essentials, i.e. artistic essentials to save expense and allow flashy and *ad captandum* unessential things to remain.

So he argues to himself, but he is evidently not quite convinced as the following letter, written the same day, shows:

To his wife.   28.3.15.

There is no doubt that this trip here has opened up all sorts of possibilities. It is a pity that I did not come when I was a bit younger. I feel torn in two ways. The opportunity of trying my hand on theatre music and dancing is very alluring to me, while on the other hand I want to complete my folk-song and -dance work in England. Whether it is possible to do both of these things or not I cannot at present say. However, these things have a way of settling themselves if left alone.

125

As soon as he had finished with rehearsals he worked hard to get lecture and teaching engagements. The dances were more popular than the songs, and so after some weeks Mattie Kay returned to England and Sharp worked single-handed. Besides New York, he visited Boston, Pittsburgh, Chicago, Philadelphia, and Pittsfield. 'I worked terribly hard at Pittsburgh,' he writes, 'taking five or six hours' classes each of the four days I was there and lecturing three times'; but this was surpassed at Chicago, where on his last day he taught for eight and a half hours and finished with a lecture of one and a half hours.

By the beginning of March he can write:

People are really beginning to rise to me and my preaching, and to be attracted by the latter, at any rate, partly because of its novelty and partly because it convinces them.

Three weeks later he recognized the probable permanence of the work in America by establishing a U.S.A. Branch of the English Folk Dance Society with Centres in New York, Boston, Chicago, and Pittsburgh. At the same time he agreed to direct a Summer School later in the year.

Sharp's initial motive in seeking engagements had been to earn a living, and he succeeded in making a clear profit of £400 in four months and, no doubt, could have made more had that been his sole, or even main, interest. On March 15th he writes to Maud Karpeles:

I believe if I had the pluck and I were keen enough—and I am not—I could coin money out here. The way to do it would be to get up a really swagger studio and make a bid for social people and charge enormous fees. But really when it comes to the point I feel I can't do it. Why, I hardly know; but to make money by charging disproportionate fees for the work done goes against the grain. . . . The whole question of making money is very much on my mind at the moment and I cannot see through it. The question has never occurred before in my life, because I have never had the chance of making it; and I feel very funny about it. I feel a sneaking satisfaction that I have proved that I could make it after all if I were to get myself to do it! I am afraid you won't make much out of this—nor can I!

And again a week later:

Sometimes I wish I wasn't making money, which is very stupid; at other times I pore over my cheque book and accounts as though I were a miser. . . . I believe I am fast becoming a horrid business-man and sordid money-grubber!

He need have had no fear! One had only to accompany him into a second-hand bookshop and hear him discourse with enthusiasm on the great value and rarity of the dance-books which the bookseller was trying to procure for him to realize that Cecil Sharp would never be a business man. He was absorbed in the songs and dances, and his first thought was to share his interest and pleasure with others.

Moreover, in spite of his irritation at some aspects of American life, he was beginning to like the people, and consequently his desire to give rather than to receive became all the greater. This liking afterwards developed into real affection, and Sharp numbered many Americans amongst his best friends. On his first visit he became acquainted with Mrs. Dawson Callery of Pittsburgh, and Mrs. James Storrow of Boston, with whom he had previously corresponded. Both became enthusiastic disciples, and 'it was worth while coming to America to make friends' with them. Mrs. Storrow, a name now familiar to folk-dancers on both sides of the Atlantic, is described as 'a woman after my own heart, as wise as she is genuine and nice . . . a fine product of this country'.

These are his impressions after a few months:

To Joan Sharp.　　　　　　　　　　　　　　　　　5.4.16.

It is a very exciting life, seeing new people and new scenes almost every day. The people interest me. They are full of vitality, consciously groping for ideals and getting somewhere, but without any clear idea of their objective. They live in a little world of their own, knowing little of what the greater world outside is doing, and caring less, but all the time determining to make a great country of the land that belongs to them. I find it very stimulating, and at times, of course, very irritating. It does not make me feel 'superior' at all; indeed, I feel very humble at times in the presence of an enormous population all striving so hard to get somewhere. Some day perhaps you will see it all with me, and perhaps with younger eyes you will see further and deeper than I can.

The aspect of American character that most irritated him was what he termed 'their old maid's delight in exercising moral control over others'. After recovering from an attack of gout, he writes:

To T. Lennox Gilmour.   6.7.18.

It was not the result of high living or inordinate drinking! Although if I did take to drink out here it would not be surprising. The superior self-righteousness of the people with regard to that question maddens me sometimes and almost forces me to get drunk by way of protest. This kind of thing makes me fear for the future of democracy. The tyranny of a majority rule may be quite as bad as the tyranny of an autocrat.

Always an outspoken critic, he at times indulged in rhetorical tirades, which gave offence to no one, for they were always tinged with good-humour; and no matter how fierce was the onslaught he usually finished with a laugh against himself. 'Well, I gave them something to think about,' he would say afterwards with the delight of a schoolboy.

On April 21st, 1915, Sharp sailed for England in the *Adriatic* with the intention of returning to America in June. He was pressed by his friends not to take the risk of the double journey, or at any rate to delay his journey for a week and sail in the *Lusitania*, which being a faster boat was felt to be safer. But Sharp, who hated a change once his mind was made up, did not 'like the idea of allowing those —— Germans' to upset his plans. So perhaps for once his obstinacy saved his life.

He returned to America in June to direct a three weeks' Summer School. This was held at Eliot, Maine, in a camp delightfully situated on the banks of the Piscataqua River. The students, of whom there were sixty, slept in wooden shacks and the class-room accommodation was provided by a barn and two large marquees with wooden floors, which had been erected especially for the purpose. But the ideal surroundings were marred by abnormally wet weather, and when at the end of two weeks the marquees were blown down and flooded, the whole School moved and took up its quarters at a Hotel and Conference Centre some few miles away. The students took to the dances with an enthusiasm which still lasts. Among them was Charles Rabold, a musician and teacher of piano and singing, who became one of Sharp's most ardent followers. He gave up his other musical work and devoted himself for many years entirely to the teaching and dissemination of English folk-music and dance. He was, unhappily, killed in an aeroplane accident in California some three years ago. Sharp was assisted at the School by three English teachers: Maud Karpeles, Norah Jervis, then residing in the United States, and Lily Roberts (now Mrs. Richard Conant), who had come to America some weeks earlier in order to teach, under Sharp's direction, the folk-dances for a pageant at Wellesley College. After the School, Miss Roberts went to live in Boston, and there by her teaching and dancing, and above all by her persuasive manner, she has persuaded many hundreds that folk-dancing is one of the good things of this life.

The Summer School did much to consolidate the interest which Sharp had aroused; but a more important event was a visit from Mrs. Olive Dame Campbell, shortly before the Summer School, when he was imprisoned in Mrs. Storrow's country house at Lincoln (Mass.) with an acute attack of lumbago. Her husband, Mr. John C. Campbell, was the Director of the Southern Highland Division of the Russell Sage Foundation, and his work had taken him through the Southern Appalachian Mountains. Mrs. Campbell had, on more than one occasion, accompanied him and, coming into close touch with the mountain people, had heard them sing. She was impressed with the beauty of the songs, which were unlike anything else she had heard, and noted down some seventy of them. Hearing that Cecil Sharp was in America she decided to seek his help and interest, and made a special journey from the south. Her first meeting with him may be described in her own words:

He was sitting very straight in an imposing high-backed chair . . . a table in front of him. He could not get up, but he greeted me with an easy apology to the effect that he was indulging in a rich man's malady—gout, but that he owed it to his ancestors rather than to any luxuries permitted by his own income. I got a quick impression of his fresh colour, high, clearly cut features and the nervous force of his personality. His eye was obviously on my bundle of papers, and I wasted no time in laying it before him.

'How did you take this down?' he asked.

I explained meekly that I was not a trained musician. I had had to learn the melodies from the lips of the singer, noting down rough helps. I worked out the whole afterwards, using a piano if I could and going back again to the singer to check myself. A long time after he paid a compliment to my exactness of memory, which I am proud to remember, but at the time: 'Of course, you know that that is a very unscientific way of recording,' was his uncompromising observation.

The moments fled by. I consulted my watch from time to time, but did not like to interrupt him. Moreover, I certainly could not detect any signs of boredom or exhaustion. When he finally laid the pile of manuscripts on the table and turned to me, it was with a keen but relaxed and almost lenient look. All the charm of his most winning mood was shed upon me as he explained how many people had brought 'ballads' to him before, but that this was the first time that he had come on any really original and valuable material. I am told he improved from that day.

Sharp went back to England in July for the immediate purpose of directing the Stratford-on-Avon Summer School. Beyond that he had no definite plans. But his great desire was to return to America and investigate the mountain regions of the Southern States, for what he had seen in Mrs. Campbell's manuscript collection made him suspect that here was 'a mine, which if properly and scientifically explored would yield results—musical, historical, literary—of the first importance'. And he was constantly turning over in his mind ways and means of carrying out this project.

The voyage home in the *St. Paul* was unexpectedly brightened by the discovery of an old shanty-singer amongst the ship's crew. Permission was given him to visit Sharp's cabin when off duty, and day by day he appeared punctually at the appointed time, equipped with a sheet of newspaper which he spread on the bed before sitting down on it.

Arrived in England Sharp was met with the distressing news of his wife's serious illness—heart-trouble, following an attack of scarlet-fever; and although she ultimately recovered enough to be able to get up and about she remained a semi-invalid for the rest of her life.

In October 1915 the family moved to 27 Church Row, Hampstead, a panelled house of the late seventeenth century, described by Sharp as 'about the time of the sixth edition of Playford', and there he tackled the publication of *One Hundred English Folk-Songs* (Oliver Ditson Co., Boston).[1] Most of the songs had already been published in *Folk-Songs from Somerset* and other collections, but he took this opportunity of revising the texts, reverting more closely to the originals, and of re-writing many of the pianoforte accompaniments. After he had finished this work he became very restive. He feared that war

[1] With some modifications the contents were later published in two volumes, *English Folk-Songs, Selected Edition* (Novello, London, 1919).

conditions had effectively put a stop to all his hopes of a permanent and widespread folk-dance revival. Furthermore he was itching to get to work in the Appalachian Mountains, and he faintly expected some financial help from the Carnegie Corporation. He expresses to Mrs. Storrow his hopes and fears:

7.12.15.

I have heard nothing from the Carnegie people, so I am almost afraid that nothing will come of that project. . . . I think that if they made any sort of offer I should take your advice and come out to America and see if I could continue the work which I started last winter. Apart from ways and means I feel that if the dances are to be firmly rooted anywhere in my life-time it will be in America rather than in England. The movement is languishing here, of course, and there seems no chance of things becoming normal again for an indefinite time. And I do very much want to see the dances thoroughly well started before I disappear, so that the tradition may not be lost. If, therefore, you can see any real prospect of my doing something in this direction in your country, and at the same time something to ease the financial strain from which I am at present suffering, I will come out at once.

Help from the Carnegie Corporation did not come, nor any definite promise of work, but he decided to take the risk, and in February 1916 he returned to America. He began by organizing classes and lectures in New York. He soon had sufficient engagements to keep him fully occupied until mid-July. In April 1916 he wrote from Kalamazoo to his friend, Paul Oppé:

I have managed somehow or other to get plenty of work since I arrived here about seven weeks ago and, what is more to the point, I have been able to send something home already to keep the family going. So the anxiety on that score, which was rather acute when I last saw you is, I am glad to say, allayed. I am selling myself for a week at a time to different cities—Asheville, St. Louis, Cincinnati and now here, and after this for a month at Pittsburgh. I charge a pretty high figure—high, that is, to English notions—and then let them get what they can out of me. I usually teach four or five hours a day and give one or sometimes two lectures, so that they get a good deal out of me measured by time and energy! I enjoy it very much, though I feel it rather a strain, especially when the classes are large—they have been as large as seventy or eighty!

After six weeks of highly concentrated work interspersed with long railway journeys the strain told on him rather severely, and on Mrs. Callery's advice he cabled for Maud Karpeles to come out from England to help with the teaching. This she did, joining him at Pittsburgh, and remained with him throughout his subsequent travels in America.

The year 1916 was, as it happened, a particularly auspicious one for Sharp's work, owing to the numerous Shakespeare Tercentenary celebrations which were being held all over the country. Sharp abhorred most forms of pageantry, but he recognized these celebrations as a useful means of introducing the English folk-music and dances. Accordingly, when the New York Centre of the English Folk Dance Society was invited to provide an English 'Interlude' in Percy Mackaye's *Masque of Caliban*, to be performed in the New York Stadium, Sharp agreed to compose the scenario and to direct the performance. The Interlude represented the celebration of an Elizabethan May-Day Festival on the outskirts of an English village, and consisted of a series of processional, country, and morris dances, together with songs, hobby-horse, may-pole, and other folk-rituals, all skilfully woven together and set off to advantage by Robert E. Jones's costume designs. The entrance of four or five hundred dancers in the Tideswell Processional (accompaniment, four unison clarinets and two side-drums) aroused a murmur of delight amongst the audience of some twenty thousand spectators, and 'This is what I should like to be *doing*' was heard on all sides. Sharp was highly delighted and wrote:

It was like a puff of fresh country air laden with the smell of the hedgerows coming in the midst of artificial, exotic surroundings. . . .

133

No country in the world can be gay in the simple, fresh way that England can—it is our contribution to civilization. I felt more proud of being an Englishman than I have ever felt before. And the spirit of the tunes and dances was such that all participants became infected by it and for the moment they became English, every Jew, German, French, Italian, Slav one of them.[1]

It was no doubt this quality of 'gay simplicity' which persuaded a judging committee of experts—actors and theatrical producers—to award first prize to this Interlude in preference to those of other European countries. The Interlude was repeated as part of other Shakespeare celebrations at St. Louis and Cincinnati, and these performances occupied Sharp until the date of the Summer School, held in this and the following year at Amherst Agricultural College (Mass.). In expressing his satisfaction at the result of the School he writes:

To Mrs. Storrow.   16.7.16.

This last School has dissipated the chief fear I have had here, viz. whether the average American student would take the trouble to acquire the complicated technique which our English dances—and indeed all dances worthy of the name—require. I was told so much about the craze for quick results demanded in this country. But so far as this particular subject is concerned I find no difference between the American and the English student, and I find it no more difficult to interest one than the other, nor to inspire one to work as hard as the other.

And this estimation of the American's capacity for perseverance was justified when at the 1917 Summer School seven of the American students gained the advanced certificate of the English Folk Dance Society, an award which is made only to those who pass the Society's final and most searching text.

At the same time there were many obstacles to overcome

---

[1] To Mr. Percy MacKaye he wrote in the same vein, adding: ' "Sumer is icumen in" [which was sung as an introduction to the Interlude] is the real motto of the English people.'

and Sharp did not always view the results of his work in such a rosy light. At a time when things were not going so well he wrote to Charles Rabold:

The average American dancer seems to me to be incurably superficial. They seem to aim at a splash and having pulled it off look out for something else. They do not seem to me to have any critical acumen . . . they like everything equally well, good, bad, and indifferent. However, there must always be a minority if only you can get hold of it.

Sharp had to convince his pupils that the English dances as presented by him had more content than the many so-called folk-dances of other nations with which the country was overrun; and he had also to overcome the objection that American citizens were not justified in devoting more time to English dances than to those of other countries. He met this by pointing out that culture is determined mainly by language, and that as Americans had adopted the English language it was only logical that English song and dance should likewise play a prominent part as a cultural subject.

Many of his pupils had learned 'aesthetic' dancing, which Sharp dubs 'a poisonous, bowdlerized form of the so-called "classical" ballet'.

This form of dancing, save the mark, has over-run the schools in this country. . . . My chief difficulty is to get them [his pupils] to do the running-step. They put out their legs in front of their bodies and fail to spring from one foot to another, which produces a peculiarly odious form of obsequious crawl.

But this fault, like many others, disappeared after being subjected to his merciless but kindly chaff. He put his pupils at their ease by making their task so absorbing that they had no time to be self-conscious. Combining enthusiasm for his subject with an appreciation of the personalities of his pupils, he could charm academic professors, refined young ladies from a 'millionaire' boarding-school, or crude young men of a physical training class.

135

Of his pupils at one of the Middle Western universities he writes:

They are good-natured and good-intentioned, very desirous to learn, but accustomed to learn only with their brains, crude in manner and cultivation, but withal something about them that attracts and fascinates me. It is raw material—very raw—but stuff out of which something is going eventually to be made.

Sharp found nearly everywhere an overweening belief in the power of education coupled with a depreciation of the instinctive faculties. At the end of a week's course of instruction at a large women's college he remarked to the Principal of the Physical Training Department on the fact that not one of the girls had a natural movement in running. Her face fell as she saw the justice of his criticism, and she said thoughtfully: 'I am afraid it is true, and it is our fault. We have never taught them how to run!' Another educational method which Sharp fought against not only in America but in England was the incitement of students to be original. On this subject he writes:

In the early period of the students' development they must be content to imitate, and this makes it incumbent on the teacher to see that none but the best models are placed before them. Originality is after all a comparative not an absolute term. All that it means is that the individual is succeeding in adding something of his own to forms already evolved in the past by others. This must necessarily be a lengthy process in any case, while for the average person, originality is but a will o' the wisp—he seeks but never attains it and has to content himself with mere repetition. But my point is that if he is ever to attain originality it will be by the road his predecessors have travelled—in other words, he must hitch himself on to tradition.

He got a great deal of satisfaction and amusement from his teaching. To his daughter Joan:

I have been taking a lot of folk-dance classes and am learning how to manage them in the orthodox Karpeles-cum-Kennedy manner!

And there were humorous incidents.

To Joan Sharp.   23.6.16.
    The other day I was coaching a Morris side made up of Univer-
sity Professors. One of them habitually omitted the hop in the
'4/3 step'. So I stood before him and showed him what he was
doing and what he ought to do. He said: 'Yes, I know that, but—
I am not hopping to-day.' I heard afterwards that he was going to
a tea-party after the rehearsal and didn't want to spoil his collar!

Sharp spent two months in the Appalachian Mountains
(see next chapter) from July to September, when he was
due at Chicago for some lecture and teaching engagements.
Whilst in the mountains he received news that three of
his dancers, Perceval Lucas, R. J. Tiddy, and George
Butterworth had been killed and George Wilkinson was
missing; and on arrival in Chicago he found cables from
his wife informing him that his son Charles had been
seriously wounded. For many weeks Charles's condition
was critical, and his father's anxiety was all the greater
because cables from Mrs. Sharp in France were subjected
to delay. He thought of throwing up his engagements and
returning home, but could not afford it.
    After leaving Chicago he gave classes and lectures in
New York, Mount Holyoke College, Pittsburgh, Philadelphia, Toronto, and Boston. About this time he writes
to his wife:

    I am very well on the whole and have hardly any asthma, which
is a great relief to me. I am in grand dancing form and am making
quite a reputation as a dancer! Moreover I have added another
accomplishment and now sing my own ballads at my lectures
unaccompanied! Maud and I sing some together and I sing some
alone! It really is a very effective way of showing them—in many
respects far better than having them sung by a regular vocalist
with accompaniment. The fact that our voices are just ordinary
is really the point of the performance.

    At the beginning of December he returned home. He

spent two months in England, paying daily visits to the Highgate Hospital, where his son was lying.

In February 1917, accompanied by Maud Karpeles, he returned for the last time to America, where he remained until December 1918. A few days before their intended departure on a Dutch liner, Germany declared her policy of submarine warfare against neutral shipping and in consequence the sailing of the Dutch boat was cancelled. After a few days' delay passages were booked in the *Baltic*, the first available British ship, and New York was finally reached after a fortnight on board ship, including a preliminary four days' isolation in the Mersey. During the early part of the voyage Sharp was strained and nervous: as usual, he was alive to physical danger, and, as usual, he did not disguise that fear. In writing to his son he owns to the strain of the voyage and ends his letter with one of his typical jokes:

There were only five women—including Maud—on board ship, and if they all behaved like Maud and a lady friend . . . their chief anxiety was how to dress for the life-boat. They were not so much concerned with the matter of comfort and warmth as with the look of things. O these women!

After his arrival Sharp fulfilled engagements at the University of Illinois, Pittsburgh, and other towns, and then spent from April to October in the Mountains, except for a break of five weeks to direct Summer Schools in New York and Amherst. On November 23rd he gave an invitation-lecture at the Hall of the Russell Sage Foundation on the current year's work in the Appalachian Mountains; and he gave the first performance of the Running Set, the dance he had recently discovered in Kentucky, taking part in it himself. His book[1] containing 323 tunes had been published the preceding day, and with

[1] *English Folk-Songs from the Southern Appalachians*, collected by Olive Dame Campbell and Cecil Sharp.

this tangible evidence of the results of his work he had high hopes that some institution would be ready to finance his further efforts. Throughout the year he had made persistent efforts to get support from various public bodies, but had met with no success, and except for some private assistance from Mrs. Storrow and other friends had been thrown back on his own resources. Whilst in the mountains he had had a serious break-down in health, and in order to avoid the double strain of earning a living and carrying on his investigations it was important to get some financial backing. An application to the Carnegie Institution of Washington, supported by the highest recommendations, was, however, refused. In April, after a winter's work in Chicago, he was again in the mountains, but made a short trip to Washington in May to lecture at the house of Mr. Henry White to many distinguished people, including M. Jusserand. The Capitol made a deep impression upon him, and although he found it possible to criticize the details of the decoration, the general effect of the group of buildings produced 'a great emotion'. He felt that the whole conception was an expression of the deep feeling which had been inspired by the ideal of a government of free people, and it gave him a better understanding of American aims and aspirations.

A Summer School and classes in New York and Boston occupied July, and after that Sharp had hoped to vary the scene of his researches by going to Newfoundland. In this way he would have escaped the intense heat of the south during August, but the expense of the journey ruled out this plan; he reluctantly gave up the idea and returned to the Appalachian mountains for his final visit.

November 1918 found him hard at work again in Boston, Cleveland, and Detroit. He had planned to spend the winter in California and to 'collect' in other parts of the States and in Newfoundland during the following spring and summer months, but as the end of the War came within sight his longing to return home became very great. Already in August he wrote:

I want to get home again. The restless life I am leading begins to tell. . . . I am too old to grow roots in a new country like this, even if the people with their vitality and exuberance do win some of my admiration.

And on November 9th:

I go nearly wild when I think of a quiet room with my piano and my books around me.

Armistice Day was passed at Cleveland, Ohio, the streets 'crammed with people, hooting, shouting, rattling and making every conceivable noise'. In his diary:

11.11.18.

A wonderful day, but I do not feel like making a noise. . . . I cannot forget poor Butterworth, Tiddy, Percy [Lucas] and the many others. Here they have made few sacrifices.

The post-War idea of reconstruction had not yet been formulated, but Sharp knew that his work in England would be needed, and so, throwing up all his engagements, he sailed from New York on December 10th. In mid-Atlantic he wrote:

To Mrs. Storrow. 17.12.18.

I find it hard to realise the happenings of the last few weeks—those stupendous events which have influenced the whole world as well as those which have affected my own little puny plans. What the future has in store for me I know not, and there is not much use in speculating—it will all be decided for me. But I believe it is going to be interesting and full of opportunity. The result of my American experiences should stand me in good stead and help me to solve some of the problems with which no doubt I shall soon be confronted. I would that I had visited America twenty years ago before my character and habits had been so fixed. Still I have learned something of which I ought to be able to make good use.

And thus, with the adventures in the Appalachian Mountains yet to be described, there ends an important chapter in Sharp's life, for he did not visit America again, although he kept in touch with his many friends and with the folk-dance organization which he had established. But the chapter has its sequel in the folk-dance activities which have gone on there continuously up to the present time. Sharp regarded the dissemination of the dances in America as a natural corollary to their revival in England. He held that in spite of superficial differences the two countries had the same ideals and aspirations, and that English folk-song and -dance belonged to both as a common culture. He believed also that the American contribution to the art of dancing was genuinely complementary in its vigour, spontaneity, and simplicity of expression.

CHAPTER XII[1]

1916

THE APPALACHIANS, I

Great things are done when men and mountains meet;
This is not done by jostling in the street.

WM. BLAKE.

CECIL SHARP had many times wished that he had been
born a few centuries earlier when English folk-song
was the common musical expression of young and old alike,
and towards the end of his life, when the song-collecting
in England was practically finished, this wish was in a
way gratified. For in going to the Southern Appalachian
Mountains it was as though he had been transported to
an England of two or more centuries ago.

The Appalachians lie in the Eastern States about two
hundred or two hundred and fifty miles from the Atlantic
seaboard, and, running more or less parallel to it, extend
from the Canadian border in the north to Alabama in the
south. The Southern Appalachians include several different ranges—the Blue Ridge, Great Smokies, Cumberland
Mountains, Black Mountains, Alleghanies, &c.—and the
region, which is an extensive one, considerably larger than
Great Britain, includes about one-third of the total area of
the States of North and South Carolina, Tennessee, Kentucky, Virginia, West Virginia, Georgia, and Alabama.
The population is over five million, or excluding city-
dwellers, about three million.

The history of the settlement of the mountains is to
some extent conjectural, but the inhabitants are descended
from colonial stock—many from settlers who migrated
from England, the lowlands of Scotland, and the north of
Ireland (i.e. the Scotch-Irish) some time during the eighteenth century. Their motive for doing so was probably

[1] This chapter and the next have been written by Maud Karpeles.

to better their fortunes; where they found coast-lands already occupied, or competition with slave-labour distasteful and unprofitable, they moved westwards. Possibly their aim was to trek through to the fertile Blue Grass region of Kentucky, of which they may have heard from the Indians, but, weary of the struggle of penetrating virgin forests, and finding abundant game, and here and there fertile valleys, they decided to make the best of their present surroundings. And there, isolated in the seclusion of the mountains, they and their descendants have been living for many generations.

During the years 1916–18 Cecil Sharp spent twelve months in the Southern Appalachian Mountains, forty-six weeks being given to actual collecting—nine weeks in 1916, and about twice as long in each of the following years. He travelled over a big area, spending about three and a half months in each of the States of North Carolina, Virginia, and Kentucky, a month in Tennessee, and a few days in West Virginia. He visited altogether between seventy and eighty different small towns and settlements.

In the spring of 1916 he had paid a short visit to Mr. and Mrs. John Campbell in order to discuss plans with them and to re-note the tunes that Mrs. Campbell had already collected. He writes shortly after his visit:

To me it is quite wonderful that any one so little in touch with any work of the kind that has been done elsewhere should have set herself such a high standard and, in effect, reached it. She has just the combination of scientific and artistic spirit which work of this kind needs if it is to be of any use to posterity. . . . What she has so far accomplished is of great value, but I gather that it is after all only the beginning. The field that has yielded what she has harvested[1] must be a very rich one, and its exploration must be thoroughly done as soon as possible, for I gather from her that present conditions are rapidly undermining and destroying the traditions.

Not only did Cecil Sharp appreciate the pioneer work

[1] Mrs. Campbell had collected between seventy and eighty tunes.

143

that Mrs. Campbell had done, but he was 'anxious not to do anything discourteous to her nor to queer her pitch in any way', and therefore, before deciding to undertake the investigation, he made certain that he had her complete concurrence. He wrote (August 15th, 1915):

It would be impossible for me or any one else to do the work without your good help. . . . The simplest scheme would be for us to form a partnership and the results of our work to be published under both our names. You would bring to the pot an intimate knowledge of the district and of the people and a certain amount of material that you have already collected, and I should supply experience in this particular kind of work and a certain amount of musical and scientific knowledge. . . . It would be a thousand pities if any personal considerations were to prevent such important work from being done.

Mrs. Campbell's reply left no doubt in his mind. She wrote:

I want the collecting done and done by the person most competent to do it, and if I could have wished for a definite result from my work it would have been to attract to this region just such a person as yourself.

Mrs. Campbell was unable to continue her collecting or to accompany Cecil Sharp on his travels, but she and her husband planned his first expedition and Mr. Campbell acted as guide for a few days.

The first half of 1916 was filled with lecture and teaching engagements and it was not until the last week of July that Cecil Sharp was free to start on his travels, and even then it looked as though they might have to be delayed owing to the damage to rail and roads caused by recent floods. His objective was Asheville in North Carolina, which he had chosen at his first base. Ordinarily it is an easy journey of less than twenty-four hours from New York, but the main lines had been washed away in several places and he was told that it would be some days before the trains would be running again. To wait, even for a

few days, was more than patience could bear; after repeated visits to railway-bureaus and persistent telegraph-
ing it was found that by making a big detour Asheville
could be reached by a small branch mountain railway. So
on July 23rd Cecil Sharp and I left New York in great
heat, and after forty-eight hours in the train and an uncomfortable night in a small and dirty mining-town in
Tennessee we arrived in Asheville and were met by Mr.
and Mrs. Campbell, who took us to their home.

On their advice he decided to explore first that region
of North Carolina which is known as the Laurel Country,
so named because of the abundance of rhododendrons
(called 'Laurel' by the mountain-people) which grow on
the mountain side: the real laurel is called ivy, the ivy
becomes vine, and our vine is distinguished as the grape-
vine, 'and after that I suppose they get straight again',
Cecil Sharp would add.

The journey from Asheville presented difficulties, for the
roads, such as they were, had been very much damaged
by the floods, and the railway which might have served
for part of the journey was out of action. The experience
is described by Cecil Sharp in a letter to his wife (July 31st,
1916):

We breakfasted at 7 a.m., then motored to a place called Weaver-
ville where we transported ourselves and our luggage into a four-
wheeled dog-cart or buggy [locally known as a Surry] with two
seats, one behind the other. Fred, the driver, and Maud sat in
front, Campbell and I behind. And then our troubles began. I
have never been so frightened in my life! The nerve-strain was
really awful. How we went over those roads to Marshall I cannot
tell you. They were at times nothing but a morass, at others a dry
creek-bed strewn with huge boulders. Of course, we never went
faster than a walk, but the road, or the track, was never level, but
always precipitous one way or the other. As C. said—and he is
thoroughly used to it—it is no use attempting to describe it, for the
more nearly you succeed in doing it the less likely it is you will be
believed. Of course, our horses—we had a pair—are quite used

to the job and the trap was specially built for it. The wheels are very thin, made of hickory with round iron tires about an inch or less in diameter. After Marshall the roads became better, but no less nerve-racking as we went round innumerable hair-pin curves with the mountain on one side and a precipice on the other. Well, we arrived at White Rock about 6 p.m. doing the 40 miles in about 11 hours with an hour off for lunch.

This experience, though mainly due to the effect of the floods, proved to be only one instance of the normal difficulties of travel, and was by no means the worst.

The valleys are narrow, and the mountains, though they rarely reach a height of more than six thousand feet, rise up sharply, so that a man will boast that he can stand erect to hoe his corn-patch. As there is but little level ground, the people are forced to live in small communities by the side of the mountain rivers, or creeks, which have descriptive names, such as Possum Trot, Owl's Nest, Dish Rag, Kingdom Come, Hell for Sartin (certain), and Devil's Fork —the last renamed 'Sweet Water' by the missionaries.

The country has undergone many changes during the last ten or fifteen years[1] and transport is no longer the difficulty that it was; but at that time there were few railroads beyond the main trunk-lines, which here and there traversed the mountain ranges, and good roads were scarce or non-existent. They were for the most part rough tracks over the mountain passes or along the creeks, or occasionally the creek-bed itself would serve as a roadway for a few miles. The mountain people rode mules, or harnessed them, if a load had to be carried, to a conveyance that was aptly named a jolt-wagon—a cart without springs which could be heard lumbering over the boulders a mile away. Whenever possible we walked, although this was a tiring business when it meant a tramp of fifteen or sixteen miles in great heat over a track so rough that it

[1] It should be stated that the present social and economic conditions of mountain life are very different from those which Cecil Sharp experienced in 1916–18.

was necessary to pick every foot-step. However, we mis-
trusted the mules, and to ourselves we excused our timidity
on the grounds that as foot-passengers we could more
easily pay informal calls, which was probably true enough.
If luggage had to be carried we hired a boy and a mule,
and hung our two suit-cases and my typewriter across its
back; or if the distance was too great or the road too much
entangled in the river we had resort to a jolt-wagon, and
sometimes—though it seemed incredible—to a Ford car.
Our particular terror was crossing the foot-logs, that is
the trunks of trees which served as bridges over the creeks.
In a letter to his wife, Cecil Sharp described one of the
many predicaments we found ourselves in:

> North Carolina,
> August 13th 1916.
> There was one [a foot-log] we had to cross on the way to
> Carmen, quite high up over a rushing stream, only about 14 inches
> wide, but 16 or 17 yards long and very springy—no hand-rail of
> course! The first time I went across I didn't like it at all, but
> didn't say anything to Maud for fear of making her nervous too.
> Coming home I felt it worse than ever, and when she followed me
> she stuck in the middle and frightened me awfully. However she
> summoned up her courage and got over all right. Then I told her
> what a funk I had been in and we decided we couldn't risk it again.
> You see it meant a bad fall on to the huge boulders—probably
> a broken leg at the least. So we tried to find a path through the
> woods, because the road crossed the stream again a few hundred
> yards further on. But we couldn't get any trail through. So we
> finally decided that as we *had* to go—the Hensleys [our singers]
> were on the other side—we would wade at a ford. Every one said
> it was too deep, but after a little prospecting we did it, and afterwards
> repeated it several times. You would have laughed if you had seen
> me cautiously picking my way across with a tall sort of Alpine stock
> in one hand and my umbrella in the other. I carry the latter instead
> of a rain-coat as it is easier to walk with and quite as serviceable.

There was certainly nothing of the adventurous, resourceful
pioneer about either of us. One morning at a missionary

settlement Cecil Sharp announced with pride that he had made his own bed and that his wife would be surprised when she heard this. 'She would be more surprised if she saw the "made" bed' was his hostess's comment.

The country, though difficult to get about in, was of surpassing loveliness. 'It is a paradise,' wrote Cecil Sharp; I don't think I have ever seen such lovely trees, ferns, and wild flowers. . . . If I had not my own special axe to grind I should be collecting ferns or butterflies or something.

At White Rock, our first resting-place, where we spent several days, we were entertained by Dr. and Mrs. Packard, and during our travels in 1916 we depended for board and lodging very largely on the hospitality of the Presbyterian missionaries, making our head-quarters with them and walking sometimes long distances to visit singers in the surrounding country.

At first Cecil Sharp was carefully shepherded and introduced to selected singers, for there was a certain amount of nervousness as to how he and they would 're-act' on each other, but these fears were soon dispelled. After three days at White Rock he writes:

There is no doubt that I am going to add some wonderful stuff to my collection. I have never before got such a wonderful lot in such a short time. The singers are just English peasants in appearance, speech, and manner. . . . Indeed it is most refreshing to be once again amongst one's own people.

And a fortnight later:

Although the people are so English they have their American quality [in] . . . that they are freer than the English peasant. They own their own land and have done so for three or four generations, so that there is none of the servility which unhappily is one of the characteristics of the English peasant. With that praise I should say that they are just exactly what the English peasant was one hundred or more years ago.

In other parts of the States little was known of the mountain people, who were—and still are—constantly referred to as 'mountain whites' or 'poor white trash'. 'White', as a distinction from the 'coloured' negro, seems in any case a little unnecessary as there are practically no negroes in the mountains. We were told by our New York and Boston friends that we should find ourselves amongst a wild and dangerous community, and we were advised to arm ourselves with revolvers. Cecil Sharp paid no heed to the warning; indeed, he said that the handling of a revolver would cause him far greater fear than encountering the wildest savage; and, as a matter of fact, it would have been hard to find any other place where a stranger—and particularly a woman—would be safer than in the mountains.

The people were mostly illiterate and had no money—serious shortcomings in the eyes of American city-dwellers—but though they had none of the advantages of civilization they had a culture which was as much a tradition as the songs they sang. 'A case of arrested development?' Cecil Sharp replied to a facile critic, 'I should prefer to call it a case of arrested degeneration.' Owing to the difficulty of transport they were to a very great extent shut off from the outside world, and so in the more secluded parts of the mountains they were very nearly self-supporting. Some had built themselves frame-houses, but they lived mostly in log-cabins, usually, but not always, lighted with windows. The following extract from a letter to Mrs. Sharp (September 3rd, 1916) gives a picture of a remote mountain home:

I wish you could have seen us at a home far up Higgins Creek where we spent the greater part of Friday. We arrived about 10.30 (we breakfast here 6.30 week-days and 7 on Sundays) and left about 4, dining with them at 11.30. There were fourteen people in the room at one time, mostly grandchildren and great-grand-children of the old lady. I don't suppose any of them had any money at all—many of them have never seen any!—they barter a little, but never sell for money. They really live almost entirely upon what they make and grow. All their clothes, blankets, etc. are made by them with the wool their sheep produce. Hardly any of them wear boots. The only meat they ever eat—and it is very little—is pig, or hog-meat as they call it. For the rest they subsist on vegetables, fruit, and corn-bread, i.e. maize-bread. At the present time they are busy preserving vegetables, fruit, etc. for use in the winter. They make their vinegar out of apples. The only groceries I saw were salt and pepper, and perhaps the latter was grown by themselves.

It may be added that one of the family was a beautiful singer and we noted seventeen songs from him that day.

Owing to the absence of roads there were no markets, and so there was no inducement for the people to produce more than they needed for their own requirements, and that was extremely little. However, the mountain people seem to thrive on their diet, for physically they are strong, well-grown, and loose-limbed, though spare almost to gauntness. But to us the food was monotonous and unpleasant, mainly owing to its greasiness. The country abounds in little black pigs of the 'razor-back' variety which run about half wild in the forests, and although little of the flesh of the animal was eaten its presence was all-pervading. Cooking meant frying, and all things, even apples, were served swimming in fat. Later on, when we lived with the people, we found it hard to keep ourselves properly nourished, for not only was the food not to our liking, but their standard of cleanliness was not ours, and the swarms of flies—the pest of a hot country—did not stimulate our appetites. Many was the time we thanked Providence for having placed eggs inside shells. As far as possible we supplemented the diet with our own provisions, but it was impossible to carry any great quantity or anything at all bulky. When Cecil Sharp left the mountains, he said, 'I feel I can never again look a raisin in the eye'.

It was not only in matters of cleanliness that the highlanders showed signs of having remained in the eighteenth century, but also in their patriarchal mode of life. In some homes the women did not eat at table until the men had finished; and one of our singers, a hoary-headed gentleman known as 'Frizzly Bill', informed us that he had 'owned three wives'.

Like all primitive people they mature at an early age and they marry young; often at the age of thirteen or fourteen and occasionally even earlier. A young wife and mother is thus described by Cecil Sharp:

Yesterday we called at a cabin and found such a lovely young, fair-haired, blue-eyed girl, fifteen years of age with a buxom seven-months-old baby in her arms. I never saw a jollier, stronger, healthier baby or mother in my life; and she must have been married at fourteen, perhaps thirteen! So much for these Eugenic people!

The first marriage is often not a success, and the couple separate, usually without any ill feeling. A boy when asked where his parents lived replied quite simply:

My mother and step-father live here and my father and step-mother live at Alleghany [a neighbouring settlement].

The characteristics of the highlanders have provided good copy for writers of a sentimental and sensational order, who have in particular enlarged upon the customs of blood-feuds and of the illicit distilling of corn-spirit. 'I always thank my stars I am not a literary man having to note characteristics of my friends and acquaintances and turn them into copy,' wrote Cecil Sharp apropos of a magazine article on the mountain people.

We heard many stories of the feuds which were often maintained between two families for generations, but we were given to understand that this barbarous custom had been discontinued. Of the whisky-making, or 'moonshining', as it is called, we saw no signs, but we wisely avoided showing any curiosity in this matter; and no doubt my female presence relieved the people of any suspicion which they might otherwise have had that Cecil Sharp was a State revenue officer. There is no doubt that the stills were often close at hand though carefully hidden. On one occasion we visited a creek with a bad reputation for moonshining. It was approached by a steep and narrow mountain pass, and before descending into the valley we called at a log-cabin to make some inquiries. The man answered us courteously enough, but after we had proceeded a few yards he fired his gun into the air—no doubt a warning to his neighbours that strangers were abroad. We saw very little drinking—in fact, but two instances. At an evening-party the men retired periodically for refreshment and came back in a merry mood; and a singer, who came to the mission-house where Cecil Sharp was staying, disburdened himself of a bottle before entering the house, out of deference to the missionaries, and hid it in a convenient spot in the bushes, where he had recourse to it during the intervals of singing.

Very few could read or write, but they were good talkers, and their talk showed that they had wisdom and knowledge. They used uncommon expressions, many of which were old English. One peculiarity which was universal was the pronunciation of the impersonal pronoun with an initial aspirate—'hit'.[1] A child who is 'ill' is not sick, but bad-tempered; a woman does not give birth, but 'finds' a baby; and 'clever'[2] folk are those who are kind and hospitable. They were, too, good listeners as well as good talkers. 'I could go on listening to him for hours,' said one woman, 'he is so—so educating.' And Cecil Sharp, who never 'talked down' to people, always had something interesting to tell, whether it might be the immediate business of song or dance, or the crops, or some more remote subject; the Pyramids, for instance, or the locks in the Panama Canal, or the Dardanelles campaign—

[1] The latest quotation in the *O.E.D.* for *hit* is 'To truste my life in anothers hand and send hit out of my owne' (Queen Elizabeth, 1586).
[2] Probably from its OE. meaning of 'quick', 'prompt'.

three subjects on which one singer sought information. Generally speaking, the people had not much knowledge of the outside world. They had all heard of the War, but they were not always certain whether England was fighting with or against Germany; and fact and fiction were sometimes strangely confused, as with the woman who wanted to know whether mermaids were real people.

Though unlettered and isolated from the affairs of the world, the social instincts of the people were highly developed, and their charm of manner was a constant source of delight. Cecil Sharp says of them:[1]

They have an easy, unaffected bearing and the unselfconscious manners of the well-bred. I have received salutations upon introduction or on bidding farewell, such as a courtier might make to his sovereign. . . . Strangers that we met in the course of our long walks would usually bow, doff the hat, and extend the hand, saying 'My name is ——; what is yours?'

And the children would greet us with 'Howdy', accompanied by a little bow or curtsy.

Strangers were, of course, rare in the mountains, but our presence never aroused the slightest sign either of curiosity or of surprise. We would call, more often than not without any introduction, at a log-cabin, first shouting 'Hullo' from a little distance, as is the custom in a country where a gun is always within reach, and we were invariably received with the utmost friendliness. We were as a matter of course invited to 'partake' with the family; and when we rose to say good-bye the frequent request was, 'But surely you will tarry with us for the night'.

Cecil Sharp had high hopes of what he might discover in the mountains, but the actual result surpassed his fondest dreams, and after a fortnight's collecting, when he had noted ninety tunes, he wrote:

It is the greatest discovery I have made since the original one in England sixteen years ago.

[1] *English Folk-Songs from the Southern Appalachians*, vol. i, p. xxiii.

There was not as in England the tiresome business of having first to listen to popular music-hall or drawing-room songs of fifty years ago before extracting the genuine traditional music, because the people knew little else but folk-music; and every one was acquainted with the songs, although, as in any other community, not every one was a singer. We endeavoured therefore to find out who were the best singers in the district and to get all we could from them. A certain amount of chance, or hard work, or both, was needed to discover them, for singing was not an accomplishment which was used for public entertainment. There was no such thing as a concert, or even community-singing, but song was just part of everyday life. 'There now,' said a woman who had momentarily forgotten a song that Mr. Sharp wished to hear, 'if only I were driving the cows home I should remember it at once.' The whole time we were in the mountains we never heard a poor tune, except sometimes at the missionary settlements, or on the rare occasions when we stayed at a summer-resort hotel.

We had not as a rule any difficulty in getting the people to sing to us; in fact, their readiness was sometimes an embarrassment, as in the case of the Kentucky woman and her three married daughters, all of whom insisted on singing their favourite songs at the same time at the top of their voices. When by chance the interest flagged we stimulated it by singing ourselves, promising an English song in exchange for every song that we received. It was in this way that Cecil Sharp first discovered the delight of singing to others, and his voice, or lack of it, did not in the least embarrass him. It was the songs he was asking people to listen to and not his singing.

One obstacle that we had to contend with was that of religious scruples, particularly with the 'Holiness' sect, or 'Holy Rollers' as they were commonly called, who thought it wicked to sing 'love-songs'. Cecil Sharp respected their scruples and never tried to overcome them, but sometimes they would of their own accord relent, saying they were sure that Mr. Sharp would do no harm with the songs. The religious-minded did not always frown upon the songs, however, as the following extract from a letter to his daughter Joan shows:

>   Kentucky,
>   June 4th, 1917.
> We had one curious experience the other day. We called on a Mrs. Talitha P . . ., who was living with her sister and a brother. Mrs. P. sang us several good songs, whereupon we rose to go, when the sister, a very grim, flat-chested, gaunt sort of person got up and said, 'You have made my house a house of songs, but it is also a house of prayer', and immediately dumped down on her knees. I with my recollection—rather dim—of family prayers turned round and put my head in the seat of my chair while she fired off an intimate talk with the Deity. . . . When she had exhausted her inspiration, her brother who was between me and her took up the strain and 'offered up' another prayer and did it very well indeed, in excellent language and ease of expression. In the middle of his conversation with the Almighty he mentioned the two strangers at his house and asked for a blessing on our work 'which I deem most profitable'. It was very funny, of course, but very sweet of him to pay us this compliment in a way which precluded any acknowledgement on our part. When he had done I was perspiring with fear lest I should be called upon to take up the strain, so I rose noisily to my feet immediately.

The majority of those with whom we came into contact were Baptists, whose preachers won fame for themselves in proportion to the carrying power of their voices in the open air; there were also Methodists, Presbyterians, and Episcopalians. We found that an austere Calvinistic doctrine was prevalent in which the devil was regarded as an object of fear and respect.

Some of the best songs were sung to us by children. One small boy edged his way into a cabin where Mr. Sharp was noting songs from an old man, a singer of some repute. 'Hullo, what do you want?' said Mr. Sharp on seeing him, and the boy answered, 'Please, sir, let me stay. I love to be where there is sweet music.' Of course, Mr. Sharp let him stay, and later on when the singer professed ignorance of a certain song, the small boy piped up, 'Please sir, I know it.' And without any persuasion he sang the long ballad of 'Young Hunting'[1] in a way, as Cecil Sharp said, 'which would have shamed many a professional singer'.

Another of our singers in whom Cecil Sharp took a great interest was Emma Hensley, a girl of thirteen, of beautiful, Madonna-like appearance, who lived with her mother and father in a remote mountain valley. Cecil Sharp writes (August 13th, 1916):

> I spent three days at the Hensleys, walking over each morning after breakfast about 8.30 (we breakfast at 7.30), getting there about 10 and leaving again about 5. We sat on the verandah of their little home amongst the mountains, surrounded by huge trees and small clearings covered chiefly with corn (maize) and tobacco. All three sang and he played the fiddle. I got about 30 tunes from them and had an awfully jolly time. I got very interested in Emma, the child, who is crazy to go to school. . . . Her mother is anxious for her to go for two reasons: (1) because she does not want her to marry as young as her sister [who married at fifteen], and (2) because she chews tobacco, which very unladylike habit she learned from an aunt; and her mother feels that school discipline is the only thing that will break her of the habit!

Her father, too, wanted her to go so that she might learn to play, having promised that if she did he would sell the cow and buy an 'organ' (harmonium). Cecil Sharp was doubtful whether the school was the best place for Emma and whether she would be able to resign herself to the loss of liberty; but he interviewed the head mistress, paid for the outfit, and helped with the fees. The day Emma arrived at the school we happened to be staying in the same small town, which is on the railway and has quite

---

[1] See *English Folk-Songs from the Southern Appalachians*, vol. i, p. 102.

a large and not unfashionable summer resort hotel, and so
we invited Emma to dine with us. She arrived at the hotel
looking very neat and demure in her grey school uniform
—she had been barefoot when we last saw her—and
although she had never left home before, she comported
herself as though dining out were an everyday occurrence.
She showed no sign of embarrassment or even surprise
at her unaccustomed surroundings. She watched to see
what I did with my napkin and the many knives and forks,
and without comment did the same with hers, conversing
the while in an easy, friendly way. Early next morning
we were standing on the bank of the French Broad river,
waiting for a ferry to take us across—the floods had washed
away the bridge—when whom should we see but Emma
and a schoolfellow, both carrying suit-cases. Emma looked
slightly flushed, but otherwise her usual dignified and
composed self. 'Good-morning,' she said sweetly, 'we
have just run away'; and before we could find a suitable
reply they had jumped into a boat. We shouted to them
to wait for us on the other side, which they did. Cecil
Sharp, though secretly rejoicing, felt it his duty to try to
persuade Emma to go back; but Emma was quite decided.
'No,' she said, 'I am going to my mother. Perhaps later
on I may return—I don't know: I haven't yet made up
my mind.' And then, just a little crestfallen: 'I'm sorry,
because you have been so good to me.' But the next
moment she had brightened up and asked if we would not
go back with her. We declined the invitation, and the last
we saw of Emma was as she started off for her twenty-mile
walk across the mountain. She did not return to the school,
and no doubt our gifts of clothes formed an attractive
trousseau. 'I am filled with admiration for her,' Cecil
Sharp wrote to his wife. 'She is just unique; and it seems
awful, nothing less than barbaric, to spoil her and turn her
into an ordinary respectable half-educated American girl.'

Cecil Sharp acknowledged the hospitality and friendli-

ness of the missionaries towards himself, but he thought
that much of their work amongst the mountain people
was misguided and harmful, particularly their educational
methods. He writes of it:

To Mrs. Storrow.
13.9.16.

Some of the women [missionaries] I have met are very nice
and broadminded. But I don't think any of them realize that the
people they are here to improve are in many respects far more
cultivated than their would-be instructors, even if they cannot read
or write. Take music, for example. Their own is pure and lovely.
The hymns that these missionaries teach them are musical and
literary garbage. . . . The problem, I know, is a very difficult one.
For my part, I would leave them as they are and not meddle. They
are happy, contented, and live simply and healthily, and I am not at
all sure that any of us can introduce them to anything better than
this. Something might be done in teaching them better methods
of farming, so as to lighten the burden of earning a living from their
holdings; and they should certainly be taught to read and write—
at any rate, those who want to, ought to be able to. Beyond that
I should not go.

The singers took the greatest interest and delight in our
noting of the songs. Cecil Sharp used the phonograph
for a short time when collecting in England, but found
it unsatisfactory, mainly, I believe, because he thought it
made the singers self-conscious. In any case, the transport
of phonographic apparatus would have presented insuperable difficulties in this mountain country; so he noted the
tunes in ordinary musical notation as they were sung,
whilst I took down the words in shorthand. The singers
regarded this process almost as a conjuring trick, especially
when by looking at our books we could sing the songs back
to them. An old man, who could neither read nor write,
was shown the musical notation of the song he had just
been singing. 'Look, there's your song,' said Mr. Sharp,
handing him his little note-book. The old man looked
thoughtfully at the page of manuscript for a few moments,

then, shaking his head, said: 'Well, I can hardly recognize it.' Another singer, the father of nineteen children (not all by the same wife), commended our efforts in these words: 'Singing is a great power in the world and you are doing a noble work.'

The first eight weeks were spent mostly in Madison County, North Carolina, and Unicoi County, Tennessee. Then, having only a week to spare before we were due to leave for Chicago, we decided to spend it in the university town of Charlottesville, Virginia, partly in order to sample the Blue Ridge section and partly to get into touch with Professor Alphonso Smith, the founder of the Virginia Folk-Lore Society, who, as Professor of English at the University of Virginia, had aroused an interest in balladry amongst his students and had encouraged them to collect.

Inspired by the monumental work of Professor Child of Harvard, the universities of America have taken great interest in the English and Scottish popular ballad; but until recently the subject has been viewed almost entirely from the literary standpoint, and such collections of mountain ballads as had hitherto been made by the State folk-lore societies, universities, and other individual efforts were with a few exceptions restricted to the texts, and the tunes had been ignored. It is, however, of interest to note that shortly before Cecil Sharp went to North Carolina a similar quest had been made, unbeknown to him, by Miss Loraine Wyman and Mr. Howard Brockway, who had spent April, May, and June collecting in Kentucky.[1]

Cecil Sharp, as we have seen, was unwilling to poach on other people's preserves, and so before venturing into Virginia he wrote to Professor Smith:

. . . I have an idea, though it may be a wrong one, that in the majority of cases it is the text only and not the tune that has been

---

[1] See *Lonesome Tunes* (25 songs) (H. W. Gray Co., New York, 1916) and *Twenty Kentucky Mountain Songs* (Oliver Ditson Co., Boston, 1925). The songs in both volumes are arranged with pianoforte accompaniment.

noted. If I am right, it seems to me very important that the investigation, initiated by your students, should be followed up by some one, like myself, who can take down the tunes; for I am sure you will agree with me that the tune is every whit as essential a part of the ballad as the text. So it occurred to me that it might be . . . profitable for me to spend my last fortnight in your neighbourhood. . . . But I should not wish to do this without your approval, or unless I felt assured of your co-operation. . . . Apart altogether from the question of collection it would be a great pleasure to me to visit Charlottesville, show you the tunes and ballads that I have already taken down and discuss them with you.

Professor Smith extended a cordial welcome and the last week was profitably spent in exploring the country around Charlottesville.

We had our disappointments, of course, and there were some long weary trudges with no results; but sooner or later the luck turned, sometimes quite unexpectedly, as at the end of a tiring and fruitless twelve-hour day in Tennessee when without hope we paid yet another call and were instantly rewarded by hearing 'The False Knight on the Road'. On the whole, there was certainly no cause for dissatisfaction, for in the first nine weeks Cecil Sharp noted nearly four hundred tunes, reaching the high-water mark with seventy in one week.

CHAPTER XIII
1917–1918
THE APPALACHIANS, 2

When I travelled, I took a particular Delight in hearing the Songs and Fables that are come from Father to Son, and are most in vogue among the common People of the Countries through which I passed; for it is impossible that anything that should be universally tasted and approved by a Multitude, though they are only the Rabble of a Nation, which hath not in it some peculiar Aptness to please and gratifie the Mind of Man.—STEELE, *Spectator*.

IN 1917 we were in the mountains during April and May and again during August, September, and the first half of October. The first three weeks were spent in Tennessee and the rest of the time mostly in Kentucky.

This was our first experience of the mountain country in Spring and it appeared a real fairyland. Cecil Sharp wrote to his wife (May 6th, 1917):

I wish you could see this country in its fresh Spring green. The trees are almost fully out now, and there is plenty of shade and the country looks wonderful. I miss the singing birds of England, and the woods sound very quiet for the time of year, but the flowers and flowering trees are just wonderful. The dogwood tree is very lovely, a pure white Christmas-rose kind of flower, which covers the tree before its leaves come out like the blackthorn. Then there is the magnolia, which they call the wild cucumber, because of the scarlet, cucumber-shaped seed it bears in autumn. It grows very freely from twenty to forty feet in height and is thick with blossom. Then there is a small purple iris which grows pretty well everywhere. Lots of violets, but no primroses; and a lot of flowers I have not yet named.

Our travels throughout the year were fraught with anxiety owing to Cecil Sharp's poor state of health. He managed to do a fortnight's collecting, and then, whilst staying at the Lincoln Memorial University, at Harrogate, Tenn.—a school for mountain boys and girls—he had a severe attack of fever with delirium, which kept him in bed for three days. Even then he could not put the collecting aside, but took down twenty-four tunes from students, whom I first tested and then brought to his bedside.

Whilst he was still painfully weak we moved on to Pineville, a railroad town of some three thousand inhabitants in Kentucky, where there was a comparatively comfortable hotel, and singers were to be found in the neighbourhood; but after a week he felt he had for the present exhausted the district, and so, leaving creature comforts behind, we moved on to Barbourville, a small town, also on the railway, where oil had recently been discovered. Although the prospects did not at first seem very good, we soon struck a 'nest of singing-birds'; but our satisfaction was short-lived, for after a few days Cecil Sharp had an alarming return of the fever, which the local doctor diagnosed as 'probably typhoid'. As soon as they heard of his illness Mr. John Campbell and Dr. Packard came to his assistance, making a two days' journey over the mountains. When they arrived at Barbourville the fever had subsided and Cecil Sharp, though barely strong enough to sit up in bed, was taking down songs from a woman-singer, whom I had brought to his bedside in the hopes of dispelling the acute mental depression from which he was suffering.

The journeys into the 'wilds' which he had planned were now quite out of the question, but, as he could not be persuaded to give up the collecting completely, we compromised and, with the assistance of Dr. Packard and Mr. Campbell, made the journey to Berea, in the foothills of Kentucky, where there is a College for mountain students and a comfortable hostelry run by the College. We remained there a fortnight, and during that time Cecil Sharp added another hundred tunes to his collection, but the field was not a very good one, for the people had become sophisticated, and the singing of traditional songs was apt to be despised as belonging to a past and discarded mode of existence. We were told that the singing of love-songs was only practised by the rough, common people, and an earnest young College student was reluctant to sing a version of 'The Swapping Song', as he cared only for songs which contained 'great thoughts'. On another occasion, though not in this district, Cecil Sharp was told by a woman that she and her husband made it a rule never to sing love-songs nor to swear before the children. 'What the connexion between the two was, I don't know,' Cecil Sharp wrote to his daughter Joan; 'I do both to *my* children, as you know!'

In the meantime his health continued to give cause for anxiety. He suffered from extreme weakness and ex-haustion and seemed on the verge of a nervous collapse. So after a few days at Pineville he gave up the collecting, and at the beginning of June took a ten days' rest at Ashe-ville, in order to fit himself for the work of his Folk-Dance Summer School.

At the end of July we were back in the mountains. We first spent a few fruitless days in North Carolina, on the Asheville–Murphy line (which had been our first approach to Asheville in the preceding year), trying in vain to com-bine song-collecting and physical comfort.

To Mrs. Storrow. 30.7.17.

The fact is we are too close to Waynesville, a large industrial centre, and the inhabitants have been partly spoiled, that is from my point of view. The log-cabins are primitive enough, but their owners are clean, neat, and tidy, looking rather like maid-servants in respectable suburban families! It is sad that cleanliness and good music, or good taste in music, rarely go together. Dirt and good music are the usual bed-fellows, or cleanliness and rag-time! So we move further on tomorrow and in a day or two shall be roughing it pretty badly, I expect

—an expectation that was fulfilled.

We decided to continue our researches in Kentucky, which had been cut short two months earlier by his illness. The train journey from Asheville was a trying one. 'I have never felt the heat so much since my last trip through the Red Sea,' he wrote in his diary.

A terrible experience waiting for the train, herded—about 150 of us—like pigs in a sty, not even with the information that we were in the right sty! After nearly half-an-hour of this purgatory the train drew up and we were let out one by one through a narrow opening. The windows so dirty in the train that we could not see the mountain scenery. Heat almost unbelievable—no air. There we remained till 9 p.m. when we reached Knoxville and decamped to the hotel. How we lived through that night I shall never know. I am feeling very seedy—headache, asthma, and general lassitude.

From Knoxville we proceeded by train to Barbourville, and after a few days there we made our way to Manchester (Clay Co.), a small county town in the heart of the mountains, by an insecure branch railroad. 'And such a railroad!' writes Cecil Sharp.

The cars swayed to and fro and creaked and wheezed like an old sailing-ship riding out a severe storm. They say it is safe because they travel so slowly—about nine miles an hour—but I don't look forward to the return journey.

Manchester (pronounced Manchéster) was enjoying a new-born prosperity due to the opening of coal-mines and the running of the light railway.

To Mrs. Storrow.   August 26th, 1917.

Manchester, though the County seat, has no made roads nor water (except very doubtful wells—shallow at that) and no system of sanitation. The hotel faces a vacant square with a dry creek running across it covered with large boulders. Residents just throw the contents of their dustbins out upon the streets where the hogs which are numerous eat of it what they can! ...

And to Mr. John Glenn, the Director of the Russell Sage Foundation, a kind and much valued friend, he writes:

September 2nd 1917.

This trip is causing me to modify the opinion that I first formed that the singing of folk-songs was universal in the mountains. . . . Primitiveness in custom and outlook is not, I am finding, so much the result of remoteness as bad economic conditions. When there is coal and good wages to be earned, the families soon drop their old-fashioned ways and begin to ape town manners, etc. And where the land is rich and the valleys broad and it is easy to accumulate surplus wealth the same thing follows. I found, for instance, that Clay County despite its remoteness was quite sophisticated. Frame-houses were the rule along many of the creeks, rather than the cabins; and here the inhabitants received my remarks about the log songs with a superiority of air that was almost contemptuous. Still even in country of this sort it is possible to extract songs, and often very good ones, but only with difficulty, and then mainly from the older inhabitants. . . . Here is a curious instance of superficial sophistication. A young girl was staying at Manchester . . . who had come from a very remote part twenty-five miles back. She was so ignorant that she imagined that England was a province of Germany and that America was at war with both. Yet she apologised one morning at breakfast because she had omitted to use her face powder.

This sophisticated air of superiority was well described by a singer, one of the 'really nice people' with whom Cecil Sharp made friends. 'Those people have got rich before they have any money,' she said. We spent many long hours with her and a friend who lived with her, delighting in her racy talk and enjoying the songs that the two women gave us. They both smoked pipes, although when we visited them they had only one between them. She told us she had married three times: the first husband had killed a man and was serving a long sentence in a penitentiary; the next one drank, so she kicked him out; and the third wouldn't work and so had to depart in the same summary fashion. She had a three-roomed house and each room contained an enlarged framed photograph of one of the husbands which she showed us with great pride.

She had always been the same to everybody: 'I've just got one face and I've worn it out—that's why it's so ugly,' she said. Two months after our visits she wrote to thank Mr. Sharp for some snapshots and books he had sent her, for she could read and write. Her letter is given as she wrote it, except for the correction of a few spelling errors and the addition of punctuation:

I received your letter yesterday and all our pictures. And I have no words to express how well pleased I was to hear from you and dear little Maud, for I know there is something in your lives as well as mine that brings grief instead of pleasure. Well, I received the novels you sent me and you can guess whether I was pleased or not. Bet your life I was more than pleased. Well, you spoke of the pipes, it is impossible to get them and I had rather have a pair of spectacles, as a pipe I can smoke in most any kind of pipe and I can not see through any kind of glasses. Well, I truly hope you and Maud will get back to Manchester some day and that before long, for it would do my heart good to see you. Excuse paper and pen and hand.

The pipes referred to were meerschaum pipes. When Cecil Sharp asked her what she would like as a present from New York, she said 'A pipe made of the foam of the sea'.

At the end of August we visited the Pine Mountain Settlement School in Harlan County. There was then no road to the school and it was reached by a steep, rough trail over Pine Mountain. Cecil Sharp was enthusiastic.

To Mrs. John C. Campbell.

2.9.17.

There is a mountain-school—if you can call it a school—after my own heart! It is just a lovely place, fine buildings, beautiful situation, and wisely administered. Miss Pettit and Miss de Long are cultivated gentlefolk, who fully realize the fine innate qualities of the mountain children and handle them accordingly. And the children, many of them little more than babies, are just fascinating, clean, bright, well-behaved little things, who come up, put their hands in yours, and behave like the children of gentle-folk—which is, of course, just what they are. This settlement is a model of what the mountain-schools should be. Everything is beautiful. . . . Flowers are grown everywhere and large bowls of them in every room. They do not emphasize the school side of things, nor, I am glad to say, the church side. They sing ballads after dinner and grace before it.

The visit was a memorable one, not only to Cecil Sharp, but to the members of the school staff. One of them, Miss Evelyn Wells, writes (1931):

I remember what a hot August day it was when Mr. Sharp and Miss Karpeles came walking in across Pine Mountain. Most visitors from the outside world were heralded by the guide, who came ahead to open gates for his mule-passengers; not so these two, who were quietly at our door-step before we knew it. . . . There are many highlights on that visit of five days. . . . There was the hour after supper in our big dining-room, where after the day of farm-work and canning and other vacation occupations, we settled back in our chairs while those two sang to us—'The Knight in the Road', 'All along in the Ludeney', 'Edward', 'The Gypsy Laddie', and many nursery songs. I can remember the twilight creeping in on us, the youngest children falling to sleep, dropping on their crossed arms at the table, as if they were being sung to by their own firesides, the voices of the singers getting more and more impersonal in the dusk as song after song was finished.

There were the two noon hours when eight workers from the staff learned 'Rufty Tufty', 'The Black Nag' and 'Gathering Peascods' on the porch of Laurel House to Mr. Sharp's teaching and Miss Karpeles's singing of the tune. I always think of that when I watch a Pine Mountain May Day now with its four or five sword teams, its varied country dances, its early morning morris. . . . All the work of the day stopped during those lessons—children stopped weeding the vegetable gardens, girls stopped washing the clothes, even the workmen stopped building the school-house. And this was in the days when we worked incessantly to put roofs over our heads and to can food against the winter, and every minute counted.

I remember the first morning when Mr. Sharp came to our six o'clock breakfast late, having lost his way to the dining-room in the thick mountain mist that filled the valley—suffering terribly from an attack of asthma, which to my inexperienced eyes seemed highly alarming—and then going off down the valley within the next hour, walking miles to get songs from Singing Willie Nolan. I remember tea under the apple-trees, where again we let the Pine Mountain world stop, while he talked of his mountain experiences, and of collecting in England and the dancing there. . . .

Mr. Sharp summed up for Pine Mountain much that till then had been implicitly taken for granted. That he found there the right soil in which to plant again the native crop of songs and dances made us realise our responsibility as never before and we have never since let the heritage of the children die out.

Another mountain school that Cecil Sharp thought and spoke well of was at Hindman (Knott Co.). We spent a happy week there and Cecil Sharp noted sixty tunes, which included some first-rate songs. Although only twenty miles from the railway, the journey by mail-hack took about ten hours. The return journey is described by Cecil Sharp in a letter to an American friend.

To Miss Peggy Scovill.

26.9.17.

Travelling here is an arduous affair. . . . There aren't any real roads, merely dirt-tracks strewn with boulders and plentifully be-sprinkled with large cavities. We had seven people in the mail-hack, the driver and his cook on the front seat, Maud, self, and another female jammed tight like sardines on the back-seat, and two stalwart men standing on the mail-bags behind us. The cook was of 'cookly' proportions or I should have shared the front seat with the driver, but for Maud's sake I sacrificed myself and placed my thinner body on the back seat—but all the thanks I got was an acid remark to the effect that, though larger, the cook would have probably made a softer companion! There is no pleasing some people.

This letter was written at Hazard, where we stayed a few days in order to rest after our journeys, and Cecil Sharp, finding that he could have the use of a piano which was not too badly out of tune, spent his time in harmonizing, and made the first draft of all the songs in his *American-English Folk-Songs*.[1]

Hazard, which, as Cecil Sharp said, should have been called 'Haphazard', he describes as

A noisome little place, new, crude, dirty, unkempt, insanitary, a mass of people, diligently dollar-hunting with no other ideas in their heads. These mountain places that get exploited by financial and business men because of the presence of coal and oil are as horrible as the unexploited places are beautiful. But there is a fairly good hotel here, and I can eat the food, and to tell the truth when we arrived here on Monday we were both nearly at the end of our tether.

Our next journey was from Hazard to Hyden, the county town of Leslie. Again the distance was about twenty miles and it took the whole day to do. 'The journey', writes Cecil Sharp, 'was the worst we have yet experienced.'

The waggon was without springs or cushions on the seat—a tumbledown affair which rocked and creaked and bumped most ominously all the way. Indeed, so impossible was it to sit in that we walked all the way except for the five miles or so when the road went down the middle of the creek. . . . We crossed five mountains on the way and were just dead when we arrived.

Hyden he described as 'the most primitive county town I have struck'.

We hadn't been there more than a day or so before every one in the place knew us and knew our business and everything about us. It was like entering a family party.

They all spoke of him affectionately as the 'old gentleman', and they followed our movements in search of songs with the greatest interest. It was an excellent centre for collecting, and the songs in Cecil Sharp's note-books were rapidly increasing, but after a week he was again stricken without any warning with a sharp attack of fever, which was

[1] Published by Schirmer, New York, 1918, and reprinted as *Folk-Songs of English Origin*, vol. i, by Novello, 1919.

alarming, as we were two days' journey from a big town.
Happily, it did not last long, and after five days we decided
to risk the journey and move to a more accessible place.

A few days before he was taken ill, Cecil Sharp saw and
noted the Running Set, a form of country dance which is
now popular all over England. We had seen the dance
first at Pine Mountain, and the scene is thus described
by him:

It was danced one evening after dark on the porch of one of the
largest houses of the Pine Mountain School with only one dim
lantern to light up the scene. But the moon streamed fitfully in
lighting up the mountain peaks in the background and, casting its
,mysterious light over the proceedings, seemed to exaggerate the
wildness and the break-neck speed of the dancers as they whirled
through the mazes of the dance. There was no music, only the
stamping and clapping of the onlookers, but when one of the
emotional crises of the dance was reached ... the air seemed literally
to pulsate with the rhythm of the 'patters' and the tramp of the
dancers' feet, while, over and above it all, penetrating through the
din, floated the even, falsetto tones of the Caller, calmly and un-
excitedly reciting his directions.[1]

The dance had on that occasion been sprung upon us
unawares, and we were unable to make more than a few
casual notes. We saw it again at Hindman at a party
which had been arranged for our benefit, but the dancing
was not good, and it would in any case have been difficult
to note the dance owing to the crowded state of the room.
There is no such thing as a private party in the mountains, but all come who wish, whether invited or not. At
Hyden we were fortunate enough to see undisturbed a
good set of dancers, and a few days later, after Cecil Sharp
had been taken ill, I went to a 'bean-stringing' in the
neighbourhood, where I witnessed and took part in the
dance. It was performed in a small, unventilated room
about twelve feet square into which thirty to forty people

[1] Introduction to *The Country Dance Book*, Part 5.

besides the dancers managed to squeeze themselves. Set-running has a bad name in the mountains, possibly because of Puritan prejudices, but more probably because it leads often to drinking and sometimes to shooting. Whatever the cause, all but the most sternly religious-minded continue to dance, only they speak of it as 'playing' and not dancing.

After leaving Hyden we remained in Kentucky for a few days and then proceeded to Asheville. An entry on October 17th in Cecil Sharp's diary reads:

So now this tour is finished. I am feeling rather sad but greatly relieved to know that I have reached a haven of rest without mishap where I can eat, sleep, write music, and, I hope, get flesh and strength again. . . . And there are the 600 tunes in my trunk collected this year—not without some expenditure of physical vitality.

In 1918 we again had two periods of collecting in the mountains: the first from April to June, and the second from July to October. The whole of the first period was spent in Virginia, except for a few days in West Virginia, and we returned to Virginia for the first five weeks of the second period, spending the remainder of the time— about six weeks—in North Carolina. Living conditions were at times very primitive and there was some rough, hard travelling, but Cecil Sharp had no return of the fever, and although he often felt ill and exhausted he got through without any serious collapse.

The mountains of Virginia—or at any rate those parts that we visited—were free from the industrial towns of mushroom-growth which were an objectionable feature of Kentucky, and on that account our travels were plea-santer, but the singing of the songs was no more general than it was in Kentucky. Cecil Sharp sums up the situa-tion in a letter to Professor Alphonso Smith (September 1st, 1918):

The tradition [in Virginia] is steadily approaching extinction owing to the establishment of schools and the contaminating influence of what is usually called modern progress. In North Carolina every one sings and the folk-song is still vital. In Kentucky the tradition was, I imagine, in full blast up to a few years ago, and still is in some of the most remote districts, but is now being rapidly killed in its prime by industrialism. In Kentucky it is a case of sudden death; in Virginia of euthanasia.

In the same letter he states:

I have found the tunes in Virginia extraordinarily beautiful; I think of greater musical value than those that I have taken down anywhere else in America.

Sometimes we were able to stay at an hotel or a school, but generally there was no alternative but to live with the people themselves, and however poor might be the accommodation they were always ready to 'take care' of us and to give us of their best. One of the pleasantest times was that which we spent in the Tye River Valley with a family consisting of our host, his wife Salina, and three children. As is usual in mountain homes, there was only one wash-basin, which was kept on the back-porch and there did duty as might be required, but the hospitable instincts of our hostess led her to suspect that we might prefer to perform our morning ablutions in the privacy of our own rooms; and so with great courtesy the basin was handed in each morning first to me and then to Mr. Sharp.

It was whilst staying in the Tye River Valley that we first heard the rumour that we were German spies, a suspicion which we afterwards had to contend with in other places. We were told that after an evening prayer meeting the whole congregation stayed and discussed us, and it was generally agreed that we were highly suspicious characters, and that noting tunes was merely a blind to hide our nefarious actions, which included the poisoning of springs amongst other things. All this we heard from our host and hostess, who enjoyed the joke, and other friends, including the postmaster. He was convinced that we were not Germans for he had once seen one, and neither of us bore any resemblance to that specimen of the race. Whether or not they believed us to be spies, every one seemed glad to see us. Some neighbours, an old man of the name of Philander, who gave us many good songs, and his blind wife, did their best to persuade us to come and live with them in their tiny log-cabin, and every time we visited them the old blind lady would anxiously inquire: 'And is Salina still familiar?' hoping that if we fell out with Salina we might be willing to change our lodging.

The tunes came in apace, but there were some disappointing periods, as for instance a short stay in the Shenandoah Valley, where the population proved to be very largely of German extraction, and a tiresome journey into West Virginia, where we found that the continuity of rural life had been disturbed by the coal industry. On September 1st, 1918, Cecil Sharp wrote to Mrs. Storrow:

This is to let you know that we are both alive, though somewhat chastened by the heat and the buffetings of a rather unkind fate! For the last month we have struck a rather unproductive patch, but in this work it is necessary to explore all the ground and every now and again we must expect to meet with failure. It was rather disappointing in this case because we had expected the last two counties in Virginia—Franklin and Patrick—to be especially productive as the railways are very few and the mountain districts more than ordinarily isolated. We had built many hopes upon a place with a thoroughly bad reputation for illicit stills, shootings, etc., but when we got there (it was twenty-five miles from the station) there was a Missionary revival going on and in the evening the residents crowded to the 'preaching' dressed in fashionable garments, low-necked dresses, high-heels, and well powdered faces. . . . The fact is the price of whisky has so gone up that 'moonshining' has been exceedingly profitable and they are rolling in money. Songs were, of course, out of the question and we retired next day somewhat crestfallen. . . . Then again, we had set our expectations on the Meadows of Dan, partly because of its delightful name, but mainly because of its extreme isolation and altitude of 3,500 feet. And it was certainly one of the most arduous and dangerous journeys we have ever undertaken. We motored to the county town, Stuart, and then, after many refusals, prevailed on a driver to take us up to the Meadows in his motor, a matter of seventeen miles. The road which is ordinarily a very steep, narrow, and dangerous one was far worse than usual on account of some recent thunder-storms which had washed it clean right down to the native rock. In some places the inclination of the car was so great in turning a corner, with a sheer fall of five or six hundred feet over the side, that the driver himself suggested that we should get out while he negotiated it—which we did with alacrity! How a car could have driven up at all I can't imagine. I am sure nothing but a Ford could have done it. And then when we got to the top of the ridge we found a large plateau of rolling meadows and fertile land occupied by a thoroughly respectable, church-going, school-attending population, making money at a great rate owing to the advance in food prices, and many of them housed in comfortable frame-dwellings and sporting their own motor-cars. . . . Still we did get some songs and a few rather good ones, but nothing like the bag we had expected to make.

Then there were the day-to-day difficulties and disappointments. On two separate occasions we toiled up a steep mountain in tropical weather to call on an old lady of eighty-nine who had a great reputation as a singer, only to find on the first occasion that she had gone out visiting, and on the second that she was preparing to receive the preacher for dinner and was in such a fluster that she would scarcely talk to us. It was on one of these occasions that we proved with bitter experience the fallacy of the 'nigh-way'. The directions were clear: we had only to walk up to the top of the mountain and then drop down to our destination on the other side—a matter of six or seven miles; but the mountain was densely wooded, and after having walked for several hours we made inquiries at the first log-cabin and discovered that we were only a mile from whence we had started. We had walked up the mountain and down again on the same side.

However, such difficulties and hardships only served

to throw into relief the pleasant experiences of our journeys—the beautiful country, the musical atmosphere, and
the charm of the people.

An incident that lives in the memory was that which
occurred in a poor home in Virginia. We were noting
songs from a woman who was surrounded by her family
of thirteen children—seven of her own and six step-
children. Eagerly but quietly they watched the strange
proceedings, and then as their mother began to sing a
beautiful modal tune[1] they softly joined in, almost without
consciousness of what they were doing, enhancing the
beauty of the tune by the haunting loveliness of their young
voices.

Cecil Sharp's relationship with the people can, perhaps,
be best understood by quoting a remark made by a singer
whom we called upon to say our last good-byes. 'My
husband and I are sorry you are going,' she said, 'we like
you both—you are so nice and common.' Cecil Sharp
considered that the greatest compliment he had ever
been paid.

The last six weeks which were spent in North Carolina
were very productive. During the last month we were
more or less comfortably housed in a little summer hotel
in Burnsville, Yancey Co., and the field was so rich—
Cecil Sharp noted two hundred songs in the district—
that there was no need to move elsewhere.

From the Grove Park Inn, Asheville, our haven of rest,
he writes to Mrs. Storrow (October 13th, 1918):

Here we are at last. We arrived yesterday safe and sound, I am
glad to say. . . . I am dreadfully tired and worn, but a week's rest
here and good feeding will I am assured make me quite fit again. . . .
I am sorry to have said good-bye to the mountain people, but I
suspect I have seen the last of them. There is enough work left,
which might be well worth doing, that would take perhaps another
year, but I am satisfied with what I have done, and the rest can be

1 'The Green Bed.'

left to others. Without your active assistance the work would never have been done, and I am deeply grateful to you.

It would seem that Cecil Sharp had every reason to be satisfied. He had collected from 281 singers a total of 1,612 tunes, including variants, representing about 500 different songs and ballads. Of the artistic and scientific value of his work he had no doubt. He regarded it as the coping-stone to what he had done in England.

Practically all the songs and ballads can be traced to English or Lowland-Scottish sources, but the tunes are very different in character from those which have been noted in this country in recent times. Whether they have suffered a sea-change, or whether they represent English folk-music of an earlier period is open to argument. A large proportion are cast in the pentatonic scale. They are more rugged and austere than the English tunes; less mellow, but no less beautiful, although their beauty is not perhaps so obvious. Whether one prefers the Appalachian or the English type is a matter of taste, and there is happily no need to make a choice, but taken in the aggregate most people would agree that the general average of the Appalachian songs is higher than that of the English collections. From the scientific standpoint the value of Cecil Sharp's Appalachian collections lies in the fact that it is an expression of the innate musical culture of a homogeneous community.

To Cecil Sharp the mountain community was an outstanding example of 'the supreme cultural value of an inherited tradition'.

Their language, wisdom, manners, and the many graces of life that are theirs are merely racial attributes which have been acquired and accumulated in past centuries and handed down generation by generation, each generation adding its quota to that which it received.

It must be remembered also that in their everyday lives they are immune from that continuous, grinding, mental pressure due to the attempt to make a living, from which nearly all of us in this modern world suffer.... In this respect, at any rate, they have the advantage over those who habitually spend the greater part of every day in preparing to live, in acquiring the technique of life, rather than its enjoyment.[1]

His experiences in the Appalachian Mountains strengthened his belief that 'the hope for the future of art is that the leisured class may become the whole community and not one small part of it'.

When Cecil Sharp lectured about the mountain people and stressed their charm of manner and their culture there were usually some sceptics in his audiences. 'Surely', they said, 'he is looking at these people through rose-coloured spectacles.' Yet he was only describing human beings in their natural state; but in our ordinary lives the real person gets so covered over with the veneer of civilization that when he is shown us naked and unadorned we do not always recognize him.

With the eye of the artist Cecil Sharp saw beneath the surface, and where some might have seen only poverty, dirt, and ignorance, he saw humanity, beauty, and art. To Cecil Sharp it was axiomatic that any natural and sincere human expression must be beautiful, because human nature is beautiful. Or, as a woman in Kentucky put it, on hearing that the ballad of 'The Death of Queen Jane', which she had just been singing, was founded on historical fact: 'There now, I always said it must be true because it is so beautiful.'

[1] Introduction to *English Folk-Songs from the Southern Appalachian Mountains*.

CHAPTER XIV

1918–1923

PICKING UP THE THREADS

Lorsqu'un homme a commis un manquement dans sa conduite, soit
aux affaires de sa famille, ou au gouvernement d'un état, ou au com-
mandement d'une armée, ne dit-on pas toujours, Un tel a fait un
mauvais pas dans une telle affaire? Et faire un mauvais pas peut-il
procéder d'autre chose que de ne savoir pas danser?

MOLIÈRE, *Le Bourgeois Gentilhomme.*

AFTER an absence of nearly two years Cecil Sharp returned in 1918 to 'a new England but a very nice
one all the same'. With Maud Karpeles he joined his
family in their new home at 4 Maresfield Gardens, Hampstead, where he spent the rest of his days. After 'perhaps the happiest and most peaceful Christmas' within his
memory he plunged straight into work, the immediate
business being the direction of the Stratford-on-Avon
Christmas Vacation School, which was attended by seventy
students. The majority had learned their dancing before
the War, and the coming together of these fellow-dancers,
after the upheaval of the last four years, established a sense
of continuity which was not without its poignancy.

Cecil Sharp found the change of climate—'the dull
sunless cold winter after the exhilarating air of America'
—very trying. He felt 'more or less collapsed, as a man
would feel who had lived on stimulants for some years
and then had suddenly given them up'. But to others he
seemed rather to be charged with dynamic energy; now
that he was back again, the dances pulsated with new
life. His teaching experiences in America had given him
a deeper understanding of the art and technique of the
dances, and as usual he was longing to impart it to others.
Then there was the breathless Running Set dance to be
taught, experiences of the Appalachian Mountains to be
told, and ballads and songs to be sung. But perhaps the

most stirring occasion of all was one in which Cecil Sharp took no active part, but listened together with the rest of the 'School' to four members of the staff describing how they had taught folk-dancing to the troops in France.

Folk-dancing was introduced into the Army in May 1917 by Miss D. C. Daking, entering under the auspices of Miss Lena Ashwell's concert-parties and the Y.M.C.A. It was extraordinarily difficult to know how to begin. No one would learn till he had seen the dance, and there were not numbers enough to show him it. Then the halls were wanted in the evenings for entertainments, and the men had work in the mornings. Miss Daking began in the Convalescent Depot, where the morning was free, with a Northumbrian Sword Dance, 'because a man likes the feel of a tool in his hand'. Every one crowded round; no one laughed; some one said, 'That's the stuff to give 'em'. No. 5 danced it through with an amputated toe in a new boot; No. 3 sat down looking pale and shiny (a heart-case); but the thing went. At last 'The Granary' was found, with puddles in the floor and holes in the ceiling, but at any rate dancing room. Men came in slowly, with whole limbs; a paper and comb provided music, then a fiddle, then a piano. The thing made fame: neighbouring commands heard of it and indented upon the instructress for an evening or a week of evenings. The E.F.D.S. sent out more to teach. The dance was put on parade, with squads of men and the band playing. By Christmas there were twelve happy people with every minute occupied in teaching the most popular side-show in France.

The fact that folk-dancing had been tried in France with success in particular circumstances did not, as might have been expected, cause it to attract greater numbers at home; and only a handful of those who danced in France actually joined the Society. But this experience changed the attitude towards it; the dance was now seen to be a sane and intelligent thing, not merely a pastime for children

179

and cranks. In 1914 interest in it was to make; in 1919 it was made, partly because every one was dancing something just then, partly because the War had altered our values. 'Nationalism in art,' said Sharp, 'which before the war was an academic subject, has become a vital one.' In writing from New York to congratulate Miss Daking on her progress and success, Sharp had said:

I have always felt sure that although the War would disrupt and sweep away many things it would not affect our dance and song movement except perhaps to strengthen it. The stuff we deal in is as genuine and real as anything in the world; reality is just what an upheaval such as the present will make every one demand— things that are insincere and untrue are the things that it will alone destroy.

At the beginning of 1919 the Right Hon. H. A. L. Fisher, President of the Board of Education, 1916–22, decided to emphasize the musical side of teaching. He asked Sharp to call on him and discuss the best way of instilling into the minds of children 'a sense of rhythm and a love of our old English national songs and dances'. He saw that Sharp was 'marked out by his great knowledge and single-minded enthusiasm for the task, and that the place where his peculiar gifts would tell most, and soonest, was the training-college'. It may be mentioned that two other presidents of the Board thought highly of his work. In 1923, when a special performance of folk-songs and folk-dances was shown to members of the Imperial Education Conference, Lord Irwin (then the Rt. Hon. Edward Wood), speaking for the Government in the House of Commons, mentioned Mr. Cecil Sharp as one 'to whose work in this field British education owes an almost irredeemable debt of gratitude'. Sir Charles Trevelyan has also called him 'one of the greatest educational influences of the time'.

In April 1919 Sharp was offered and accepted the

work of 'occasional' inspector of Training Colleges in Folk-Song and Dancing. An initial difficulty cropped up in that Sharp would have to use his own publications as text-books because, as Mr. Fisher said, there was 'happily no alternative'. In view of this difficulty the permanent officials suggested that Sharp should get rid of his rights in the books; however, the matter was dropped after discussion. More serious was the proposal that his work should be made a branch of the Medical Department. Sharp's view was that to appoint a physical expert to inspect the dancing would be as ridiculous as to appoint a throat doctor to inspect the singing. He gained his point eventually, and held the appointment from 1919 to 1923. Sharp was the only Occasional Inspector of Folk-Dancing appointed by the Board with the single exception of Mrs. Douglas Kennedy, who held the position during the whole of 1920; but the Board has shown itself to be continuously in sympathy with the movement (see App. C).

In his Report to the Board of Education (1920–3) Sharp thus describes his aim:

To present the dance to the students at the Technical Colleges as a Fine Art with technical principles and possibilities, and to prevail upon the College authorities to make it one of the regular subjects of study.

To each College he made (or repeated) his visit at the express invitation of the Principal. In the lecture-lesson, from one and a half to two hours, he would see, discuss, or criticize any folk-dance that the students could show him, or teach them a new one. This would give an opportunity for inculcating principles, such things as poise of body, elimination of superfluous action, interpretation of the music by the dance, and so forth. The interest of the students was soon secured, and the College authorities were not unwilling to make room for the dance in a crowded curriculum. Sharp advised that the folk-dancing be made a voluntary subject and associated wherever

possible with the social activities of the College. He
pointed out that little time need be spent upon technical
instruction so long as the teaching was in the hands of a
really efficient instructor.

The Board of Education appointment came just when
the English Folk Dance Society needed much time and
attention. The sudden and rapid increase in the number
of people who wanted to dance made it imperative to
strengthen and extend the organization of the Society, and
so Sharp had his hands full. One difficulty was that the
Society had no head-quarters. In January 1919 a public
meeting, organized by Mrs. Shuldham Shaw, was called
by Lady Mary Trefusis, to see if this could be remedied;
Sharp spoke, Sir Arthur Somervell, Mr. Granville Barker,
Mr. Plunket Greene, Sir Henry Hadow (in the Chair),
and others. Nothing came of it, and the Society hugger-
muggered along in a one-room or two-room office, hiring
various halls for the dancing, an irritating and expensive
process. Meanwhile the number of dancers grew, and it
was hard to find enough halls or teachers for the many
classes that had to be arranged. During 1920 the average
weekly attendance at London classes rose to nearly seven
hundred, and by 1924 it was a thousand.

The organization of the dancing in London was, however, the least part of Sharp's work, for all the time he
was keeping in touch, by correspondence and by constant
visits, with the local branches which were scattered all
over the country. At the end of the War there were
twenty-three provincial branches, which now had to be
reconstructed; by 1924 there were forty-three. He did
not make the organization rigid; each branch was responsible to the parent society for the artistic standard,
but otherwise managed its affairs in its own way. Sharp
was always ready and was constantly called on to give
advice, but his suggestions were usually accompanied
with 'Of course, you know your own local conditions

better than I do'. The branches began in towns and their areas were extended as occasion demanded; in 1923, partly in consequence of a grant from the Carnegie United Kingdom Trust, Sharp devised a county basis.

The Vacation School was one of the best and pleasantest ways of spreading a knowledge of the dances. In 1919 the Schools which had hitherto invariably been held at Stratford-on-Avon began to be taken elsewhere, e.g. Cheltenham, Aldeburgh,[1] York, Exeter. The Christmas Schools from 1920 onwards were in London: of one of these Sharp writes (27.12.22):

We open tomorrow with 578 students, 21 teachers, and 21 accompanists, a motor-bus service between the outlying rooms and the central building, and a rotten Director doubled up with lumbago, coughing and spluttering with bronchitis, and otherwise displaying symptoms of galloping senility.

By July 1921, after two and a half years of steady work, Sharp thought it was time to appeal to a larger public, so the King's Theatre, Hammersmith, was taken for a week's Festival, and performances were given every evening and on two afternoons. Sharp orchestrated most of the tunes and conducted, Miss Elsie Avril leading. There was little doubt of the impression made on those who watched these performances: 'open-air sweetness', 'cleanness', 'wholesomeness', were the expressions.

I found myself [wrote Mr. Ernest Newman] growing more and more interested in the dances as an art, . . . astonished at the variety, and enchanted with the perfect harmony between the steps and the music. . . . However cosmopolitan a man's culture may make him, there always remains deep down in him a love for the ancestral things of his own race.

And the change of attitude (see p. 66) was very welcome.

Sharp probably did as much work during the last few years of his life as at any other period, inspecting, judging, lecturing, &c. Mattie Kay being abroad, he usually

[1] See *Music and Letters*, October 1923.

illustrated his lectures on the Appalachian songs himself with the help of Maud Karpeles. Even after twelve years Sir Michael Sadler can say:

A romantic tale and a great adventure—so told that it left a deep mark in my memory and became a landmark in my mind.

At his first public lecture on the subject in London, at the Aeolian Hall (May 1919), the songs were illustrated by Mr. Owen Colyer; and in the second part of the programme, Sharp, having changed into flannels, danced the Running Set with seven other members of the Society. He appeared, too, on many other occasions as a dancer; a favourite form of propaganda was the 'quartette'—usually Sharp, Maud Karpeles, Douglas and Helen Kennedy —in which Sharp lectured and joined in the country dances for two couples.

This would be the natural place to say something about his lectures. His main tenets were that beauty is not the aim of art, but the proof of it; that it comes of work for a clear purpose, and of economy;

that every human being is a potential artist and that all forms of artistic utterance are natural and inborn; that technique and artistry —body and soul, matter and spirit—are two aspects of the same thing, and nearly all the troubles in the world come from the attempt to divorce the one from the other; that technique is not the enemy of enjoyment, but the condition precedent of it; and that self-forgetfulness is the measure of the higher forms of enjoyment.

What he has to say of the peasant and his art may be summarized as follows:

You must first understand the peasant, the sole survivor of a homogeneous society, with few class distinctions; and what we think of as conscious arts were to him unconscious occupations. Looking back on twenty years' contact with him, I should name as his chief characteristics reserve, personal detachment, and dignity. He is gentle, unobtrusive, unassertive, both to his fellows and to cockneys like myself. He believes [with Steven Guazzo, 1594, whom he quoted] that 'as words well uttered shewe eloquence and learning, so silence well kept showeth prudence and gravitie'. This quality has been misinterpreted as proceeding from a low intelligence, a restricted vocabulary, or churlish manners. No; his mind moves slowly, but give him time; he is considerate to a fault, and has a quiet natural courtesy of his own.

This comes out in the song and dance he invented and performs. His song has no superfluous words; it repeats stock phrases 'gay gold ring', 'pretty fair maid', 'skin as soft as silk', 'milkwhite steed'; the tune has few ornamental notes. In his dance he cuts out the unnecessary and suppresses his individuality. He learned both song and dance as he learned his speech, from his parents, and takes them for granted; he enjoys them for what he gets out of them, not for anything he might put into them, and in this respect he contrasts strongly with the professional singer, who is all for an 'original' reading. Such exhibition of personality may be necessary with poor music; it is to be deprecated with Bach—or with the Bible. Folk-song and folk-dance contain within themselves potential expression and our problem is to extract it.

Sharp's position as Director of the English Folk Dance Society had been an honorary one until the end of 1919 when he accepted a salary of £400 a year from the Society. This addition to his income, though it did not make him a wealthy man, did at least relieve him from financial anxiety, and three years later—at the end of 1922 —he relinquished his Civil List Pension on the grounds that his books were beginning to provide a fairly adequate income. To his friend, Paul Oppé, he confided (24.11.22) that the consideration which had prompted him to take this action was

the fact that W. H. Hudson resigned his pension in similar circumstances and for the same reason. . . . The matter has been on my mind, as you know, and I found it perpetually troubling me because my instinct told me I had no longer a right to it.

And in reply he was congratulated on a relinquishment which did him even more honour than the original award.

Though the last few years brought relief from poverty,

that other handicap ill health was greatly increased. The story is that of a sick man fighting against time. After apologizing for the delay in answering a letter on account of stress of work, he writes:

To Mrs. John Campbell. 20.5.1920.

I really hardly know how I have got through this last winter. I have worked—slaved—like a pack-horse, fighting all the while against indifferent health. How I am going to survive another winter I really don't know! This country is the most beautiful in the world but its climate is the most detestable. I have coughed incessantly for nearly six months and shall continue to do so till the weather gets warmer. . . . And all the time the drafts on my time and energy have been and are steadily increasing, and I do not see any way in which I can lighten my work. The men who would by now have shouldered the responsibilities I am bearing were, as you know, killed in the war and as yet no one has come forward to take their place. I am just longing to retire from active work and get back to my books and writing, but I do not see how it is to be done in the circumstances. It is really a very dreary look-out for me and I am getting very depressed. Perhaps I shall buck up again when the weather gets warner. If I could only get away for a month's holiday I might get better, but I do not see any chance of being able to do so. The vacation schools occupy my time in the regular holidays, and they have grown enormously.

It was not only asthma and bronchitis with which Cecil Sharp had to contend, but recurring spells of fever similar to those he had had in the mountains. The fever would attack him suddenly and sharply, producing a short period of high temperature, often accompanied by delirium, and a subsequent condition of extreme exhaustion which lasted for several weeks. He consulted doctors and submitted to a course of inoculation; but the fevers persisted, and the convalescence after each attack became more and more laborious. From the winter of 1921 onwards he tried to regain strength by making occasional short stays in the country, first at Malvern and later on at Sidmouth. 'The enforced and unaccustomed leisure' which he had on these occasions and during periods of convalescence at home was not spent in idleness. He kept up his voluminous correspondence and took the opportunity of working at his songs and dances.

He now had in his possession four editions of Playford's *Dancing Master*, the fourth edition (1670) having been presented to him in January 1920 by some friends and admirers on the initiative of Mrs. Shuldham Shaw, and this enabled him to study the work more closely than he had done in the past at the British Museum. He deciphered another fifty dances, 'some of them really beautiful ones set to the jolliest tunes imaginable', and these were published in 1922 in the sixth (and last) part of *The Country Dance Book*.

Although he had neither the time nor the strength to do much collecting he could not bear to give it up altogether, and he managed to do a little each summer.

To Miss Priscilla Wyatt-Edgell.   30.9.22.

I am just back—with the faithful Maud, of course—from a strenuous collecting expedition in the Midlands—Bucks., Northants, Oxon., Warwickshire, Berks., etc.—chiefly after survivals of morris, but getting songs incidentally. We instituted definite enquiries in 45 villages. I got a few more dances and several songs. I enjoyed it very much and am feeling very downhearted at having to return and take up routine work again. I am better at collecting than anything else; it suits my health as well as my temperament—for one thing the only people who seem really to understand and enjoy my jokes are the old peasants. I suppose my sense of fun is not very subtle—at least that is what my daughters and others seem to insinuate!

During the years 1919–24 he added only another 190 tunes to his collection, but he got some interesting morris dances from Adderbury (Oxon.) and Brackley (Northants) which he published in a revised edition of Parts 2 and 3 of *The Morris Book*. The last tune he collected—a version of 'Three Maids a-milking'—was sung to him on September 13th, 1923, by an old woman of eighty-three in the Headington Union, only a few hundred yards from the spot where his first folk-tune was noted on December 26th, 1899.

On February 25th, 1923, Sharp was offered the honorary degree of Master of Music by the Vice-Chancellor of Cambridge. On June 8th this was conferred on him, with the following speech by the Public Orator:

Haec credo invenietis si generis humani velitis annales investigare: primum gentes omnes suis artibus vigere, mox dum vitae cupidi dignioris alienas sectantur homines suas fastidire, omissas tandem frustra revocare. Vixisse quidem ante Agamemnona fortes, auctorem habemus Horatium, sed omnes una nocte obscuratos esse. Nemo Homero, nemo Vergilio vitio verterit quod civium animos sibi devinxerint; dolebunt omnes carmina simpliciora temporis antiquioris et apud Graecos et apud Italos omnino periisse. Hoc apud Anglos quam paene vidimus accidere! Hic tamen, quem vobis praesento, ubique in villis et in vicis rusticos seniores ita amicitia et concordia permovit ut carmina antiqua recitarent; immo inter montes Appalachicos, inter montanos illos moris aviti et linguae tenacissimos, carmina patriae conquisivit invenit servavit. Descripta in ora virum redeunt, et quae incuria rusticorum et oblivione paene deleta erant, jam tandem florent omnium amore. Unus homo nobis, dicemus, cantando restituit rem.* Ergo gratis animis honoramus Cecilium Sharp.

Duco ad vos Cecilium Jacobum Sharp.[1]

[1] You will find, I think, if you care to examine the earliest records of mankind, three stages. People first made much of their own arts and crafts; then they began to worry about the 'ideal', and to adopt those of their neighbours; lastly, they despised their own, and were sorry for it afterwards. For, if we may trust Horace,†
        many a man was brave
        Long before Agamemnon's day,
        But one and all have gone their way
        To silence deeper than the grave.
Without wishing to blame Homer and Virgil for binding their compatriots

---

    * Cf. *Enn. Ann.* xii. 1.   † Hor. *Od.* IV. 9. 25.

CHAPTER XV

1923–1924; 1924–1933

LAST DAYS

Thyme, thyme, it is a precious, precious thing;
It's a root that the sun shines on;
And Time it will bring everything unto an end;
And so our time goes on.

Folk-song.

DURING 1923 Cecil Sharp's health became worse; the fevers increased and he had thirteen separate attacks in that year. In October he reluctantly decided to take a rest.

I do not want to live—especially in such a world as the present one—unless I can recover my strength. I hate having my wings clipped and dragging along as an invalid.

He went to Montreux, accompanied by Maud Karpeles, and remained there two months. After two attacks of fever he consulted a doctor who diagnosed it as malaria and treated him accordingly, and he did not have another attack. His general health improved and he enjoyed the two months of rest and quiet.

He tried to improve his 'public school' French by

---

with a spell, we may regret the total disappearance of the old Greek and Roman folk-songs. A little more, and that would have happened in England too. That it did not, we owe to the man I am presenting to you. He went round the farms and villages, and by his friendliness and sympathy induced the elder generation to sing him their songs. And it was the same in the Appalachian mountains: he sought, found, and preserved the songs of a countryside where they had never forgotten the language and customs of their forefathers. These live again in his description and on our lips, and now everybody loves singing what by the indifference and forgetfulness of the peasants was all but lost. We shall say with the poet:

One man with a song at pleasure
Shall go forth and conquer a crown.*

And so with grateful hearts we honour Cecil Sharp.

I present to you CECIL JAMES SHARP.

* O'Shaughnessy, *The Music-Makers.*

having lessons with a French lady, but this was not very successful. At the end of the two months his French conversational powers were hardly greater than those of an unfortunate fellow traveller whom he once tried to assist. This was an English nun who, having found herself in the wrong train, wounded the feelings of the French guard by exclaiming, 'Ce train n'est pas *propre*'. However, although his conversation was halting and inadequate, he had on a former occasion been able to muster a sufficiently large vocabulary to explain, much to the perplexity of a French customs official, who was looking suspiciously at the E.F.D.S. 'properties', that the bundle of swords was needed for a 'danse rituelle et sacrificielle'. But he could read French (even old French), and he employed his time at Montreux by translating, with the help of Maud Karpeles, Arbeau's *Orchésographie*, 'the first really elaborate treatise on dancing that was printed'.

It is curious that hitherto no English translation of so important a book as the *Orchésographie* had been published, and it is even more curious that in the year 1923 two men should, unbeknown to each other, have been engaged in making one. On his return to London Sharp had occasion to visit Mr. Cyril W. Beaumont (till then a stranger to him) in his book-shop in the Charing Cross Road, and during the course of conversation it was casually revealed that both had just completed a translation. Whatever complications might have arisen when it came to publication,[1] the immediate thing was the delight of discussing a common interest. Sharp invited Mr. Beaumont to dinner and met his inquiries about the interpretation of certain obscure passages by placing his manuscript in Mr. Beaumont's hands; an act of generosity which Mr. Beaumont accepted with the remark that he felt as though he had his hands in another man's till.

---

[1] Mr. Beaumont's translation was published in 1925; Sharp's manuscript has remained unpublished.

Sharp approached the study of folk-music with a previous comprehensive knowledge of the art and history of music in general, but with the dance the process was reversed; it was his interest in the folk-form which led him to study and acquire a knowledge of the general history of dancing. This was undertaken with a folk bias, that is to say, his chief interest was in the correlation of the folk-dance with other forms. He desired rather to trace and follow up the folk forms in other dances, rather than to pursue the study for its own sake. However, when, early in 1924, it was proposed that he should write a short history of the dance in collaboration with Paul Oppé, who was to be responsible for the illustrations, he agreed to the suggestion. This he did partly that he might unburden himself of the mass of knowledge that he had accumulated (and so prepare the way for a book on the Folk Dance, which unhappily he did not live to write), and partly from a sense of obligation and a pride in making, as a folk-dance expert, a contribution to the general subject.

The Dance: an Historical Survey of Dancing in Europe was published after his death without his final revisions. Throughout the writing of it he was worried for fear he would not be able to finish it by the appointed time. The book is an ingenious marshalling of sparse and sporadic data, and every opportunity of tracing development is taken. Although it does not present a connected view to the ordinary reader, it may well fire the imagination of a dancer. Every one will delight in the illustrations, abundant, various, well chosen, and well executed. These have been assembled by Mr. Paul Oppé, who writes the Preface.

The subject is treated of under three headings—Folk Dance, the Social Dance, and the Spectacular Dance, which means principally ballet. In the concluding paragraphs Sharp deplores the fact that technical development in the ballet has been achieved at the expense of expressive quality. He refers to the Russian dancers who, under the direction of M. Diaghilev, have tried to bring about a reformation, and quotes M. Fokine (*The Times*, 6.7.14), who says that the conventions of the older ballet with its artificial form of dancing on the point of the toe, with the feet turned out, have been rejected. How far the Russian dancers have been successful in translating their ideals into practice, Sharp is doubtful. In fact, he questions whether reform can come from within, and believes that the better way is—as the Florentine reformers of music did three centuries ago—to revert to first principles, start afresh, and endeavour to create a ballet which shall be founded on the folk-dance technique.

Sharp gave a further exposition of his views on folk-dance development in one of his lectures at the Aldeburgh Summer School (1923).

The ballet, throughout its history, has been a highly specialised and conventional form of art, divorced from popular tradition, and artificial and exclusive in both its nature and its appeal. . . . In every other art, . . . there is a place for the amateur. . . . The ballet, however, has got a complete technique, a distinction which it shares with the folk-dance alone. The other forms of dancing which have become rampant in the last twenty years, 'aesthetic', 'rhythmic', 'natural', 'Greek', and so forth, are either bowdlerised versions of the ballet, or have no real technical content of their own, no vocabulary out of which a dance language could be created.

His view was, in effect, that the fundamental change which an English ballet founded on folk-dance would bring about is the rejection of miming. The greatest art creates its own form and content. Although dancing must rely on music, yet each should express itself in its own way without drawing on anything external. English ballet would satisfy this condition: it would dispense with mime. And this would be more in accordance with the English character, for English people do not use gesture in daily life. But it would be a counsel of perfection to expect all this to happen at once: it will take time.

Reviewing what had already been done, Sharp referred to his own tentative effort with *A Midsummer-Night's Dream* (1913); to Mrs. Shuldham Shaw's far more successful and ambitious attempt in 1920; to *Old King Cole* by members of the Cambridge Branch of the E.F.D.S. (music by Vaughan Williams) in 1922, which marked a great advance; and, finally, to Mr. Douglas Kennedy's skilful attempt to create a ballet of 'absolute' dance to Haydn's quartet in G (Op. 64, No. 4), which opened up 'immense possibilities'. These experiments show what can be done when people have acquired a fully developed technique.

The E.F.D.S., as a Society, cannot itself do anything, because dance development is not within its province. But its individual members can and have already done much, while the Society can indirectly assist—and will do so.

Before leaving Montreux Sharp had a talk with his doctor, and the following day he reports the result:

To Paul Oppé.
                                                              9.11.23.
It looks to me that if I want to prolong my life I shall have to live mostly out of England. The question is: Is it worth doing? A difficult problem to decide—probably it will be decided for me.

He returned in time to direct the Christmas Vacation School at Chelsea, and managed to keep fairly well for the first winter-weeks of 1924 by seldom going out. On the whole he felt better than he had for the last few years, and he was full of plans for the future. He wanted above all a time of quiet and leisure in which he hoped, among other things, to write a comprehensive book on English folk-dance and to publish the remainder of his Appalachian collection.

For twenty years I have been accumulating facts, first-hand, and have had no time properly to digest them,

he wrote; and six months before his death,

I seem to have spent my life in making a largish heap of raw material, and now have but a short time to sift it and display its value.

Whether he would ever have been content to be cut off altogether from this business of collecting and organizing is doubtful. He was considering another visit to America in order to strengthen the organization of that branch of the English Folk Dance Society, and was constantly thinking of Newfoundland. Only a few weeks before his death Mr. Percy Grainger had asked to be allowed to place a proportion of the royalties on his arrangement of 'Country Gardens' at Sharp's disposal for the assistance of his work, and Sharp in accepting this generous offer had written (8.5.24) that he was planning to

make a dive into Newfoundland next year and prospect for songs and ballads. . . . It is a beastly climate, but I think I might manage the three or four summer months with the help of Miss Karpeles.

None of these plans was fulfilled, but the time immediately preceding his last illness was spent in full activity, as the following diary of events shows:

April 20–4.	Harrogate—directing the E.F.D.S. Vacation School.
24–6.	Exeter Vacation School.
May 2–3.	Torquay—judging competitions.
6.	General Meeting of E.F.D.S.
7.	E.F.D.S. Committee meeting and conference of E.F.D.S. Branches.
9–10.	Sheffield—folk-dance examinations.
14.	Cardiff—lecture.
15.	Newport—lecture.
16–17.	Bath—folk-dance competitions.
20.	Birmingham—E.F.D.S. meeting.
21.	Lincoln—Inaugural Meeting of E.F.D.S. Branch.
23–4.	Norwich—folk-dance competitions.
25.	Visit to a Watford School.
27–8.	Ilkley—folk-dance competitions.

On May 25th he wrote:

I am flying about all over the country, and all my literary work is at a standstill. I go away again tomorrow till June 3rd; then, a slight respite I hope!

His next engagement after Ilkley was at Newcastle, where he was due to judge a three days' competition from May 30th to June 3rd, but whilst at Ilkley he got what seemed to be a severe cold and felt very ill. He managed to get through his work and came on to Retford, where he had arranged to stay the night with Mr. Hercy Denman, in order that he might investigate a hobby-horse ceremony in the neighbourhood. On his arrival he had to go to bed. On June 3rd he travelled back to London with Maud Karpeles. On the journey he felt mortally ill and nearly collapsed. On June 23rd—just three weeks later—he died.

From the beginning there was little chance of recovery, for an X-ray photograph showed that he was suffering from a fatal illness. At first he managed to get up for a few hours every day, but as he got gradually weaker this became impossible, although within quite a short time of his death he was still working at his history of the Dance and dealing with his correspondence. He was strangely incurious about the nature of his illness. He knew that he could not get well and his only fear was a long illness. He did not mind dying, although there were things and people that he was sorry to leave; but he felt his work was unfinished and that worried him. As soon as he realized that the end might be very near, he began to make plans for the future organization of the English Folk Dance Society and expressed the wish that Douglas Kennedy should direct it.

During the last few days he was semi-conscious for most of the time, and lucid intervals became fewer. He was restless and troubled. 'So many questions,' he murmured; and then after a while, 'But there is no need to ask them—they answer themselves,' and with that he became more peaceful. When given an injection and told that he would feel no more pain, he added, 'Never again'; after that he did not speak. Death came in the early morning of Midsummer Eve.

His body was cremated at Golders Green on June 25th, and a Memorial Service was held at St. Martin-in-the-Fields on June 27th. By his wish no memorial tablet was set up. He left his manuscript collection of songs, tunes, and dance-notes to Clare College, Cambridge, and his library to the English Folk Dance Society, appointing Maud Karpeles as his literary executrix.

The folk-dance revival was to all intents and purposes a one-man show, but as in other cases in which the man is showing not himself but what he believes to be the truth, the show is not dependent on his physical presence.

When he died the three immediate projects which he had to relinquish were the writing of his history of the English folk-dance, the publication of the remainder of his collection of Appalachian tunes, and research in Newfoundland. The first is still to do. The Appalachian material has been edited by Maud Karpeles and a two-volume book with 971 tunes has been published.[1] Newfoundland is not now the fruitful field of research which it might conceivably have been in 1918 when Cecil Sharp first intended to go there, but during two visits in 1929 and 1930 Maud Karpeles noted about two hundred tunes, amongst which there are some good songs and ballads.[2]

With the exception of the cancelling of the week's Festival at Hammersmith and an open-air country dance party in Hyde Park, the work of the English Folk Dance

[1] *English Folk-Songs from the Southern Appalachian Mountains* (Oxford University Press, 1932).
[2] Thirty of these, with pianoforte accompaniment by R. Vaughan Williams and others, will shortly be published (Oxford University Press).

Society continued without interruption after Cecil Sharp's death.

A Board of Artistic Control was appointed consisting of Dr. Vaughan Williams, Douglas Kennedy, and Maud Karpeles, and the following year the direction of the Society was put into Douglas Kennedy's hands.

The number of dancers is now about four times as many as it was at Cecil Sharp's death, and the influence of the Society is felt not only in the Dominions and the United States of America, but in many countries of Europe, where great efforts have recently been made in the direction of preserving the traditional arts of the people. The Society has participated in Congresses organized by the International Commission of Folk Arts (*Arts Populaires*), which is under the auspices of the League of Nations. It is, in fact, very noticeable in how high esteem the work of Cecil Sharp is held on the Continent.

In 1932 the English Folk Dance Society which he founded, and the Folk Song Society of which he was for many years a member of committee, amalgamated under the title of the English Folk-Dance and Song Society. We may take it that the work of collection is nearly finished, but the new Society has before it a wide field of activity in organization and maintenance of standard, to which it vowed itself at its coming of age on December 11th, 1932.

A month after Cecil Sharp's death a special meeting of the English Folk Dance Society was called by its President, the Lady Mary Trefusis, and at this meeting it was resolved that 'a memorial should be raised to Mr. Cecil Sharp and that if practicable it should take the form of a central building in London as the head-quarters of the Society'. As Miss Margaret Bondfield has said:

The only kind of Memorial that Cecil Sharp would cherish is one in which all who will may share: not a museum to preserve something that was once alive—not a perpetual reminder of loss—

197

but a home of joy, a place from which can flow the living waters of merry dance and song.

For six years a committee under the chairmanship of the Rt. Hon. H. A. L. Fisher worked for the establishment of the memorial. The Honorary Secretary of the committee was Mrs. Shuldham Shaw.

Honorary secretaries may be defined as people who work all day and every day and receive *ex-officio* thanks on state occasions. For Winifred Shuldham Shaw that occasion never came; indeed, she never even saw the completed work for which she had toiled during six years, as she was too ill to come on June 7th, and on August 14th she died; but all her life she had run away from thanks. She had a quick mind and a merry soul. With her full share of actual suffering, she never complained; she was too busy thinking about others. She put heart and soul into the building of this house out of a deep-seated admiration for Cecil Sharp's character and work; she divined in these the high quality that some others have discovered only by reflection on their results.

The foundation-stone[1] of the building in Regent's Park Road was laid by Maud Karpeles, with William Kimber assisting, on June 24th, 1929.

Among the sums [she said] given to our fund was one sent by a boy in the north of England—the pennies he had collected among his schoolfellows: he wrote, 'We did not know Mr. Sharp but we feel he was a friend of ours.' And two years ago I spoke with Charlie Benfield, who had given Mr. Sharp many a song and dance, and asked if he remembered him. He nodded, and then said very slowly: 'Ah yes, Mr. Cecil Sharp. I see in the papers they are going to put up a memorial to him. Well, he deserved it. He was a good man.' A friend! A good man! Perhaps they mean the same. I know that

---

[1] The inscription reads:
   This building is erected in memory of Cecil Sharp who restored to the English people the songs and dances of their country.
                                        Midsummer Day 1929.

these simple people felt at home with him: I think it was his sincerity and utter selflessness that appealed to them.

The building was declared open by Mr. Fisher on June 7th, 1930, and called 'Cecil Sharp House'. As Mr. Granville Barker said, 'In so far as a building can be like a human being, it is like Cecil Sharp himself—classical without being severe, and pervaded with an extraordinary sense of gaiety.'

The opening of Cecil Sharp House marks a definite stage in a long creative process. The songs and dances that have matured through generations have here a seal set upon them. The folk-period has passed and cannot be recalled, but the life of folk-music, so Cecil Sharp believed, is not dependent on the conditions which brought it into being. That which was unconsciously evolved is now being grafted on our conscious culture. Even those who are in the direct line of tradition are affected by the changed conditions. The songs and dances which they alone treasured have been given an added significance and security, and there are many who can say with Miss Margaret Bondfield, 'I owe an immense debt to Mr. Cecil Sharp for having re-discovered and explained to me the memories of my childhood.' From the daughter of one of Cecil Sharp's best singers in the Appalachian mountains we hear:

I do not keep mother's songs in mind as I used to, but I know I have only to look at them in Mr. Cecil Sharp's book, and then they will come back to me just exactly right.

And William Kimber, who needs no book to remind him, seems to share Cecil Sharp's faith in the power of this music to endure the changes and chances of time when he tells us:

I read the *Radio Times* every week for one reason only. Just to see if there is any of my dear old friend's tunes there. And when there is one I must hear it and by myself too. Then and then only do I seem to be with him once more.

CHAPTER XVI

SUMMARY

Like a New Moon's exquisite Incarnation
  In the Ebb and Flow of a Surging Sea,
Wave-breasted Beauty, the whole Creation
  Wanes, and waxes, and rocks on thee!
For we rise and fall on thy Bosom's Billow
  Whose heaving Swell is our Home Divine,
Our Chalice at Dawn, and our hot Noon's Pillow,
  Our Evening's Shrine.

F. W. BAIN.

OF the lives of all who have devoted themselves to music
in this country, Cecil Sharp's life was the least to be
prophesied by others or foreseen by himself. What he
regarded as the turning-point of his life happened on his
forty-first Boxing Day, and his true vocation was not clear
to him till he was forty-five. His whole work was, therefore, packed into the relatively small space of twenty years.
One's first thought is to regret that so much time was
wasted before he got to his real work; one's second is to
reflect that the time was by no means wasted, but was,
though he did not know it, a very good preparation for
what he was going to do and be.

After four years at the University in which, as we have
seen, he took hold of life with both hands, and, without
any exceptional powers of mind or body, yet made himself
felt by his companions as a man of character, goodwill,
and open intelligence, he spent ten in seeing the world in
a colony, far removed from the accepted standards and set
conventions of home. He took things as they came. He
was a hand in a mews, a clerk in a bank (wielding the then
new typewriter), articled to a lawyer, and secretary to a
Governor; and he made such music as he could, unpaid
or paid, on pianoforte or organ, establishing a choir,
writing an operetta, and founding a music school—more
or less, but rather more than less, as an amateur. The last

twelve years of this preparation he gave to strictly professional duties. He taught, with fixed hours, in a school and in a conservatory, he conducted a choir, and gave a series of lectures on musical subjects.

He married for love, and love stood the strain of poverty and ill health. His honest work made him many friends. His determined character brought him some testing opposition. His constant asthma depressed him and made him irritable, but it never finally damped his spirit, which, as Mr. Fisher said, had the qualities of a good folk-song—gaiety and lightheartedness.

Some men become early immersed in their profession and never see life. Some swing through life's ups and downs without the steadying influence of a profession. Cecil was happy in having both the outlook of an amateur and the discipline of a profession. He emerged from them a scholar, who knew when he knew a thing, and a man, who could be all things to all men; and those are precisely the qualities that were needed for his life's work.

Two things in particular were noticed about Cecil as a boy. He was always able to turn his hand to the thing that happened to be wanted. Besides the pianoforte, his life-long friend, and the violin and organ with which he did not go far, he taught himself the cornet and banjo (when he was ill in bed), made a xylophone, and used whittle and dub for his lectures (until his daughter Joan eclipsed him). He could act a bit, sing in a musically unmusical voice, dance enough to illustrate his point, put you wise on cathedrals, and beat you at chess. He wrote a good letter because he had a great deal of practice in answering them at once and at length; but he was not a writer of prose. He read and knew his books, not merely collected them. His mathematics had made him a logical thinker, and that prevented his art from running away with him.

The fact is, he had an overwhelming curiosity about the world he lived in and was, therefore, good company, conversing easily and well. And his lectures, of which no one has spoken ill, and which many have praised, were this conversation mounted on a platform with a glass of water in front of it. He was genuinely interested in other people because he was not thinking particularly about himself. He liked to know how they lived their lives, how they came to be what they were, and what they hoped to make of it all. He did not want to analyse any one or to search for motives; he was not introspective, and he hated anything beginning with 'psych-'. He tried various plans of life—spiritualism, Fabianism, Christian Science—as settings for the gay world of fact and idea. He was opposed for a long time to Women's Suffrage by prejudice, and was a vegetarian by conviction. In politics he called himself a Conservative Socialist.

Another thing that is spoken of by those who knew Cecil as a boy is his generosity. After all these years there are certain bunches of fruit and boxes of chocolate bought with his pocket money that are not forgotten. He took the trouble to think what people would like—an ounce of tobacco, a photograph, a Christmas dinner, a visit if sick, an outing if well—and to give it to them. And it was true giving, because he had to go without something himself sooner or later. That was, no doubt, one of the points that drew him to Marson, who took the precept of his Master literally, and when he possessed two coats gave one of them away. But he did not learn it at Hambridge. Later on, also, when his traffic was rather in the less obviously good things of life, in ideas rather than in facts, he could leave an attractive field untilled because some one else had a better right there, or when he had carried his harvest, could empty his voice of any note of triumph.

He always thought, and with good reason, that what he had to give was especially fine. One great gift—or rather, two at different times, folk-song and folk-dance— he set before himself as worth making. He intended, at whatever cost to himself, to give these back to the rightful owners, the English people. There have been, there are—besides the utilitarians who will admit no non-self-regarding act, the Gallios who care neither for these nor any other form of art, and the cosmopolitans who having got rid of the family now look askance at the nation—those who doubt both the value of the possession and the magnitude of the cost. Cecil had no doubt; and it is his mind we are trying to understand. E. V. Lucas calls this gift 'a piece of the most exquisite patriotism'.

Exquisite patriotism: not the half-baked conception of 'England for the English', which underrates the benefits of a true *commercium mentis et rerum*; nor the hasty misconception of 'Homes for Heroes', which tries in a phrase of the moment to balance a century of neglect. It was finer things than those that Cecil saw and loved and remembered at his homecoming after ten years' absence. He did not idolize the men nor idealize their homes; he did not exaggerate their virtues nor excuse their defects. He could have taken on his lips these words, if he ever saw them, written thirty years ago:

Put things at their lowest, it was worth while for me to belong to a country like ours. No other country could have given me such a portrait to paint, so full of contrasts and opposing moods. I could have painted them all—the vulgarity, the snobbery, the hypocrisy, and the greed. But anyone can see all that, and, you know, it is only the difficult that counts in art. . . . In our country I saw hidden things very difficult to discover—a flicker of generosity in spite of greed, a gleam of honour in the midst of vulgarity, and somewhere in the very depths of hypocrisy some little grain of faith. These were the things I painted in her portrait, being her lover, and caring only to paint what is so difficult to see, and my reward would have been to see her grow more and more like the picture I had drawn. For the meanest begins to straighten up when you call him the soul of chivalry, a girl will grow in beauty directly you call her beautiful, and certainly it would be the same with one's country.

(H. W. Nevinson.)

Summary

The picture that Cecil drew, 'being her lover', was this corpus of folk-song and dance that he collected and promulgated. He was not the first by any means to collect the songs, nor the first to promulgate the dance; but he was the first to do both for both of them, because he saw that both were emanations from the same spirit, and that until they became vocal and articulate neither could properly be said to exist. He knew them as a man knows the voice and gait and gesture of his friend, and he loved them with a passion that few have ever felt, and none have expressed but Shakespeare:

> I saw, but thou couldst not,
> Flying between the cold moon and the earth,
> Cupid all arm'd; a certain aim he took
> At a fair vestal throned by the west;
> And loos'd his love-shaft smartly from his bow,
> As it should pierce a hundred thousand hearts;
> But I might see young Cupid's fiery shaft
> Quench'd in the chaste beams of the watery moon;
> And the imperial votaress passed on,
> In maiden meditation, fancy-free.
> Yet mark'd I where the bolt of Cupid fell:
> It fell upon a little western flower,
> Before milkwhite, now purple with love's wound,
> And maidens call it, Love-in-idleness.
> Fetch me that flower.

It is easy to see the prose of everyday lives, hard to read the poetry behind them. Though he would have winced at being called a poet, which implies a gift he did not possess, his faith and insight were of that quality.

In the Introduction to the third series of the *Folk-Songs from Somerset* occurs this passage:

No one man, even if he were a Beethoven, could compose tunes of such good general level, and at times of such surpassing excellence, as those which have been evolved or composed communally by many generations of men in the long period of the racial life. If any one questions this, let him compare the folk melodies of England, not with the harmonic compositions and the orchestral pieces, symphonies, and sonatas of great writers, but with the melodies, the sheer melodies, of any one man he chooses to name.

This is signed by Marson, but presumably endorsed by Sharp, in 1906. It conveys possibly to the average reader some false ideas—that the general level of folk-song is higher than that reached by any individual composer, that some specimens are better than any that even the greatest composers wrote, and that comparison between harmonic and non-harmonic melodies is possible.

What I believe Sharp meant was this: that the qualities which make communal song good are precisely those that make individual song good. In the broadest sense there is their obedience to instinct, which Robert Bridges raised to a high plane when he bade us listen to 'those small folksongs' of the 'thoughtless' birds, and

> see then how deeply seated is the urgence whereto
> Bach and Mozart obey'd, or those other minstrels
> who pioneer'd for us on the marches of heav'n.

And in a narrower sense there is their conformity with certain basic tendencies, such as the maintenance of an established point, the alertness to modifying circumstance, the avoidance of anti-climax, and the like; all of which are the principal marks of any good music whatsoever.

But the training which produces the result is different. Training proceeds by imitation and criticism. Of imitation, as far as folk-song is concerned, we can say nothing, because not only do we not know the date of the songs, but we do not know where they come from. (From Somerset, for instance, you will say: yes, but where did Somerset get them from? Some of the phrases are found in old Dutch songs, some in the songs on the Bayeux tapestry, and so on.) Of criticism we can say more. The individual composer is his own critic, and if he listens to his critical self, may modify his work accordingly: after

that, he fixes it, by writing, from further modification. But
with communal song the criticism comes after the maker of
the song is buried, and is delivered not in words but in
the act of singing, and without appeal, because nothing
is in writing. So, when Sharp says that even a Beethoven does no more than this, he means that we have
in this simple instance the principles on which all the
great men have worked. And he means probably a little
more: that though great works are complex, we apprehend
them only as elaborations of the simple; and, if they are
new to us, we look in them for the simple in order to
clarify and bring home to ourselves the complex. How
often has one noticed this in talking to 'the folk'! They
are surprised at the number of words we seem to think
necessary to explain an everyday matter. To them it seems
to be all summed up in an aphorism, or a trite quotation
from some piece of poetry or the Bible; to us it seems that
in so doing they miss half the 'points'. Similarly, a folk-
tune has in it something aphoristic, and we turn to it as
being not wiser, but simpler and deeper, than our more
highly organized music.

Some confusion has been introduced by thinking of
folk-song as 'archaic', or as a process of 'unlettered' minds.
The point is neither the age of the song, which, though
implied by the modal texture, we are not in a position to
affirm or deny, nor the musical or literary status of the
singer, who is no more than the mouthpiece of the race;
but its rejection of the elaborate. The whole communal
doctrine supposes an eloquence which has discarded the
purple patch and ornament of any kind, and is content
with no more than everybody may hope to understand.
And what drew Sharp to it, and may draw others, was his
rooted belief that 'in the long run the mob is generally
right'.

A folk-song, then, is more alive than printed music;
as much more alive as an heirloom is (which has passed

206

through many hands, has been put to many uses, and has acquired many associations) than a will, which may be interpreted but not altered. A will gives us pleasure or displeasure; we can judge it: but we are usually too fond of an heirloom to be able to say whether it is beautiful or ugly; we accept it, and leave the judging to others. That was what Sharp felt about these heirloom-songs—that they were alive, and that they were objects of deep affection. He knew, of course, as we all do, that some were more beautiful than others; otherwise he would not, out of a collection of five thousand, have published only five hundred. But he felt, as every collector does, that their beauty lay in their genuineness, though the conviction of this genuineness cannot easily be conveyed to other ears.

The accompaniments he wrote were partly an attempt to convey this; but they had also the practical object of getting the songs quickly and widely known. For this purpose of bringing the tunes to the cognizance of everybody, they have not often been surpassed. The accompaniment never interferes with the tune. The tune is not overlaid with bits of imitation or pianistic devices or compelling harmonies. It is not ornamented or corrected or sophisticated. The 'mode' was strictly followed in the accompaniment, after the first few experiments, not as a piece of purism, but so that nothing should obscure the tune. The technique in the best of them is that of Schubert—the invention of a flowing figure, capable of adapting itself to environment, and consonant with the general style of tune and words. When Sharp failed, which was not often, it came of his being afraid of the education authorities, who might not wish to put forth the unconventional as the norm, or of the harmony professor, who might not like to see his rules broken, or of the limitations of executants, who might defeat his ends by putting the song aside as too difficult. He told me once what a comfort it was to him when Vaughan Williams said to him one day, 'Take any chord you want'. He loved harmonizing these songs, and taught himself much in the process.

It was a revelation to hear him play them himself. He made every one want to sing them, from Mattie Kay downwards. And the same with the dances: his fingers seemed to pull it all together. This is generally called rhythm; but so many things are called rhythm that a word or two more seems necessary. The only positive direction he seems to have given is 'Play them as if they were music'; and the worst of that is that, though those who would have played them so in any case will be fortified by the prescription, those who would not will be left in the dark. He played definitely: definitely loud or soft, definitely fast or slow; no 'subintents and saving clauses'; nothing tepid; no wily rubatos, no gushing crescendos. He never thumped. You felt the beat, rather than heard it. He seldom drew attention to single points, least of all when they were his own. He did not, like an executant, beautify ornament, nor, like a composer, exhibit structure. It was all simple, unobtrusive, right.

Absorbed in the songs and ballads, Sharp, when one friend drew his attention to carols and another to the dance, rather put these aside as not being his job. What he valued most in the dances, like many who see them for the first time, was their simple invigorating tunes. He changed his mind when he saw the instantaneous effect the morris had on Miss Neal's girls. But to get hold of these dances was a much more difficult matter. The dance is and must be concerted, and the few complete 'sides' left in the country were hard to find; and there was no available notation. The dance he pieced together often from fragmentary indications; the notation he invented with a friend's help. He would rush off to any part of England to get a new dance, or merely to verify a detail of an old one. The practical knowledge thus acquired enabled him to interpret with some certainty the brief indications in Playford's *Dancing Master*, a riddle no one had yet solved.

On the strength of this knowledge he became the only real authority on the subject, and when he saw the dance being used as a handmaid to philanthropic, antiquarian, or dramatic, or even sartorial projects, he was driven to protest. This position was difficult to maintain, since he had as yet no visible credentials. He saw that unless the river was to run underground and be lost in the sands an authoritative course must be made for it, and that, in point of fact, he must make that course. So after half a dozen years he created the English Folk Dance Society. He set himself to the task of organizing this society with its members scattered over England, no light matter for one who suffered from two tiresome ailments—asthma and penury. As the Society was getting into its stride, the War came. During that the Society was in abeyance, there was nothing for it to do, though it took its part, later on, with other agents of recuperation at the rest-camps. For himself, in poor health, at fifty-four, there was also nothing. He decided to work on at his job, but that being impossible in England, he carried the gospel to America, and he spent three summers (1916–18) in the Appalachians collecting, with Maud Karpeles, many songs and the only dance they had. He loved the adventure of it, but felt the expatriation, endured some illness and much discomfort, and suffered the several pangs of the death of his dancers and close friends at the front. His expeditions added a new chapter to the history of folk-song, and the friendships he made there did something to foster the friendly feelings between the two countries.

After the War the Society went ahead again. Its numbers grew year by year, helped greatly by the Vacation Schools held two or three times a year at some likely centre. At these Sharp was a kind of self-effacing tyrant. He got his way without ever seeming to lay down the law:

every one knew he knew, and there was no more to be said. Besides, dancing is so amazingly good for body and soul that querulousness cannot exist with it.

A man of such distinct flavour could not fail to make some enemies. If we look for a moment with their eyes, we find that they saw in him one who claimed more limelight than they liked to concede to him, and who maintained his artistic principles, which were not theirs, with a tiresome obstinacy. The limelight he secured was not for himself but for his subject. He never disparaged the work of others in the same field; he helped them where he could. But obstinate: yes. It was annoying; but obstinacy can usually be forgiven in people who do in the end get their own way. In fact, if they believe in what they profess, it is a little difficult to see what they are to do in an imperfect world but fight for it. The obstinacy which is difficult to forgive is that which makes a fuss without making its point, and no one accused him of that. With this obstinacy went something of irritability, bless him. One has seen him rate a porter when the train had missed its connexion as if the poor man bore through the wilderness of that particular junction the sins of the whole railway company. A man must have some safety valve. Others again thought him arrogant in the way he monopolized the conversation; and even his best friend called him 'confoundedly dogmatic'.

Of these objections the only one that matters is the question of artistic ideal. Were they right in holding that the dance was a social amenity, to be pursued only for the pleasure of doing it, and not to be made into a task or a toil? Or was he right in holding that the standard set by tradition must be upheld and that the pleasure is only to be got by a dancing which combines, in a single sweep, both accuracy and imagination. This question is vital: it is still the question for the Society he left behind. Each must settle it for himself. All that this book has tried to do is to detail the history of the question as impartially as might be.

This was the rough and tumble of life. But a man is to be judged less by his average performance than by the heights he can reach. His love for folk-art, whether it was 'told' or sung or danced, has been spoken of; it proceeded from a love of themselves and a respect for their attitude towards life. But it was always a real enjoyment of utterances that are in themselves beautiful, and what was rare about it was his power of finding uncommon beauty in common things. To find that is to be in spirit an artist— to know that it is on beauty that 'the whole Creation wanes and waxes and rocks'. With that knowledge in his heart, the troubles he was called upon to endure seemed light.

He approached this task of getting to understand simple human nature, which turned out to be his life work, through music; he was indeed, primarily, a musician. Although the editor of 'Grove' was not alert enough to recognize him as one in 1911, his University conferred on him a year before his death the degree of Master of Music. It is possible that the music of this country owes him more than it yet knows. It is not a small thing to have set the elementary schools and the factories singing songs that no one doubts to be true music, that are their own songs, and that they take kindly to; and to have made from twenty to thirty thousand people happy and contented with dances that are their own, and that combine two virtues by which they set much store—an absence of swagger, and the skill of playing not for themselves but for the side. The song is melody; the dance is rhythm; àll that there is else in music is, however desirable, an adjunct. If then some future historian writes of our period as a time when music took a step forward, he will have to put in a high place the name of Cecil Sharp, who, more than any one, prepared the soil in which the seed should grow. This is not in the least to belittle the labours of others, but it is indisputable that he alone, without any lowering of the standard—a thing which the Folk-Song Society feared and the Guild of Morris Dancers desired—made folk-song and folk-dance available to all.

He did all this as looking beyond the present to the future. He was convinced, not, as has sometimes been supposed, that a native music would eventually be made out of folk-song, but that if a large part of England, especially the young, had the songs and sang them, it would not be long before the true composer would come from among them. He believed that all men have something of the artist in them, and that to 'lead that out' is an 'education' worthy the name. He believed that when we say all souls are equal in the sight of God, it is not a mere theory for Sundays but a truth to be lived; and he held therefore that this song and dance whose beauty goes straight to the soul, short-circuiting, as it were, the mind, would be the simplest and best means of bringing about that equality. He was more, then, than a musician. He was an artist in humanity and a patriot. Just as the great doctor used his medical experience to reclaim poor little waifs and start them in life with a new hope, or the great soldier seized upon the imagination of boys and girls with his 'to-day's good deed' to remind them that unselfishness, too, is a power, so Cecil Sharp, the musician, found and used with the young the words and melodies and rhythms which all can grasp, to help them to simple sincerity. What can we call these three men but artists in English humanity?

APPENDIX A

The Place of Folk-song in Music

THE collection of folk-songs is a pursuit which has many and highly varied attractions. No man would expend his skill, patience, and persistence in tracking down and identifying what may be no more than the uncertain vestige of a half-forgotten art, unless his appreciation of even a small success amounted to a passion. What fires this ardour may be a strong local or national devotion, and this may be chiefly antiquarian or social, rather than musical or aesthetic. Relics of past customs, of names and places, of dialects and stories, can illumine many an obscure tract of social history, and these gains alone might well suffice to urge the collector. Folk-song is something very much more than music, and a man for whom the music is to some extent a by-product might yet give generous time and labour to the task of collection. Indeed it is doubtful if any of the great collectors, and of these Sharp was certainly one, would have pursued their calling, often at great personal sacrifice, for the sake of a purely musical result. Most collectors of folk-music have been equally interested in local speech, local verse, local dances, and habits of life, and the tunes they rescued from oblivion were but one more evidence of a vivid social past which they had learnt to recreate with affectionate enthusiasm. This is not to belittle the musical product. The music is itself a part of the social order. It cannot lightly be divorced from its own natural environment.

Similarly, when the collectors present us with their discoveries, we may approach them with a judgement essentially complex. Folk-tunes and folk-verses, like all other tunes and verses, vary greatly in merit. The tune may save the verse, the verse the tune. Both may be aesthetically poor in themselves, yet be quaint enough or crude enough to give us a true and pleasant glimpse of more primitive tastes. The sheer contrast with sophisticated arts may be in itself a main attraction. Local affections, phrases, and customs may capture our hearts. We may admire folk-songs for any number of reasons other than the normal musical or poetical values by which we appraise music or poetry in general. And it is very difficult to extract the purely artistic appeal from work so composite in association.

213

Appendix A

Theoretically, folk-songs ought to have for us a measure of inherited response. These echoes of our own past should have a special significance. We ought at least to have traces of the same artistic predispositions which our forefathers expressed in old songs. Yet the fact is that our present folk-music, the songs and tunes which our populace accepts and hums in its work and play to-day, are far more frequently derived from alien lands and races than from our own native past. Popular ditties may be nearer to the American negro than to the English country-side. Old folk-songs, as preserved and revived by the collectors, are the food of a comparative handful of people, and most of these are in one way or another musical specialists. There is a great deal of indirect propaganda and practice in schools, but we have yet to see how far the general taste will be changed.

Put thus into its true perspective, folk-song becomes a matter for the musician as such to handle. If it is ever to become the prevailing standard of popular taste, it will have to be disseminated in the first place by musicians. What should be their reactions to this wealth of native material?

A glance at our neighbours may be helpful. No one would deny that there are melodic inflexions characteristic of Russia, and that Russian music is full of them. There is equally a local flavour in Italian and Spanish melody, both specialized, and both permeating their respective musical literatures. The Hungarian, the Czech, indeed every country which has made homogeneous contributions to the art of music, has fostered and developed a melodic dialect which it also spontaneously created. Cosmopolitanism in music is generally the overwhelming prestige for the time being of a particular national brand. In the eighteenth century it was mainly Italian, in the nineteenth mainly German.

History is equally illuminating. The flavour of Bach is the flavour of the Lutheran Chorales, of the older German songs and dances. His most characteristic phrases and inflexions are thus derived, and only our ignorance of his most formative influences obscures for us these constant reminiscences. Haydn was simply a Croatian peasant of musical genius, and what we call the Haydn melodic idioms are literally the idioms of Croatian folk-music. Mozart and Beethoven, in their most intimate melodies, speak the music of German song. Schubert and Brahms carried the use of

214

their natural Austro-German vocal inflexions to such a degree of assimilation that they almost convinced the world that these local phrases were uniquely expressive. Music almost became, and for some people completely became, music of this German species.

Technical skill, power of development, and mastery of design may come in many ways. Melodic style is often the germ of them. What concerns us chiefly for the moment is the fact that when Schubert and Brahms wrote melodies they were not English or French or Italian, least of all were they cosmopolitan melodies; they were German melodies, through and through, and the more intimate and spontaneous they are the more they reflect the strength and depth of this native source. Their work is most convincing just when these fundamental elements colour both the subject-matter and the design.

The body of English folk-song given us by Cecil Sharp, and by his predecessors and followers, is thus not merely a present contribution to our repertory, not merely a collection of new and quaint flavours, above all not a mere museum of the past, however interesting. If musical history means anything, if the study of antecedents explains the nature and provenance of masterpieces, then English folk-song is intimately related to all permanently and specifically English music. An English Bach would have used these idioms just as his predecessors the Tudors had done. Purcell knew of them, and his best melodies are English in precisely this sense. Even Handel, in some suites and dances, caught a touch of our musical climate. There have been a few echoes in subsequent times, but the decline of our music and the virtual loss of our folk-songs were probably but two aspects of the same process. With our present renaissance our folk-songs have come back.

But there should be no self-conscious artifice in their use, no strings of disconnected quotations, no incongruous technique. An Irish rhapsody written in a German technique will not do. A Scotch symphony in which the tunes are mere interludes will not do. English opera setting English words to French or Russian music will not do. The relation between melody and words is vital. True English opera will defy the translator just as the best foreign operas do. We make ingenious transliterations, but most of the original intimacy of words and tunes is gone. English speech has its own unique cadences. They will not properly fit German or Italian tunes. They will fit English tunes. Folk-song shows us the way. The natural accents of communal poetry are paralleled by the applied cadences of native melody. Indeed to the musician genuinely inspired and technically mature the two things are one. The tune *is* the words. Greek drama knew this, and Italian recitative, and Wagnerian declamation. The best of our vocal English music knows it too. When we are instinctive masters of all the native idioms which Sharp discovered and revived, we shall have the proper background for music of all kinds, pure in source, inexhaustible in fertility, original in thought, yet characteristic of our own natural reactions and spontaneously consistent in that style. On these terms we can add to English songs English operas and symphonies. Our music need be no more externally derived than is our poetry or our drama. We can learn from the thoughts of others, yet steadily express our own. Our masterpieces will rank with the greatest, not because they borrow a foreign method, but because they are both native and sincere. That is the possibility before us. That is the horizon which Sharp's work has so finely opened for us.[1]

G. DYSON.

August 1931.

[1] This essay and the next were especially written for this book.

APPENDIX B
Cecil Sharp's Acccompaniments

IT has sometimes been questioned whether Sharp had the creative impulse in music, but his accompaniments to my mind clearly show that he had. His creative impulse came from the tune he was setting. That is why his settings are often better than those of more technically gifted arrangers, because they come to the task as composers and let the suggestions started by the tune run away with them, and so forget the tune itself. This is especially bad when the arranger deliberately sets out 'to make something of' the tune. In all the best of Sharp's accompaniments it is the tune that counts and the arrangement falls into its proper background. In some cases his accompaniments look wrong, and sometimes even when played by themselves seem awkward, but they stand the important test, that they make the tune sound right. It is true that Sharp had little of the conventional technique of pianoforte accompaniment, as taught by professors of composition, but he developed a technique of his own whose complete success was only hindered, I think, by his fear of the harmony professor. He was so anxious for the songs to get known that he sometimes did not venture to produce an accompaniment which would be considered 'not correct'. And as he was not able entirely to assimilate this 'correct' style his accompaniments sometimes seem to halt between two opinions. If he had let himself go regardless of this more of his work might have been up to his best standard, but it might not have been so acceptable to the education authorities.

Occasionally, and only occasionally, his accompaniments seem to be bad. When this is so I put it down to the fact that he was so anxious for people to sing the songs, that he feared to provide an accompaniment which was beyond their mental, emotional, and technical equipment. As examples of first-rate accompaniments I suggest 'The Cuckoo', 'The Drowned Lover', 'The Water is Wide', the morris tune, 'Leap Frog' (Field Town), and 'Jenny Pluck Pears'. Of the second class, not entirely satisfactory for reasons I have given, 'Searching for Lambs' and 'A Rosebud in June'. Among those I presume to condemn are 'The Trees they do grow high' and 'Sellenger's Round'. But in nine cases out of ten the total result is satisfying and beautiful, and this after all is the only valid test.

R. VAUGHAN WILLIAMS.

APPENDIX C

Folk-dance in the Elementary School[1]

IN connexion with Sharp's appointment in 1919 as Occasional Inspector to the Board of Education (p. 181) some extracts from the opinions expressed in 1928 and 1933 by the Board themselves of the value of folk-dance in the schools and of the difficulties yet to be surmounted will be of interest.

No. 55, 1928. *Report on music, arts and crafts and drama in Training-Colleges.*

The dances are almost invariably taught by the lecturer responsible for physical instruction and for games, usually in the last ten minutes of the periods allocated to physical education. Music is supplied either by gramophone or a piano or fiddle. Where the dancing is mainly or entirely recreative the lecturer may be present as a sort of master of ceremonies.

For folk-dancing to be of any value . . .

(1) the teacher must not only know the technical details of the dances, but must also be able to appreciate the music.

(2) The accompanist must be a musician with a knowledge of the dances.

(3) The piano, if a piano is used, must be reasonably good.

(4) The floor must not be so slippery that the dancers cannot move without fear of falling.

(The last two are more easy, the first two more difficult to secure.) . . .

Folk-dancing is not a substitute for a regular system of physical education. It does not set out deliberately to cultivate every muscle of the body and every physical activity. It originates from the natural instinct for, and enjoyment of, rhythmic movement, and while satisfying that instinct very fully, adds the stimulus and discipline of music. The teacher of folk-dancing, therefore, while knowing something of the physical basis of movement, requires in addition not only a thorough knowledge of the principles of folk-dancing, but enough equipment on the musical side to be able to analyse a tune,

[1] Quotation is here made by permission of the Controller of H.M. Stationery Office from Pamphlets No. 55 and No. 95 of the Board of Education.

218

to recognize its parts in relation to the steps and figures, and to judge the speed and character of the dance as indicated by the tune— in a word to feel the tune, and in feeling it to appreciate that tune and dance are only different aspects of the same artistic conception.

The problem of the accompanist is even more difficult. . . . To play folk-dance tunes really well is no mean accomplishment. . . . Their execution requires rhythm, the absence or presence of which makes the whole difference between merely laborious plodding and the living movement. The accompanist must be able to phrase his playing and to express by appropriate turns the alternate lightness and solidity of a tune. It is a great help if he has actually danced the dances which he is to accompany. . . .

There is folk-dancing in more than two-thirds of the Training-Colleges, and at several of them it is well done. . . . In a College containing men-students Morris and Sword are of real value. . . . It may be felt by some that the inclusion of folk-dancing among the activities of a Training-College needs justification . . . yet the number of Local Education Authorities . . . who require folk-dances to be taught in their schools is large and annually increasing. . . .

Folk-dancing . . . exercises the brain and develops memory and quickness of thought, . . . it develops the body by free and yet controlled movement, . . . and it stimulates the mind and trains the emotions.

No. 95, 1933. *Recent developments in school music.*

Country-dancing can scarcely be termed a recent development. It is now some years since it took root in schools, and it has flourished and become widespread. . . . It is now generally accepted that the dance is an art springing direct from the music of its tune. . . .

Unfortunately the dances are rather beyond the powers of the ordinary pianist. It is unreasonable to expect that all teachers shall be good pianists, but it is not unreasonable to expect that all who teach country-dancing shall discountenance bad pianoforte playing. . . . One method is that of playing only the melody of the dance; . . . and as the strength of these matchless tunes is truly melodic, no wrong is done them by this. Gramophone records . . . have proved most useful. At several schools some children hum the tune while others dance.

It must be said that this indigenous art is so suitable for school use that it is not surprising it has so strongly taken root. The tunes alone are a priceless national heritage; allied to the grace and natural beauty of the appropriate movements and gestures they must surely be a lasting pleasure and benefit to the children who have learned the dances.

CECIL SHARP'S PUBLICATIONS[1]

FOLK-SONG COLLECTIONS

With pianoforte accompaniment:

Folk Songs from Somerset, 5 pts. (Pts. 1–3 with C. L. Marson) (*Wessex Press, Simpkin, Schott*) Parts 1, 2, 3, *and 5 out of print*   1904–19

Songs of the West (with S. Baring Gould) (*Methuen*)   1905

English Folk Songs for Schools (with S. Baring Gould) (*Curwen*)   1906

English Folk Songs: Lord Rendal, O No John, The Keys of Canterbury, My Bonny Bonny Boy (*Schott*)   1908

The Sheep Shearing, arr. for S.A.T.B.   1908

Folk-Songs from Dorset (coll. by H. E. D. Hammond, arr. by C. Sharp)   1908

Folk-Song Airs, coll. and arr. for pianoforte, 3 pts.   1908–11

Novello's School Songs, 11 pts. (including Folk-Songs from Dorset, coll. H. Hammond, arr. C. Sharp)   1908–22

Children's Singing Games, 5 pts. (with Lady Gomme)   1909–12

Four Folk-Airs, arr. for violin and pianoforte   1911

English Folk Carols (*Wessex Press, Simpkin, Novello*)   1911

Folk-Songs from Various Counties   1912

English Folk-Chanteys (*Wessex Press, Simpkin, Schott*)   1914

One Hundred English Folk-Songs (*Oliver Ditson, Boston*)   1916

Folk-Songs of English Origin, collected in the Appalachian Mountains, 2 pts. (*pt. 1 also published as American-English Folk-Songs, Schirmer, New York, 1918*)   1919, 1921

English Folk-Songs, Selected Edition, 2 pts.   1921, 1923

Nursery Songs from the Appalachian Mountains (illustrated by Esther B. Mackinnon)   1921, 1923

Without pianoforte accompaniment:

Journal of the Folk-Song Society (*The Folk-Song Society*):

Vol. 2, No. 6   1905

---

[1] Published by Novello & Co. unless otherwise stated.

Publications

Vol. 5, No. 18   1914
Vol. 5, No. 20   1916
English Folk-Songs from the Southern Appalachian   1917
    Mountains (with Olive Dame Campbell) (*Putnam, New York*). *Out of print, but nearly all included in the edition* (1932) *noted below*
and posthumously,
Journal of the Folk-Song Society, Vol. 8, No. 31   1927
English Folk-Songs from the Southern Appalachian   1932
    Mountains, 2 pts. (edited by Maud Karpeles) (*Oxford University Press*)

FOLK-DANCE COLLECTIONS

Dance notations:
The Morris Book, 5 pts. (Pts. 1–3 with H. C.   1907–13
    MacIlwaine, Pt. 5 with G. S. K. Butterworth)
    Pt. 1 revised and re-written   1912
    Pt. 2   ,,   ,,   1919
    Pt. 3   ,,   ,,   1924
The Country Dance Book, 6 pts. (Pts. 3 and 4 with   1909–22
    G. S. K. Butterworth, Pt. 5 with Maud Karpeles)
The Sword Dances of Northern England, 3 pts.   1911–13
An Introduction to the English Country Dance, con-   1919
    taining the description together with the tunes of twelve dances

Music with pianoforte accompaniment:
Morris Dance Tunes, 10 pts. (Pts. 9 and 10 with   1907–13
    G. S. K. Butterworth)
    Pts. 1–6, revised edition   1912–24
Folk-Dance Airs   1909
Country Dance Tunes   1909–22
The Sword Dances of Northern England. Song and   1911–13
    Dance Airs, 3 pts.

ON FOLK-SONG AND FOLK-DANCE

Book:
English Folk-Song: Some Conclusions (*Wessex Press*,   1907
    Simpkin, Novello)

Pamphlets:
Folk-Dancing in Schools (*E.F.D.S.*). *Out of print*   1912
Folk-Singing in Schools (*E.F.D.S.*)   1912

VARIOUS

Book:
The Dance. An historical survey of dancing in   1924
Europe (with A. P. Oppé) (*Halton & Truscott
Smith*). *Out of print*

Music:
A Book of British Song for Home and School (*John   1902
Murray*)
The Songs and Incidental Music arranged and com-   1914
posed for Granville Barker's production of
A Midsummer Night's Dream (*Wessex Press,
Simpkin, Novello*)
Reprinted with dance notations: A Midsummer
Night's Dream,—Songs, Incidental Music,
Dances (*Oxford University Press*)   1930

ORIGINAL COMPOSITIONS

Nursery Ditties . . . for 4 voices, 3 pts. (*Metzler   1891–3
[Cramer]*). *Pt. 3 out of print*
Menuet . . . pour piano (*Laudy*)   1895
La Fileuse . . . pour piano (*Laudy*)   1896
Two Songs: Cradle Song. The Banks of Doon   1898
(*Laudy*)

ARTICLES IN PERIODICALS, ETC.

English Review. July 1912. 'The Folk Song Fallacy.' A Reply.
(*See also* May 1912 and August 1912.)
E.F.D.S. Journal, 1914. 'Some Notes on the Morris Dance.'
Musical Times. November 1915. 'English Folk Dance; the
country dance.' (*See also* correspondence, December 1915,
January 1916.)
The Vineyard. Easter, 1919. 'Folk Song Collecting in America.'
Music Student. August 1919. 'The English Folk Dance Revival.'
The Dancing Times. October 1919. 'Folk Dancing and the
Ballet.'

Publications

Harmsworth's Universal Encyclopedia. 'Folk Song.' *Amalgamated Press*, 1920–2.

Encyclopaedia and Dictionary of Education. 'Dances, Sword, Morris and Country.' *Pitman*, 1921, 1922.

E.F.D.S. News, November 1923. 'The Development of Folk Dancing.' (A *précis* of two lectures given by Cecil Sharp at the Summer School, Aldeburgh, 1923.)

INDEX

Index

Index

Index

PLATE I

CECIL SHARP AS A BOY

From a photograph by the late John Davies,
Weston-super-Mare

By kind permission of Walter
John Davies, Esq.

PLATE II

CECIL SHARP IN MIDDLE AGE

From a photograph by Lena Connell

PLATE III

CECIL SHARP IN HIS LIBRARY AT ADELAIDE ROAD

PLATE IV.

(a) CECIL SHARP PLAYING PIPE AND TABOR

(b) CECIL SHARP PLAYING THE PIANO

PLATE V

CECIL SHARP IN 1922

From a photograph by Debenhams, Longman & Co.
Cheltenham

PLATE VI

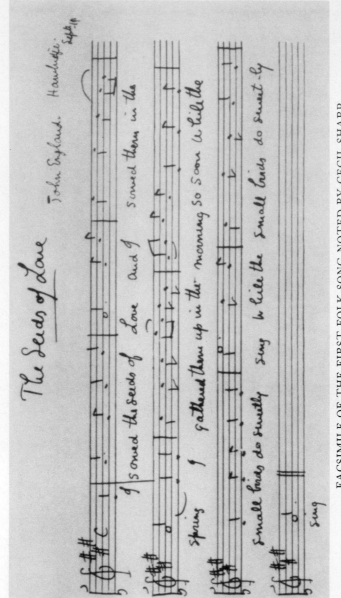

FACSIMILE OF THE FIRST FOLK-SONG NOTED BY CECIL SHARP

PLATE VII

(a) MRS. LUCY WHITE
(see pp. 40 and 45)

(b) MRS. OVERD
(see p. 36)

(c) JOHN ENGLAND
(see p. 33)

FOLK-SINGERS

PLATE VIII

(a) MRS. REBECCA HOLLAND
(see p. 42)

(b) WILLIAM BAYLISS
a Gloucestershire carol-singer

(c) MRS. LUCY CARTER
(see pp. 37 and 38)

FOLK-SINGERS

PLATE IX

(*a*) JOHN SHORT
of Watchet
(see p. 44)

(*b*) SHEPHERD HAYDEN
of Bampton-in-the-Bush

FOLK-SINGERS

PLATE X

WILLIAM KIMBER
of Headington

PLATE XI

WILLIAM WELLS, of Bampton
From a drawing by SIR WILLIAM ROTHENSTEIN
By permission of the artist and The English Folk Dance and Song Society
(see p. 95)

PLATE XII

(*a*) HENRY CAVE
a Gloucestershire fiddler

(*b*) *Another Gloucestershire fiddler*

(*c*) HENRY TAYLOR, of Longborough
Morris dancer

PLATE XIII

CHARLES BENFIELD, of Idbury, Oxfordshire

A portrait drawn by A.VAN ANROOY, R.I., *for 'The Countryman'*
which is published at Idbury

(see pp. 96 and 198)

PLATE XIV

THE BAMPTON MORRIS SIDE

PLATE XV

LEAP-FROG, MORRIS DANCE BY E.F.D.S. TEAM
in the Shakespeare Memorial Theatre Garden

From a photograph by F. J. Spencer, Stratford-on-Avon, by kind permission

PLATE XVI

KIRKBY MALZEARD SWORD DANCE
by Winchester men
From a photograph taken in 1915. By kind permission of Dr. M. J. Rendall

PLATE XVII

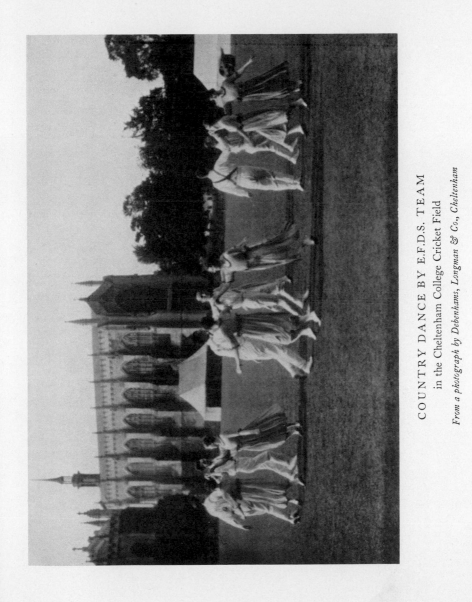

COUNTRY DANCE BY E.F.D.S. TEAM
in the Cheltenham College Cricket Field

From a photograph by Debenhams, Longman & Co., Cheltenham

PLATE XVIII

(*a*) CECIL SHARP WITH AUNT BETSY

(*b*) CECIL SHARP NOTING A SONG
By kind permission of Mr. Wm. A. Bradley

THE APPALACHIANS

PLATE XIX

(*a*) MRS. BROUGHTON
who with her three daughters, sang many songs to Cecil Sharp

(*b*) MILLER COFFEY
the singer of *Arise, Arise*

(*c*) MRS. WHEELER AND HER
FAMILY
who sang *The Green Bed*
(see p. 175)

APPALACHIAN SINGERS